Women and Media in the Middle East

Power through Self-Expression

Edited by
Naomi Sakr

I.B. TAURIS

LONDON · NEW YORK

Published in 2004 by I.B. Tauris & Co Ltd
6 Salem Road, London W2 4BU
175 Fifth Avenue, New York NY 10010
www.ibtauris.com

In the United States of America and Canada
distributed by Palgrave Macmillan a division of St Martin's Press
175 Fifth Avenue, New York NY 10010

HB ISBN 1 85043 485 9
PB ISBN 1 85043 545 6

HB EAN 978 1 85043 485 6
PB EAN 978 1 85043 545 7

A full CIP record for this book is available from the British Library
A full CIP record is available from the Library of Congress

Library of Congress Catalog Card Number: available

Library of Modern Middle East Studies 41

Typeset in Garamond by JCS Publishing Services

Printed and bound in Great Britain by MPG Books Ltd, Bodmin

Contents

List of Tables and Figures

Tables

Figures

Note on Sources, Citations and Transliteration

Two methods have been adopted for citing sources, depending on their type. Primary sources, such as interviews, internal reports, newspaper or magazine articles, press releases, speeches and talks, are treated as archival material and cited in full in the endnotes but not the bibliography. Books, monographs, conference papers, journal articles, academic theses and published reports are cited in both the endnotes and the bibliography. Arabic names and sources are transliterated following an informal and flexible method that omits diacritical marks, generally representing only the hamza by an apostrophe. Apostrophes are also used as aids to pronunciation of names (e.g. Fat'hi) or elision of a conjunction or preposition with the definite article (e.g. wa'l, fi'l). Where the letter 'jeem' appears in Egyptian names it is represented with a hard 'g', as in Gamal, in accordance with Egyptian pronunciation.

Where copyright material has been reproduced, every effort has been made to obtain permission from copyright holders.

Acknowledgements

The idea behind this collection originated with Sonia Dabbous. She shared it with Annabelle Sreberny and me in February 1999, during a workshop on satellite television in Cairo. I did not know then that, within a year, I would be commissioned to write a research report for a non-governmental organization (the Centre for Media Freedom – Middle East and North Africa), bringing together information about initiatives and good practice adopted to improve women's representation in and through the media around the Arab world. Through that project I met scholars and activists whose work has had an important impact on developments in this field. I would like to thank Sonia and Annabelle for introducing me to some of them and for having the confidence to delegate to me the job of assembling and editing the present volume. They and all the other contributors to the book have been a great pleasure to work with.

As editor I also wish to name a number of people to whom I owe a personal debt of gratitude that is linked in one way or another to the process of turning the idea of the book into a reality. They are Nadje al-Ali, Mahasen al-Emam, Angie Biegler-Turner, Nadia Hijab, Jill Hills, Islah Jad, Lena Kara, Awatef Omar Ketiti, Reem Obeidat, Christa Salamandra, Martha Sara and Susannah Tarbush. Philippa Brewster at I. B. Tauris provided warm encouragement from the beginning. In the middle and at the end I could not have managed without the help of my husband Ahmad.

About the Contributors

Magda Abu-Fadil is Director of the Institute for Professional Journalists at the Lebanese American University in Beirut. She is an Arab-American veteran of international news organizations in Washington and the Middle East.

Haya al-Mughni is an independent scholar residing in Kuwait. Her book, *Women in Kuwait: The Politics of Gender*, first published in 1993, is now in its second edition. She is the author of many articles and book chapters on Kuwait, including some co-authored with Mary Ann Tétreault.

Benaz Somiry-Batrawi is a Palestinian media practitioner who was previously Director of the Gender and Media Department at the Institute of Modern Media, Al-Quds University. In the academic year 2002–3 she was a Hubert H. Humphrey Fellow at the School of Journalism, University of Missouri.

Sonia Dabbous is Affiliate Professor of Journalism and Communication at the American University in Cairo and Assistant Editor-in-Chief of *Akhbar al-Youm*. She has written on Egyptian media for edited collections published in the UK and US.

Victoria Firmo-Fontan is a Post-Doctoral Research Fellow at Sabançi University in Turkey. She was previously a Research Associate of the Centre for Behavioural Research at the American University of Beirut, Lebanon, and an EU Marie Curie Research Fellow at the University of Deusto, Spain. She specializes in issues of armed resistance, human trafficking and media development.

Sahar Khamis is Assistant Professor in the Department of Mass Communication, Faculty of Arts, Ain Shams University, and faculty member in the Department of Mass Communication, American University in Cairo. She has published widely in Arabic and has been a reporter for the US media.

Lina Khatib is Lecturer in World Cinema at the Department of Media Arts, Royal Holloway, University of London. Her research interests include post-colonial theory and media representations of Middle Eastern politics and her most recent publications have appeared in *Visual Communication* and *Journal of Communication Inquiry*.

Gholam Khiabany teaches at the Department of Applied Social Sciences, London Metropolitan University. He has published on the Iranian press and civil society in *Gazette* (co-authored with Annabelle Sreberny) and on media theory and Orientalism in *Media, Culture and Society*.

Naomi Sakr teaches in the School of Media, Arts and Design at the University of Westminster. She is the author of *Satellite Realms: Transnational Television, Globalization and the Middle East*, also published by I. B. Tauris, which won the 2002 Middle Eastern Studies Book Prize. Her numerous monographs, book chapters and journal articles deal with aspects of media development in the Arab world.

Zahia Smail Salhi is Lecturer in Arabic Literature and Culture at the Department of Arabic and Middle Eastern Studies, University of Leeds. Her published work includes *Politics, Poetics and the Algerian Novel* (1999) as well as book chapters and journal articles on women, culture and national identity.

Annabelle Sreberny is Visiting Professor in Global Media and Communication Studies at the School of Oriental and African Studies, University of London. She has co-authored and edited many books, including *Gender, Politics and Communication* (2000) and *Small Media, Big Revolution: Communication, Culture and the Iranian Revolution* (1994). Professor Sreberny was guest editor of *Gazette*'s special Middle East issue in May 2001.

Mary Ann Tétreault is the Una Chapman Cox Distinguished Professor of International Affairs at Trinity University in San Antonio, Texas. Among her books are *The Kuwait Petroleum Corporation and the Economics of the New International Order* (1995) and *Stories of Democracy: Politics and Society in Contemporary Kuwait* (2000). She writes regularly on Kuwaiti politics, gender issues, and international oil.

Deborah L. Wheeler teaches in the departments of International Studies and Near Eastern Languages and Civilizations at the University of Washington, where she is also a Faculty Fellow at the Center for Internet Studies. In 2003–4, as a Visiting Research Fellow at the Oxford Internet Institute, she worked on a book on the Internet's impact in the Arab world. Her work has appeared *in Communications Research, Middle East Journal, Gazette* and the *Encyclopedia of International Communication*, among others.

1
Women–Media Interaction in the Middle East: An Introductory Overview

Naomi Sakr

When women's rights are discussed in a Middle Eastern context, customs and regulations in Saudi Arabia invariably come to the fore. So when a Saudi broadcaster airs a phone-in discussion programme on FM radio, aimed directly at Saudi listeners, addressing not the broad topic of women's rights in general but the specific issue of women's rights inside Saudi Arabia, something important would seem to be afoot. Exactly how important becomes apparent from closer examination of whose voices are heard in such a programme and the range of views they represent. A particular item in June 2003 was broadcast by MBC-FM, a company closely allied to a key branch of the Saudi ruling family and holder of the only private FM radio licence in the kingdom.[1] It featured Nahed Bashatah, one of Saudi Arabia's sizeable contingent of freelance women journalists, advocating further empowerment of Saudi women. When a woman caller to the programme said that the Saudi women's situation was already fine, Bashatah countered with criticism of the treatment of widows and divorcees. A male religious scholar followed up by saying that Saudi women needed to know more about their rights. A few days later a commentary on the programme appeared in *Arab News*, a newspaper connected to the same central branch of the ruling family.[2] In line with the paper's regular coverage of women-related topics, this commentary protested at what it called the 'horrendous' pressure suffered by Saudi women who dare to discuss their situation in public.

There are many ways to analyse this example of women–media interaction, all of which can illustrate the themes and purpose of this book. Women's position within media power structures and media representation of women are persistent concerns in every society, because negative stereotyping and lack of female input both reflect and reinforce wider gender inequalities. It is axiomatic that, as Peter Golding and Graham

Murdock put it, media industries play a 'pivotal role in organizing the images and discourse through which people make sense of the world'.[3] In today's changing media landscape in the Middle East and North Africa, questions arise as to whether the changes are empowering women. Each chapter in the present volume pursues these questions by scrutinizing aspects of media production, media consumption and media texts. Since each has its own introduction and conclusion, the aim of this introductory chapter is to highlight some common threads within the book and the wider literature, and to consider whether research on women and media in other contexts can be applied to the Middle East. One way to begin this task is to delve a little deeper into the Saudi Arabian example already discussed.

Lines of enquiry

For decades, ruling elites in Arab countries and Iran have monopolized the media to disseminate complimentary publicity about themselves. Government control over the press and broadcasting prevented demands that were not on governments' own agendas from being expressed, let alone debated, in public. That was what made the rise of satellite television in the region seem so significant. In theory, the technology of cross-border broadcasting allowed viewers to see material critical of governments and to take part in uncensored public debates. In practice, there was no sudden rush to exploit such freedom, as the resources required for transnational broadcasting initially put the activity out of reach of almost everyone outside the existing ruling elites. During the late 1990s, however, more players with a greater range of objectives entered the scene, contributing to an unfamiliar degree of competition.[4] Viewers' increased choice stepped up the pressure on media producers to vie for viewer loyalty with programmes that were more relevant and interactive.

It becomes apparent from this background that the MBC-FM programme about women's rights, which appeared to question the status quo, needs to be considered from a political economy perspective before its significance in terms of Saudi women's empowerment can be judged. If the Saudi authorities were obliged to rethink established policies on gender at the start of the millennium, it was because they were also forced to acknowledge that the oil boom was over and that Saudi women salary-earners were an enviable asset to families, not a source of shame. That was the context in which Saudi Arabia signed up, with reservations, to the Convention on the Elimination of All Forms of Discrimination Against Women (CEDAW), the UN treaty designed to guarantee equality between women and men. It was no coincidence that the signing followed unprecedented steps to attract foreign investment in projects to provide jobs and services for the predominantly young and rapidly growing population of Saudi nationals. Mid-2003, the period during which the MBC-FM programme on women's rights was broadcast, was an eventful time in Saudi politics. Unsettled by the US occupation of Iraq and a devastating bomb attack in Riyadh, the government was striving to quell US criticism that it had failed to act fast enough on political and economic reform. Understanding the setting in which the MBC-FM programme was produced means taking account of such related initiatives as the public relations campaign launched in the same month to improve perceptions of Saudi Arabia in the US.[5] Behind-the-scenes orchestration seemed the only explanation for reports appearing in newspapers dotted all over the US about another programme on Saudi women – this time a talkshow on a Saudi-owned pay-TV channel called *Saudi Women Speak Out*.[6] The newspaper reports all quoted Saudi women explaining how they were being 'given more freedom' to tackle taboos.

A link between policy imperatives and media production is not peculiar to Saudi Arabia. It just so happens that, in this case, an increasingly urgent media preoccupation with women's empowerment can be rather easily traced to the very same power structures that excluded women for so long. That in itself does not invalidate the process of empowerment. But it does mean that other avenues also need to be explored to locate shifts in relations of power. One such avenue concerns the status of women in the media workplace. In the unusual environment of Saudi Arabia, degree courses in mass communications have not been open to women and rules against mixing of the sexes in public have had the effect of restricting women journalists to untenured jobs, with little prospect of promotion and an initially uncertain status in the nascent Saudi Journalists' Association.[7] Again, however, inequalities that are overt in the Saudi environment are not exclusive to Saudi Arabia. As will be shown below, journalists' unions throughout the region have a poor record of representing women.

Audience access to and reception of media output are other areas to be analysed to assess change. In our Saudi examples, the media output in question was carried on drive-time radio, pay-TV and in the English-language press. Of these, only the radio programme was both free and in Arabic. But listeners to that programme would have heard other controversial topics, from unemployment to religious extremism, discussed in the same slot. Like the programme on women, some of these would also have been followed up in the press,[8] discussed in Internet chat rooms and on satellite television channels. Instead of being confined within a particular programme or article, the meanings to be found in media texts circulate in the discourse of a community, thereby repeating and naturalizing particular perspectives and privileging them over others. Such intertextuality is critical in the formation of public opinion.[9] One reason for researching interaction between women and media is to explore how dominant meanings about gender are created and how audiences interpret what they see and hear. As Liesbet Van Zoonen put it, in her study of gender and media, society is 'not constituted by orderly and dichotomous divisions of oppressors and oppressed'.[10]

Recurring concerns

If the mass media form part of the apparatus through which particular gender roles and attributes are defined and assigned, it follows that the media will also be a site for negotiating changes in those definitions. The Middle East media have changed dramatically since the early 1990s and women's voices have grown in audibility over the same period. Yet it is rare to see the altered landscape for public communication analysed in terms of how it relates to the changing climate for empowerment of women. The first edition of the *Arab Human Development Report (AHDR)*, released under UN sponsorship in 2002, set a resounding precedent when it identified key 'deficits' harming the Arab region. One it described as the 'freedom deficit', revealed by a set of indicators measuring 'voice and accountability', including indicators of media independence. Second came the 'women's empowerment deficit', based on such measures as girls' enrolment in education and women's political participation.[11] While some in the Arab Middle East quibbled over the *AHDR*'s arguments and others took them to heart, one of the clearest messages to be derived from its list of deficits was that most voices are stifled and that women's voices are stifled worst of all. This was the message *Arab News* picked up when it deplored resistance in Saudi Arabia to the public airing of women's grievances.

In discriminating between male and female voices, neither the Arab world nor the Middle East as a whole are alone. Wider margins for freedom of expression in other parts of the world are not necessarily matched by equal opportunities for women in media industries or by media coverage that adequately represents women. A study of US film and prime-time television in the mid- to late 1990s described women's employment history and outlook as 'dismal'.[12] Nearly two-thirds of US women editors questioned for a study in 2002 believed they would not be promoted because their employers preferred to hire men. This was despite similarities found by the study between male and female editors in terms of their leadership traits, job satisfaction and visions for newspaper content.[13] It might be argued that female editors would make little difference to content anyway if their visions are the same as their male counterparts'. We will return to that argument later, noting here only that discrimination on grounds of sex contravenes basic human rights. Moreover, target-setting can help to eliminate discrimination. The proportion of female senior executives at the British Broadcasting Corporation (BBC) rose from 3.6 per cent in 1985 to 30.8 per cent in 1999, after the BBC took steps to achieve a workforce balance of gender and ethnicity that would reflect the UK audience it serves.[14] Unfortunately, while the BBC's efforts were in line with a wider European scheme to promote equal opportunities in broadcasting, positive employment trends in the industry as a whole were undermined by deregulation in the 1990s. Increasing casualization of labour created insecurity for freelances and independent producers, making jobs dependent on contacts rather than formal appointment procedures and making the gender balance harder to monitor or influence.[15] Where monitoring is possible, pay disparities emerge. A study of US salaries in 2000 showed that female editors and reporters stand to earn hundreds of thousands of dollars less than men over their lifetimes through lower average earnings for the same work.[16]

When it comes to comparing media sources and media content, the results of western studies show persistent male–female imbalances. Analysis of 166 hours of prime-time terrestrial television programming conducted for the British Broadcasting Standards Council in 1994 discovered that men appearing across the range of programmes outnumbered women by a ratio of 7:3.[17] A 1997 survey of US newspapers, news magazines and trade journals found that female nurses, by far the largest professional group in the US healthcare sector, accounted for only 4 per cent of the sources for all news stories about health.[18] Another study set out to assess women's visibility in stories about human rights during the fiftieth anniversary year of the 1948 Universal Declaration of Human Rights. Out of 300 stories in English and Spanish collected during the first 11 days of December 1998 (before and during the actual anniversary), only a dozen (4 per cent) included even a paragraph of information about women and human rights. Fewer still focused specifically on women's human rights as a central theme.[19]

While findings about women and media in the US and Europe have accumulated, the same cannot be said for the developing world. In 1996 Annabelle Sreberny, co-author of a chapter in the present volume, declared gender to be one of the 'blindspots' of international communication research.[20] Today, the main source of comparative international data on the visibility of women in news media is the Global Media Monitoring Project, which has so far conducted two synchronized surveys of some 70 countries, one in 1995 and the second in 2000. The 2000 survey, held on 1 February, found that women were a central focus in 10 per cent of news stories on that day. In many of these they were victims, weight-watchers or beauty queens. In Turkey the proportion of stories focusing on women was 3 per cent, with a story on heart attacks among women illustrated with pictures of bikini-clad sunbathers on a beach. A Sudanese article about problems faced by young women whose studies take them away from home contained not a single quote from a female source.[21] Comparisons such as those in the Global Media Monitoring Project provide general benchmarks and a rationale for solidarity among activists who see the media as a prime site of struggle for women's empowerment. They also underline the need for better understanding of the influences at play in regions where women–media interaction is relatively unresearched. Margaret Gallagher, a leading scholar of gender patterns in the world's media, argues that cross-border activism has become increasingly urgent as the transnational commercial interests controlling the media have continued to 'concentrate and coalesce'.[22] Her book *Gender Setting* contains references to many African, Asian and Latin American countries. Apart from Israel, it barely mentions the Middle East. The same is true of Gallagher's 1995 study of gender patterns in media employment in different parts of the world.[23]

Statistics on employment, airtime and column inches are necessary because quantitative evidence of marginalization indicates that the diversity of women's experience is being obscured. A big part of empowering women lies in ensuring that they have the means through the media to express their own opinions about inequalities on their own behalf. In the very act of obligating states to eliminate 'all forms' of discrimination against women, CEDAW requires signatory states to find out what women themselves think about laws, policies and practices. These perceptions may well reveal that 'what appears to be oppression from outside a culture may be found tolerable and even advantageous by women within it, and what they find discriminating and subordinating may not be apparent from outside'.[24] Thus, ending discrimination includes ending the invisible discrimination whereby women are patronized or prejudged. If, as a result, contradictory perceptions emerge, that is because social and cultural identities are complex, being constructed through what Stuart Hall has called 'different categories' and 'different antagonisms'.[25] Feminist theorists from the global North and the global South have together discarded essentialist notions of 'woman' or 'Third World women'. They have rejected reductionist narratives about male–female inequalities and acknowledged the power relations that also lie in differences among women.[26] It is no longer fair to say, as it was in the early 1990s, that scholars treat western women as the norm and 'Third world women as monolithically oppressed … den[ying] the complexity of Third World women's experience'.[27] Karin Werner took up the challenge of representing complexity in her phenomenology of the media practices of Islamist women in Egypt. By countering essentializing views of 'Islamic fundamentalists', Werner was able to show how some educated young women adopt Islamist practices of self-control to strive for personal autonomy and success.[28]

Making a difference

Recognizing that individuals have multiple social identities raises practical questions about approaches to activism and research. Two questions have particular relevance to the Middle East. The first may be described, in a form of shorthand, as the issue of 'critical mass'. The second may be dealt with under the broad heading of 'the public sphere'.

Theories of complexity imply that, even when the identities of 'woman' and 'media practitioner' belong to the same individual, there is no necessary fusion of the two. Even if they fuse, there can be no automatic assumption that the female media practitioner is also politically engaged, or active in support of causes that are typically linked to women. This poses the question as to what, if any, difference is made to media content by writers, editors, producers and directors who also happen to be female. In research conducted outside the Middle East, answers to this highly contested question are usually said to divide into two camps. One emphasizes structures in the form of workplace hierarchies, norms and routines. The other pays attention to human agency and the role of individuals. Significantly, however, neither sees deliberate intentions as a prerequisite of change. This is the case, for instance, in studies showing that sheer numbers of men and women can affect media output, with the number of women making a difference once it reaches a critical mass not only in the newsroom but in the workforce generally and in politics. Kay Mills's research in the US showed the incremental impact of critical mass on story selection, editorial policy, assignments and hiring of staff.[29] When measured in terms of subjects covered, the impact of critical mass could be seen in changing approaches to news stories about rape, sexual harassment, health issues and so on. Mills's findings indicated that such changes were made by both men and women because a sufficient number of women throughout the workplace hierarchy has the primary effect of sensitizing men.[30] Research in Flanders also concluded that a critical mass of women in the media workplace affects output indirectly, through collective influence on the working environment and ethics rather than the discrete actions of individuals.[31]

Intrinsic to the critical mass argument is an understanding that agents and structures interact. As a study of women in film and prime-time television entertainment in the US discovered, a purely structural approach to media industries risks overemphasizing business imperatives and overlooking the power of the creative community behind the scenes. By the same token, *auteur* theory regards the director's vision as dominant and downplays the structures within which directors inevitably work. By developing a methodology that combined the two approaches, the researchers produced statistical evidence that women writers, producers and executive producers do influence the number and portrayal of female characters on screen. Even without a common feminist ideology, women occupying powerful roles increased the representation of women in other creative positions. They in turn influenced on-screen portrayals, including the number of female characters and their dialogue, measured in terms of their propensity to introduce topics, have the last word, and interrupt.[32]

Such findings do not negate the work of scholars who see newsroom routines and organizational structures limiting the individual freedom of action of both male and female personnel.[33] Van Zoonen has deployed a structural approach to argue that we see more female journalists today because competitive pressure to attract viewers in a multichannel environment is privileging the so-called human interest angle in news. Redefinition of the news genre increases the number of openings for women who were traditionally relegated to 'soft news'. Accordingly, it is not women who change the news, but changes in the news that open the way to women.[34] Paying due regard to structures in this fashion helps in evaluating changes that appear to be increasing media visibility for women in the Middle East. There, censorship laws restricting media content limit the scope for ground-breaking input by everyone, male and female, at all editorial levels. In these circumstances, a large percentage of women in the workforce, no matter how senior, is not synonymous with critical mass. Lines of authority in the state-owned Egyptian Radio and Television Union (ERTU) can illustrate this point. The ERTU is directly accountable for its content to Egypt's minister of information. Comprehensive controls over content limit the authority of all staff and are so vaguely worded that they encourage the ERTU's internal censors and heads of department to exercise extreme caution for fear of crossing fuzzy 'red lines'. Under these restrictions, any programme touching on women's status would be prohibited from criticizing religion or traditions, 'threatening' family ties or 'disparaging' the sanctity of family values.[35] Ideas and storylines for television dramas are notoriously subject to guidance from government[36] and Lila Abu Lughod has noted the example of Fathiyya al-Assal, one of the country's well-known socialist feminist writers, whose serials have been cut by civil servants.[37] Thus prevented from challenging social mores except with government approval, the many female heads of the ERTU's numerous radio networks and television channels[38] prove that critical mass for women in censored media is not a simple matter of achieving a statistically significant presence.

At the same time, the task of gathering statistics and contesting censorship has been blocked in the Middle East by the workings of other structures, including professional unions of journalists and writers. Unions worldwide have been slow to act on gender issues. It took the International Federation of Journalists (IFJ) 75 years to get around to holding its first conference on gender equality in 2001. An IFJ report prepared before the conference showed that just over a quarter of the federation's 146 unions had adopted guidelines to make their members more aware of gender issues when selecting and presenting news. The report found the same sets of obstacles obstructed women's promotion in Asia, the Americas, Africa and Europe. These were: prejudice against seeing women in authority; lack of equality in employment conditions and a lack of support systems to facilitate juggling between family obligations and the exigencies of covering breaking news.[39] By collating information on these obstacles and ways to overcome them, the IFJ can boost gender equality campaigns in member unions. But that presupposes that unions want to work in step with the IFJ. Where a country's leading media outlets are owned or controlled by the government, and where the only accredited journalists are those registered with the statutory journalists' union, union members have to avoid antagonizing the government in order to keep their jobs. That the Jordanian Press Association (JPA), which is not an IFJ member, has other priorities than gender equality,[40] was demonstrated by its hostility to the Arab Women's Media Centre (AWMC), launched as a non-governmental organization (NGO) in Amman in 1999. The AWMC's founder, Mahasen al-Emam, was a member of the JPA for 20 years, from 1979, and the first female member to be elected to its governing council. In 1994 she became the first female editor-in-chief of *Al-Bilad*, one of many weeklies to benefit from the shortlived era of press freedom created by Jordan's Press and Publications Law of 1993[41] – and which, by doing so, clashed with the JPA.[42] Al-Emam set up the AWMC to train women journalists, help them find jobs and provide advice on work-related legal issues. But she quit the JPA when it criticized her for accepting foreign money to help fund a conference.[43] In August 2002 the JPA issued a circular banning local newspapers from covering news about foreign-funded NGOs.[44] Al-Emam now believes the AWMC is doing what the JPA should do. Her centre, the first of its kind in the Arab world, promotes women journalists and freedom of expression. Asked to name the biggest problem facing female journalists in Jordan, al-Emam said it was 'the inability to write about anything you want'.[45]

Behind-the-scenes controls like these, which are embedded in organizational structures, tend to bear out Shirin Rai's point that, however multi-layered their social identities may be, women in the 'Third World' face the state in radically different ways from women in the West.[46] When the media are aligned with the state, the experience of women vis-à-vis the media is different too. As Rai notes, and as evidenced by controls that are deeply embedded within media structures, states try to avoid visibility in confrontation. Oppositional groups, by seeking visibility, can force the coercive arm of the state to become visible too, thereby potentially exposing it to public scrutiny and media interest.[47] Whether the media in a given context actually provide a forum for public scrutiny then becomes crucially important. It is precisely because questions about oppositional activity, the media and the state are central to women's representation in the media that feminist scholars in the West have adapted Jürgen Habermas's concept of the public sphere. Their versions of the concept can help to illuminate contemporary developments with regard to women and media in the Middle East.

Craig Calhoun has argued that Habermas's account of how a bourgeois public sphere was created out of relations between capitalism and the state in the seventeenth and eighteenth centuries is both 'more original and interesting' than his account of that sphere's later degeneration.[48] Based on an actual historical phenomenon, the theoretical construct of the public sphere envisages the existence of an 'arena for discursive interaction' where discourses that are critical of the state may circulate.[49] Indeed, essential characteristics of the public sphere as a concept are that it allows free and equal participation in public debate and that debate is free of domination.[50] The concept is thus both descriptive and normative, as noted by Lisa McGlaughlin, who sees it as both a 'vital tool' for guiding criticism of existing practices and a 'social imaginary to aspire to in reshaping our lives and the world'.[51] There are difficulties, however, in either creating or even imagining a public sphere that is truly free of domination. Nancy Fraser, citing research into the unequal assertiveness of men and women in mixed-sex discussion groups, has argued that informal impediments to participatory parity may persist even where freedom to participate is formally guaranteed. In other words, subordinate groups may be silenced by subtle forms of control.[52] Fraser concludes from this that, whether in stratified or egalitarian societies, a plurality of competing 'counterpublics' is preferable to a single, dominant overarching public sphere. Multiple spheres expand discursive space, which can be used in turn to argue out what counts as a legitimate topic of public discourse. For example, Fraser points out that a 'feminist subaltern counterpublic' managed, through 'sustained discursive contestation', to '*mak*[*e*]' the issue of domestic violence a common concern.[53]

Contestation and parity of participation are ideals against which the actual practice of women's participation in the developing Middle East media can be assessed. The Saudi Arabian programmes mentioned earlier in this introduction followed a pattern of talkshows established during the latter part of the 1990s by Al-Jazeera Satellite Channel, based in Qatar, and picked up by other satellite television stations including, most notably, Abu Dhabi TV. Al-Jazeera set a precedent in the amount of airtime it allocated for live unscripted debates, to which numerous women guests were invited to discuss contentious aspects of women's legal and social status.[54] By 2002, its weekly panel debates under the title *Lil Nissa' Faqat* (For Women Only) were attracting large audiences, with male callers to the programme proving that this audience was by no means restricted to women. Subjects covered in 2002–3 included women prisoners, women servants, women in armed conflict, consumerism, the concept of gender and the sex trade. Based on Fraser's model of dominant publics and subaltern counterpublics, *Lil Nissa' Faqat* could be compared with women's debates elsewhere in the Arab media in terms of its contestatory function and the extent to which it enabled subordinate groups to express themselves on their own terms.

Themes of the book

This introduction has argued that media studies have rich potential for illuminating ways in which women are empowered or disempowered. But that potential also poses a challenge in terms of organizing the book. The material spans the region (from Morocco to Iran), spans the centuries (from the 1860s to 2006) and spans the media (from the printed press to film, television and the Internet). Yet compartmentalization on any of these criteria would be flawed, because various themes thread their way throughout. Ultimately, all the authors explore how different media have been used at different times and in different places to open up possibilities for women or to restrict them. By taking a non-essentialist approach to women that starts from individuals' multi-layered identities and their multi-faceted relations with each other, the authors uncover both differences and commonalities in the identities that have been promoted or marginalized through the media. Similarly, by taking a non-functionalist approach to the media that views media institutions and forms of mass communication as part of the wider fabric of power relations in society, the authors uncover particular purposes to which particular media have been put – and by whom. In some cases they are used to erect gender boundaries, in others to transcend them.

Sahar Khamis's chapter on audience reception of televised literacy campaigns in Egypt makes startlingly clear how the identity constructions implicit in these campaigns are accepted by some women and not by others. Zahia Salhi shows us how, in using the medium of film to break a silence that risked permanently obliterating Algerian women's history, the writer Assia Djebar stepped across boundaries laid down by patriarchy and colonization. The narratives on Internet use collated in Deborah Wheeler's study reveal how traditional boundaries limiting communication between the sexes are being crossed in cyberspace. Magda Abu-Fadil's work on women journalists shows how her interviewees constantly straddle a notional 'East–West' divide and, by doing so, demonstrate ways in which it is both notional and real. In the Egyptian films discussed by Lina Khatib lines are drawn between groups inside the nation, and between nations, through the construction and deployment of female characters. Victoria Firmo-Fontan's model of monological and dialogical communication helps in analysing how boundaries are observed or crossed in Lebanon. Her study highlights the significance of those instances in which broadcast media and women's groups together cross pre-established sectarian and gender divides.

If gender boundaries are negotiated through the media, it is also because the media provide an interface between the private and public spheres, through which the categories of public and private can be contested. In their chapter on Iran, Gholam Khiabany and Annabelle Sreberny untangle the dynamics whereby a resilient women's press has been the vehicle for a continuing struggle to force gender to the forefront of government concerns, reverse efforts to remove women from public life and open the way to new thinking about feminism. Haya al-Mughni and Mary Ann Tétreault, by focusing on the Kuwaiti press, expose the forces that continued to deny suffrage to Kuwaiti women into the new millennium. Their analysis reveals how and why the liberal press, supposedly supportive of women's political rights, began to headline an alleged lack of unity among advocates of votes for women at the very moment when women's groups were more united on the issue than they had ever been. Benaz Somiry-Batrawi shows what television can do, in the right circumstances, to promote gender awareness as part of programmes that help to build self-confident and pluralistic local communities. The vicious circle afflicting Palestinian society is that the circumstances have almost never been right.

All these struggles over rights and boundaries are put into historical perspective by Sonia Dabbous's account of women's activism and the press in Egypt before 1952. She revisits the process whereby women emerged from nineteenth-century seclusion into twentieth-century public life via a press that was emerging at the same time. Intriguing parallels exist between women–media interaction in Egypt at the start of the twentieth century and women–media interaction in Saudi Arabia at the start of the twenty-first. Such parallels give pause for thought. As noted at the start of this introduction, media discussion of women's rights and expectations may serve certain purposes at certain times. Egyptian women found that their involvement in the public sphere was not so welcome once their activism to end foreign occupation had achieved its aims. The chapters in this volume examine women–media interaction in a region of the world where power relations are under mounting internal and external pressures. The nature of the interactions examined here can provide clues about some of those pressures and where they might lead.

The women's press before 1979

The history of debates about the rights of women cannot be separated from the broader history of struggle for democratic rights in Iran. Similarly, the history of publications for women cannot be separated from the broader history of the press in Iran, which has experienced periods of great expansion as well as fierce control. The prevailing historic dynamic has been that 'when the central authority is at its weakest, a dynamic public sphere emerges ... when central authority is strong, an atmosphere of repression exists'.[2]

The first ever woman's publication in Iran was launched more than 90 years ago, some 60 years after the introduction of the press. Before that there were a number of educated middle-class women who contributed regularly to the 'general' press, sometimes under pseudonyms or more often with no name at all. The Constitutional Revolution (1906–10) and the concern for law, rights and equality all increased women's visibility in public life and expanded their role in public culture, especially in print culture. The new openness saw the establishment of new schools; according to one study between 1907 and 1913 more than 60 schools for girls were created in Tehran,[3] and associations were established as public spaces for debating and raising awareness among Iranian women.[4]

During this period women's specialist publications also emerged, with eight titles launched between 1910 and 1925. The first of these was an eight-page weekly titled *Danesh* (Knowledge) and edited by a woman activist, Dr Kahal. *Danesh* lasted for less than a year and only 30 issues were published. A year after its closure, a fortnightly pictorial entitled *Shekofeh* (Blossom) was launched. Edited by Mozin al-Saltaneh, the founder of Mazininah School, it continued until the outbreak of the First World War and the beginning of new political turmoil in Iran. The first ever publication to refer to 'women' in its title was published in 1919. *Zaban-e Zanan* (Women's Tongue), edited by Sedigheh Dolatabadi, was originally launched as a four-page fortnightly in the city of Isfahan. It later became a weekly and, after encountering problems, moved to Tehran, where it continued publication in magazine format.[5] A year later two more publications arrived. The licence holder for *Alam-e Nesvan* (Women's Universe) was Navabeh Khanum Safavi; printed in 38 pages once every two months, it lasted for 13 years. Shanaz Azad launched *Namh-e Banovan* (Ladies' Letter) as a fortnightly publication under the slogan 'Women are the first teachers of men'.

A more controversial publication was the monthly *Jahan-e Zanan* (Women's World), originally published in the holy city of Mashhad under the editorship of Fakhr Afagh Parsa. This managed to print only four issues in this original form; its fifth and final edition appeared in Tehran after a six-month delay. Mohammed Sadr-Hashemi has argued that the final edition of *Jahan-e Zanan* created a storm.[6] It was designed to educate women, teach them the history of women's struggle and encourage them to develop their potential. But it was denounced as anti-religious. The editor and her husband were exiled to the city of Arak, making Parsa the first woman editor to be punished for her journalistic activity. Two more publications emerged in the years after the Constitutional Revolution. A magazine entitled *Jameyat Nesvan-e Vatankhah-e Iran* (Society of Patriotic Women of Iran) was published monthly and lasted for three years and *Nesvan-e Shargh* (Women of the East) was a fortnightly local publication, printed in the southern city of Bandar Pahlavi.

Table 2.1
Women's publications between the Constitutional Revolution and the Pahlavi era

Title	Editor	Launched	Frequency	Place of publication
Knowledge	Kahal	1910	Weekly / irregular	Tehran
Blossom	Al-Saltaneh	1913	Fortnightly	Tehran
Women's Tongue	Dolatabadi	1919	Fortnightly	Isfahan
Ladies' Letter	Azad	1920	Fortnightly	Tehran
Women's Universe	Safavi	1920	Bimonthly	Tehran
Women's World	Parsa	1921	Fortnightly	Mashhad / Tehran
Patriotic Women of Iran	Eskandari	1923	Irregular	Tehran
Women of the East	Zarabi	1925	Fortnightly	Bandar Pahlavi

Source: Omid Massoudi, 'A glance at the early experience of Iranian women journalists', *Rasaneh*, 9/1 (1998), p 58.

These publications played a major role in bringing previously 'private' matters into the public domain and informing Iranian women about the literature, history, culture and politics of Iran as well as Europe and the rest of the world. Many titles benefited from male support, as their editors and contributors were usually wives, daughters or sisters of political notables of the time. In some respects these publications were like a family business. However, after the Qajar Dynasty collapsed and was replaced by the Pahlavi regime in 1921, there was a downturn in the liveliness of print culture in general and the women's press in particular. For more than a decade only two main women's titles appeared: *Namh-e Banovan*, already mentioned, and *Dokhtaran-e Iran* (Daughters of Iran).[7]

The 1940s brought a new wave of optimism and renewed interest in journalism as the three major forces in contemporary Iran (religious, nationalist and socialist) all established a strong presence in publishing. What has been called 'the second wave women's press'[8] lasted from 1941 until 1953, during which time Mohammed Mosadeq led a popular movement for oil nationalization that sent the British packing and led to the Shah's deposition, only to see him reinstated with CIA help. Some 373 publications, 70 of which were opposed to Mosadeq, were published during the oil nationalization movement,[9] including many women's titles. Among these were *Alam-e Zanan* (Universe of Women), a monthly magazine published by the Office of Publishing and Publicity of the British Embassy in Tehran as part of its modernization mission; and *Rastakhiz-e Iran* (Resurrection of Iran) a family-run daily published in Tehran that initially devoted three of its twelve pages to women's issues but later reduced its size and also its coverage of women.

Left-wing organizations attracted massive support and sympathy during this period by calling for justice, equality and freedom in a society ravaged by centuries of despotic rule and poverty. A monthly, edited by Zahra Eskandari and affiliated to the Women's Organization of the Tudeh Party (official communist party of Iran), appeared under the title *Bidari-e Ma* (Our Awakening) and the slogan: 'We also have some rights in this house'. It hit the newsstands in the summer of 1945 but survived only a few months. *Jahan-e Zanan* developed into a weekly publication and also became an official organ of the Tudeh Women's Organization. Now edited by Najm el-Hajiah Hoshmand, a woman activist, it was published until the 1953 coup and reappeared after the 1979 revolution. Other titles included the weekly *Zan-e Emrouz* (Woman of Today); a monthly magazine entitled *Banu* (Lady); *Neday-e Zan* (Woman's Proclamation); *Nezhat* (Purity); *Hoghugh-e Zanan* (Women's Rights) and *Jahan-e Taban* (Shining World). In 1952 alone, before the CIA-led coup, the number of women involved in the press exceeded the number of women who were active in this field in the first eleven years of the Islamic Republic.[10]

With the Shah reinstated and Mosadeq's government overthrown, many political parties were banned, as well as their organs and numerous other publications. It would take another revolution to bring back those glorious days of a free press, in which the women's press also flourished. From the mid-1950s until 1979 only a handful of publications were allowed in the market. Although women continued to work as journalists, editors, managing directors, photographers and so on, most were either employed in specialist/scientific publications affiliated to ministries, or by official women's groups linked to the ruling elite. Specialist publications had a low circulation and targeted a niche readership. The official organs of the ruling groups, despite carrying some useful material, were the mouthpieces of the regime and commanded little respect.

In time, two big publishing houses, Keyhan and Ettela'at came to dominate the market, rivalling each other in fields such as youth, sports and children. For both firms, women's magazines were important. *Ettela'at-e Banovan* (Ladies' Ettela'at) was first published in 1957, its pages full of gossip, celebrity and royal family news, cookery, health, beauty and housekeeping. This weekly magazine continued until 1979, ceased publication until 1981 and was then relaunched under the editorship of Zahra Rahnavard, a prominent post-1979 figure and wife of Mir-Hossein Mousavi, prime minister during 1981–8.[11] The other big publisher, Keyhan, launched its first women's title in 1964. This was the colour weekly *Zan-e Rouz* (Today's Woman), managed by Fourough, the wife of its licence holder Moustafa Mesbah-Zadeh, but with a male editor. It soon overtook *Ettela'at-e Banovan* to become the most popular magazine in Iran. More than half-full of advertisements and pictures, it avoided politics, concentrating instead on food, family and fashion, as well as beauty contests in Iran and around the world. Its news pages reflected the policies of the Pahlavi regime, being devoted to the royal family and foreign visitors, especially famous women visiting Iran; occasionally there was also a serious article on changes in family law.[12]

As left-wing groups became more active in Iran in the early 1970s, the regime tried to discredit Marxism and to neutralize religious groups by portraying itself as Islamic. In the same vein, *Zan-e Rouz* reported on the Shah and his family visiting holy cities, and on 'Islamic' fashions that could take the place of the chadoor (long veil). In the heat of the 1979 revolution the magazine turned against the Pahlavi regime and denounced all role models that had been promoted in the previous years as inauthentic, corrupt and commercial. Only 23 issues of *Zan-e Rouz* were published in the period immediately after the revolution. It ceased publication in 1979 and a fully Islamicized version reappeared in the summer of 1980.

Women and public life under the Islamic Republic

The absence of rights for women in many Muslim countries is usually taken as evidence that Islam is incompatible with modernity. Muslim women have often been stereotyped in the West as veiled, faceless and subordinate. It is indisputable that Islamic sharia puts men in a superior position to women. However, since patriarchy is not particular to Islam, it cannot serve as evidence of 'Islamic exceptionalism'. Islam is no different from other major religious traditions that take for granted the superiority of men over women and protect the institutions of patriarchy; indeed, the similarities between the holy texts are greater than the differences.

Nor is the idea of gender equality (often regarded as an inherent aspect of 'European values') an inherent truth divorced from space and time. The demand for gender equality can only be born with women's social awakening, which is itself a result of changes in social and material conditions. It is precisely for this reason that Islam per se and other traditional religions cannot promote this idea. Yet, if women (and men) have managed to crack the walls of patriarchy in western societies, why can they not do so in Islamic societies? This is the question that has been the subject of intense debate in Iran for a number of years, most recently within the women's press. Indeed, under pressure from the spreading women's movement, Ayatollah Khamenei, the arch-conservative leader of the Islamic Republic, was forced to say that Islam rejects any differences between men and women in their 'development of the spirit and intellect, and also in the field of social activity'.[13]

For many years, the issues of women's rights and their roles in public life have been debated in Iran in such a context. It is interesting that both secular and Muslim activists inside and outside the country have put Islam at the centre of the debate, regarding it as the main, if not the sole, reason for the condition of women's lives in Islamic countries. Secular feminists protesting at the lack of women's rights, apologists defending cultural relativism, and advocates of essential cultural differences between women's status in Iran and other countries: all have deployed explanations based on ideology.[14] Such approaches, especially those focusing on the exclusionary nature of the patriarchal policies of the Islamic Republic, overlook the possibilities of resistance. More importantly, they isolate ideology from social and economic developments. Yet one of the important characteristics of any ideology is elasticity. Faced with the hard realities of lived experience, ideologies stretch to fit the social conditions. The totalitarian programme for Islamicization of all aspects of public and private life in Iran is a good example.

The Islamic Republic's Constitution does not recognize the equality of both sexes; indeed it denies women equal rights. The Constitution itself was part of an overall policy of excluding women from public life. In the first few years of the Islamic Republic many rights women had gained under the Pahlavis were withdrawn. Measures to bring back a glorious tradition of what was perceived to be 'true' Islam included segregation of the sexes in public spaces; compulsory hejab (veil); excluding women from some professions and directing them to work as teachers, nurses and secretaries; barring them from work as judges; and reinforcing patriarchal practices with regard to divorce, custody of children, and lowering the age of marriage for girls. Women were to be accorded high respect, but only as mothers, daughters and wives. The future of the next generation as well as the future of the Islamic government was in their hands, and therefore women could not, under any circumstances, put a foot wrong. Women's rights, as well as other aspects of human rights, were overtly violated in the name of indigenous culture, self-reliance, individual emancipation and an end to all forms of domination of one human being or country over another. As one activist has argued, cultural invasion is often seen from a patriarchal point of view as a danger only to women.[15] This mirrors feminist theorizing that suggests that the nation is often discursively gendered female. In the process women are used as symbolic markers of cultural purity and national honour, so that policing women is seen as protecting the nation.[16]

However, trying to amalgamate 'Sharia with electricity'[17] was hazardous enough; implementing the contradictory gender polices of the

Islamic Republic was even more demanding. Iranian women's brave resistance and struggle proved to be an obstacle to theocratic rule. Yet women's agency is usually neglected when the ideological foundations of the Islamic Republic's repressive rules are analysed. Asghar Schirazi has noted three problems facing the theocrats. First, the Islamists themselves had to encourage women to take up the professions thought to be suitable for females. Secondly, the measures provoked persistent opposition from modern women who, at great risk to themselves, refused to conform to the moral precepts of the conservative Islamists. For example, while not daring to appear completely unveiled in public, they wear the scarf in such a way that their protest is obvious. But the third problem was also the greatest. This consists of

> … the contradictory effect that has come from the hierocracy's politicisation of women who otherwise held traditional attitudes. In contrast to the conservative quietist clergy who condemn the very appearance of women in public, the ruling Islamists quickly realised during the revolution that they could exploit for their own political ends the social importance of traditionalist women. But this presupposed that such women were snatched from their narrow social role and brought into the politically active social environment. Their inclusion in demonstrations, their active support in times of war, their mobilisation as the guardians of morality, their votes in elections, are regularly used by the regime to achieve its goals.[18]

It was women's mobilization and active participation in the revolutionary period that forced Iran's revolutionary leader, Ayatollah Khomeini, to change his stance on women's roles in public life. There had been a major confrontation between Khomeini and the Shah when the latter granted voting rights to Iranian women in 1963. Even though the right to vote counts for little under dictatorships, Khomeini objected in principle to a woman's right to be elected or to elect. In a telegram, he accused the Shah of total disregard for Islam and the ulema (religious scholars). Khomeini was exiled soon after. On his triumphant return to Iran and in contrast to his earlier stance, he declared that 'women have the right to intervene in politics. It is their duty … Islam is a political religion. In Islam, everything, even prayer, is political.'[19] Thus the revolutionary rhetoric and the Islamists' need to expand their support base had actually paved the way for traditional women to take part in politics. The politicization of these women and their increased role in public life changed their horizons.

Women's access to education, political institutions and public domains that had been generally closed to them had a big influence in making them aware of the contradictions and the existing legal and moral limits to women's wider participation. It was hard for the regime to persuade women who had been active in demonstrations and the 1980–8 war with Iraq to go back to their traditional roles and lives. The politicization of traditional women raised their expectations – of themselves, their families and of the republic which they helped to build and consolidate. So the force that was originally mobilized to undermine the secular, middle-class women's movement in Iran became important in its own right in exposing the limits of sharia in modern Iran. After the crushing defeat of the secular opposition in the immediate post-revolutionary period, the women's movement remained the only viable alternative, regaining new momentum after the end of the war with Iraq. Major changes in education and employment facilitated the increased participation of Iranian women in the public sphere. These changes show that women's status in Iran cannot be explained simply in terms of ideology, in particular Islam.

Between 1956 and 1996 female literacy in Iran rose from 7.3 per cent to 74.2 per cent, an important long-term development that has had a deep impact on political and social life. A parallel pattern can be observed in higher education. In the 1995–6 academic year over 38 per cent of the student population were women. The number of female graduates from Iranian universities increased from 3,051 in 1969–70 to 47,323 in 1995–6. If we add to these over 200,000 female students who graduate from high school it becomes clear that the government needs to create 250,000 new jobs for women every year.[20] The growing demands for a free press and for a diverse range of cultural products are partly a result of a wider social transformation and rise in educational standards, especially for women.

This transformation has happened despite an early, and in some respects still continuing, attempt to impose gender segregation in education. Just four months after the collapse of the Pahlavi dynasty in February 1979, the new ministry of education banned co-education and declared many university courses to be unsuitable for women. In 1980, when conflict between the student movements and secular opposition and the Islamic Republic first reached boiling point, all higher education institutions were closed in what was dubbed the 'Cultural Revolution'. The staging of Friday prayers at Tehran University and attempts to

Islamicize the universities were important parts of a general plan to rid Iran of all modern, secular and 'inauthentic' culture. After the universities were reopened in 1984, women were excluded from many science courses and a year later the Majlis (parliament) passed a law banning single women from studying abroad in order to safeguard them from the allegedly corrupting influence of western values. Apparently the same danger did not apply to men. Nevertheless, women took up all possible opportunities and often surpassed their male counterparts. Inauguration of the all-women Al-Zahra University and the private Azad (Free) University opened up new opportunities. The Majlis finally lifted the ban on single women studying abroad in September 2000 after more than a decade of bitter struggle. It had previously twice rejected the bill.

Employment has been another crucial site of struggle and change. In 1976, women accounted for less than 14 per cent of the total number of employees. This figure dropped dramatically after the revolution when many women were forced out of jobs. The Islamic Republic Constitution clearly stated that women should be freed from 'multifaceted foreign exploitation' and that they would 'regain their true identity and human rights' within the family as the fundamental unit of society. All female judges were sacked. Many nurseries in factories were closed. Provisions of the 1967 Family Law on polygamy, divorce and custody of children were reversed and men were authorized to prohibit their wives and daughters from paid employment.[21]

The regime's sexual apartheid policy met with resistance. The policy maintained that female students, patients and children should be attended by female teachers, doctors and carers. As war with Iraq aggravated the country's economic crisis, many households were unable to survive on one income and women needed to work. The rising death toll in the war increased the number of female heads of household. For all these reasons, the government simply had to allow women to take paid employment. Thus, despite the constitutional rhetoric of the 'Islamic economy' that aims at the 'fulfilment of the material needs of man', Iran remained part of world capitalism, ultimately even perpetuating the modernization policies of the Shah. The reconstruction phase that followed the end of the war with Iraq signalled further liberalization. Policies on structural adjustment and privatization arrived together with World Bank loans in 1991 and 1994, and so too did further changes in family law. Contraception and abortion, previously denounced as un-Islamic, were

During the revolutionary upheaval of 1979 a large number of women's groups sprang up all over the country. Women who took part in demonstrations and helped to bring down the Shah gathered together in organizations with nationalist, Islamist and leftist tendencies. The biggest Islamic organization to emerge in this period, the Women's Society of the Islamic Revolution, gradually took over the Women's Organization of Iran, which had been established in the 1960s and was led by the Shah's sister. The new organization did not last long since the government refused to provide a budget, but many of its well-known members set up other bodies. As noted earlier, Zahra Rahnavard took over as editor of *Ettela'at-e Banovan* and changed its title to *Rah-ye Zaynab* (Zaynab's Path). She played a role in Islamicizing the whole Ettela'at publishing house during this period.[26] Azam Taleghani, a political prisoner under the Shah and daughter of Ayatollah Taleghani, a respected cleric, set up the Islamic Institute of Women and launched the monthly *Payam-e Hajar* (Hagar's Message). She was among the first Islamist women to call for a radical reinterpretation of Islamic law. A central concept among Islamic movements in Iran is *ijtihad*, signifying independent reasoning about, or interpretation of, religious texts. More prominent in Shia than Sunni Islam, *ijtihad* has been used effectively by reformists in Iran to push forward arguments for modern readings of Islamic principles that are more appropriate in the contemporary world. The battle between different factions in Iran since 1979 and especially after 1997 has revolved around this concept and its conflict with the concept of *taqlid* (emulation).

Meanwhile, some of the biggest women's organizations were part of the secular opposition. The first women's demonstration took place on 8 March 1979, International Women's Day, triggered by Khomeini's revisions of family law and imposition of hejab. The demonstrators chanted: '*Dar tolu-e azadi, ja-ye azadi khali*' ('At the dawn of freedom, the place of freedom lies empty'). The National Union of Women was then established and produced its own organ, *Barabari* (Equality), a bi-weekly publication that was replaced after just three weeks by a monthly magazine, *Zan dar Mobarezeh* (Women in Struggle). It was affiliated to the biggest left-wing organization of the time, Sazeman-e Fadayan-e Khalgh (Fedayyin). Most of the existing left-wing organizations spawned their own women's section and paper. *Sepideh Sorkh* (Red Dawn) was the organ of the women's section of the Maoist Communist Party of Workers and Peasants; *Bidari-e Zan* (Woman's Awakening) was the organ of another pro-China organization; *Rahaie-e Zan* (Emancipation of Woman) was the product of yet another communist organization and the women's organization of the Union of Iranian Communists produced *Zanan-e Mobarez* (Militant Women).

The period following the outbreak of war with Iraq in September 1980 was different from the immediate aftermath of the revolution in that it was marked by the clear absence of any independent women's movement and by the passage of major anti-women legislation. After consensus within the broad anti-Shah alliance collapsed and the Islamist nationalist groups became more isolated, the state came to rely more on grassroots support, including that of women. Their support, however, was not rewarded. This period saw a massive campaign to raise the profile of women as mothers and wives, a campaign in which state-sponsored television and cinema played crucial roles.[27] The few women parliamentarians shared the same view as their male counterparts; since all were associated with their well-known husbands or fathers, they were part of the established elite and the occasional cry about raising 'women's issues' was not met with enthusiasm. All but one had only elementary and religious education. Table 2.2 indicates that there was a sharp decrease in both the number of women candidates and those elected at the time; however, both these indices have since improved.

Table 2.2

Female parliamentarians in Iran since 1979

	1st Majlis 1979–83	2nd Majlis 1983–7	3rd Majlis 1987–91	4th Majlis 1991–6	5th Majlis 1996–2000	6th Majlis 2000–4
Total candidates	3694	1592	1999	3223	5366	6853
Men	3628	1564	1962	3152	5046	6340
Women	66	28	37	81	320	513
Women as % of total candidates	1.79	1.76	1.85	2.51	5.96	7.49
Elected men	95	118	176	133	131	262
Elected women	4	4	3	9	14	12
Women as % of total elected	4.04	3.28	1.68	6.34	10.53	4.38

Source: Compiled from www.iranwomen.org/zanan/charts/politics/majlis.

The end of the bloody war with Iraq and Khomeini's death in 1989 marked the beginning of a new phase, the Second Republic. The gender debate, which had already resurfaced and contributed to a relaxation of restrictions on the subjects that women could study at university, now became prominent. Family planning became official policy in 1988. The divorce law was amended and women judges were allowed back in court, although only in advisory capacities, in 1992. In 1988 the state established the Social and Cultural Council of Women to encourage further participation of women in the social and economic spheres; the Council soon began to produce its own quarterly publication *Faslnameh*. The Office of Women's Affairs, part of the new-look presidential office, was also created.

Segregation remained a contentious issue as did the compulsory hejab. In the new wave of Islamic reformism, calls for a more radical rethinking and re-reading of Islam were published in newly established cultural and political journals. Gender was now a hotly contested area. Of the 81 women who stood for election to the Fourth Majlis in 1991, nine were elected. The corresponding figures increased to 320 and 14 in the 1996 election. The 2000 election signalled a marginal decline on both counts, but this had more to do with the further polarization of the reformist movement than with gender issues. Changes among women MPs during the 1990s included a lowering in the average age of women elected and an increase in the number with formal education and university degrees. They included a surgeon, a gynaecologist, and women trained in French literature, planning, Islamic philosophy, health and engineering.[28] In 1992, for the first time, women were elected from outside the capital city. In the 1999 local council elections, 1,120 women were elected. The combined effect was to force the government to pay more attention to the issues raised by women activists. After the landslide victory of Mohammed Khatami as president in 1997, many ministries took on women advisors. Khatami himself chose Massoumeh Ebtekar, the editor of *Farzaneh* (Wise), as the vice-president in charge of environmental affairs. His culture minister at the time, Mohajerani, selected Azam Nouri as deputy minister. The interior minister Abdollah Nouri, another well-known reformist and editor of the now defunct *Khordad*, appointed Zahra Shojai, a professor at Al-Zahra women's university, as director-general of women's affairs.[29] The fact that gender had been forced onto the policy agenda was attributable in large part to sections of the women's press.

The women's press and Islamic feminism

Nowhere is the exposure of religion to modernity so evident and publicized as in the press. Changes in the political process under the Islamic Republic and debates about home-grown solutions to gender issues have often been linked to the women's press in Iran. They are part of a wider movement for a modernist reading of Islam that surfaced immediately after the end of the 1980–8 war and Khomeini's death. Many accounts of the gender debate in Iran since this period have been more or less studies of the women's press.[30] One of the central debates, and also one of the most contentious, is whether Islam is compatible with feminism and whether the gender consciousness movement and campaigns for changes in the law can be regarded as feminist. Ziba Mir-Hosseini clearly thinks it can,[31] whereas Shahrzad Mojab and Haideh Moghissi find the term 'Islamic feminism' misleading and inaccurate and criticize those who use it for falling into the trap of cultural relativism and backing away from feminist ideals.[32] Valentine Moghadam criticizes Islamic reformists who insist that changes will only arrive through the 'modernization' of Islam and thus seek a 'religious' solution. At the same time, however, she takes issue with the secular feminists, particularly Moghissi, for offering a narrow definition of feminism. Moghadam argues:

> Feminism is a theoretical perspective and a practice that criticizes social and gender inequalities, aims at women's empowerment, and seeks to transform knowledge – and in some interpretations, to transform socio-economic structures, political power, and international relations. Women, and not religion, should be the centre of that theory and practice. It is not possible to defend as feminist the view that women can attain equal status only in the context of Islam. This is a fundamentalist view, not one compatible with feminism. And yet, around the world there will be different strategies that women will pursue toward empowerment and transformation. We are still grappling with understanding and theorizing those diverse political strategies.[33]

Most of those identified as 'Islamic feminists' are publishers, editors, journalists, university professors and activists. It is interesting, as Moghadam suggests, that the term was coined outside the country by those who have lived in exile. Many activists inside Iran to whom the label attaches have hesitated and sometimes, as in the case of Shahlal Sherkat, refused to call themselves feminist. Those who have followed such debates have done so by analysing arguments developed within the pages of the women's press.[34] Among the most celebrated examples of the new women's press are *Zanan* (Women) and *Farzaneh*. Of these, *Zanan* has been by far the most influential in recent years.

Zanan, first published in January–February 1992, has been regarded as the twin sister of its more influential and now defunct brother, *Kian*.[35] The main cadres of these two monthly publications embarked on their 'modernist Islamist' project in the 1980s while working on two magazines published by Keyhan. Shahla Sherkat, who became *Zanan*'s first editor, edited *Zan-e Rouz* in the 1980s; those who later published *Kian* used to run *Keyhan-e Farhangi* (Cultural Keyhan). Many early ideas and polemics of the modernist Islamists first appeared in these two Keyhan papers at the time when Khatami, who later became president, was managing director of Keyhan.[36] The papers published early articles by influential thinkers such as the religious intellectual Abdolkarim Soroush – who has been called the Luther of Islam – as well as conservative responses. If *Keyhan-e Farhangi* could not publish a certain article, *Zan-e Rouz* took it, and vice versa. These intellectuals, activists and journalists were among the early circle of the reformist grouping in Iran.[37]

As managing director of *Zan-e Rouz*, Shahla Sherkat rapidly transformed it. Cookery and needlework pages were replaced with hard-hitting analysis and commentary about physical punishment in schools, the problems of widows, women's domestic and unpaid work, women's employment and participation in public life and critical analysis of the portrayal of women in state-controlled television programmes. After a critical review of the renowned film-maker Mohsen Makhmalbaf appeared in *Keyhan-e Farhangi*, written by its managing director under a pseudonym, Sherkat published a rebuttal by Makhmalbaf. This provoked a showdown with Keyhan, which gave Sherkat three options: accept supervision over the content of her magazine; create an editorial board; or abolish the role of managing director. Sherkat refused all three, correctly seeing them as a ploy to 'cleanse' (*paksazi*) the staff of Keyhan.[38] Many people involved in these and other publications were sacked or left. *Keyhan-e Farhangi* stopped publishing for a year and a half, and *Zan-e Rouz* continued under a new editor.

Zanan was born in early 1992. Its first editorial stated that the magazine had a clear mission to debate gender-related issues in four areas: religion, culture, law and education. *Zanan* was to achieve financial stability by targeting a wide readership and thereby subsidize its more intellectual companion title, *Kian*. With a circulation of nearly 120,000 of mostly urban, educated readers,[39] *Zanan* became the most popular women's publication in Iran. It has tried to offer alternative readings of the Qur'an and sharia in the current context. Contested areas have ranged across the issue of equality between men and women in Islam, family law, political participation, individual freedom, employment and civil law.[40] Men wrote many of the articles in the early stages, but what is most celebrated is the way in which *Zanan* paved the way and opened up a space for contributions by secular writers. Two of its best-known contributors were Mehrangiz Kar, a legal attorney, and Shirin Ebadi, a jurist. In *Zanan* these writers managed to explain legal issues to a wider readership, and *inter alia* exposed the patriarchal nature of the existing laws on education, marriage, divorce, custody of children and employment. They thus paved the way for more informed challenges to the ruling conservatives.

Cooperation between secularists and modernizing Islamic feminists was put in doubt, however, by the now infamous Berlin conference in April 2000.[41] Mehrangiz Kar and the publisher Shahla Lahiji attacked the repressive policies of the Islamic Republic in their speeches and were arrested on returning to Tehran. This provoked a conservative backlash, aired and supported by Iranian television and some conservative titles including *Keyhan*, and ended the collaboration between secular and Muslim activists that had seemed so successful and creative. Sherkat, the editor of *Zanan,* was among the participants in Berlin but avoided arrest and made no effort to support the cause of Kar and Lahiji. In an interview with the Iranian feminist online magazine, *Badjens* (Disreputable), Kar said:

> We always sensed there was a gap. It simply became very clear after Berlin that the reformists would never take any risks for us, pay any price for us, or defend us. They used us. Especially after our imprisonment, we felt this with our body and our soul.[42]

The publication of Lily Farhadpour's book on women's experiences in Berlin, *Zanan-e Berlin*, has been regarded as an important step towards renewing that partnership.[43] But it seems unlikely that *Zanan* will again provide a platform for critical engagement of these diverse views of Iranian women activists. A desire to remain on news-stands at a time when a large number of publications have been banned has proved to be the determining factor for Sherkat. Asked in an interview in 2001 why the magazine has survived for ten years, she said:

> One reason is that *Zanan* is a women's magazine and is not a political magazine. The magazines and newspapers that were closed down may have had a strong political side, and in dealing with political issues of the day they ended up with problems. I prefer for *Zanan* magazine to remain a trade and women's magazine that can solve women's problems that are not necessarily political.[44]

The trouble with this argument is that there are almost no women's problems that are not explicitly political in Iran. In a country where even holding your partner's hand in public is regarded as un-Islamic and by definition anti-state, nothing is ever outside of politics. This represents a major retreat from the original mission statements of *Zanan*, announced more than a decade ago.

Another celebrated women's title, *Farzaneh*, began publishing in the autumn of 1993 as a bi-annual journal. The licence holder was Massoumeh Ebtakar and its editor-in-chief Mahbobeh Abbas-Gholizadeh, both members of the Women Studies Centre in Tehran, which was headed by another influential woman, Monir Gorji. Abbas-Gholizadeh had previously been a member of the editorial board of *Zan-e Rouz*, and later *Keyhan*. She was famous, at least among secular Iranian feminists outside Iran, for writing a series of five articles for *Zan-e Rouz* in which she examined the impact of feminism and the possibility of Islamic feminism. With an educational background in religious philosophy, she triggered some of the early debates about Islam and gender. As Ardalan reports,[45] in order to attract the attention of traditional thinkers, the content and the tone of her articles were openly critical of feminism but still far removed from the official stance that saw feminism as a disease and a corrupting western influence. *Farzaneh*'s editorial board was quickly invited by the president's advisor on women's affairs to help in future planning. They clearly saw themselves, as revealed by Ardalan's analysis, more as *karshenas* (experts) than as feminists or even activists. *Farzaneh* was never a campaigning journal, but a platform from which to engage in theoretical/theological debate and a bridge between policy-makers and experts/intellectuals, as well as between traditional thinkers and modernists. Published in both Persian and English, the journal clearly wanted to appeal to 'experts' both inside and outside Iran.

The first ever daily paper devoted to women, *Zan* (Woman), was launched in August 1998 by Faezeh Hashemi, daughter of the previous president, Ali Akbar Hashemi Rafsanjani, and a member of parliament in her own right. In its short life, *Zan* managed to create considerable controversy by raising some key issues at the height of conflict between different factions of the ruling elite. Hashemi's high profile allowed the paper to challenge the conservatives on a number of fronts. It campaigned for women to stand as candidates for the Majlis Khebreghan (Assembly of Experts) and resulted in ten women putting forward their names as candidates, all of whom were rejected. From early on *Zan* attracted the wrath of the conservative faction. It was banned for two weeks in January 1999 for 'assaulting' security forces and was fined 250,000 tomans. The actual charge, as Shadi Sadr has explained,[46] was unlawful since the article of the Penal Code that was used by the judge to condemn *Zan* only applies to 'real persons' and not general categories such as 'security forces'. *Zan* was finally ordered to cease publication on 3 April 1999 for publishing an interview with Farah Diba, the widow of the Shah (although this had already been reprinted by conservative dailies and gone 'un-noticed'), as well as for publishing a satirical cartoon criticizing the *ghesas* (retribution) law. According to the 'eye for an eye' policy of *ghesas* law, the blood money for a murdered woman is only half that for a man. The cartoon showed a gunman pointing at a couple and the man shouting 'Kill her, she is cheaper!'.

In a matter of months, *Zan* had developed a circulation of 40,000. Hashemi also helped to create women's committees in a number of cities to organize women activists better and to create sustained pressures on local government. But in the 2000 parliamentary election, despite having had the second highest number of votes in Tehran in the previous election, she lost her seat. Her association with her father who had become, more than ever, a hate figure even among Islamists, cost her dearly.

The groups and publications labelled 'Islamic feminist' are not exactly the same, do not share the same ideas and certainly do not have the same approach; the three different types that Ahmadi-Khorasani usefully analyses are distinguished mainly by their involvement with the state apparatus.[47] The first are independent writers such as Shirin Ebadi who have no links with any factions of the ruling elite. The second group have tight-knit links with the political elite; they know only too well that repression of societal needs is impossible and certainly do not want to disregard international pressure. *Zan* clearly belonged to this group and focused on issues of central concern to the international community such as stoning, human rights abuses and elections. The third type is not independent, but no longer has the same level of access to the centre of power as the second type. Thus *Zanan* has focused more on the urgent needs of Iranian women and has been instrumental in gathering women's support for the reformists and forcing some legislative reform. In other words, despite some clear openings, establishing an independent publication is still extremely difficult, especially for women. Even so, the most prominent publications do not reflect the current diversity in the women's press.

The conservatives' response to such publications also needs greater attention. The mainstream conservative press not only maintained attacks on the reformist press, but also established three women's publications to challenge the modernist interpretation of Islam. *Payam-e Zan* (Woman's Message), a monthly, is the attempt of the Qum religious seminary to engage more systematically with the gender-conscious movements of recent years. Unlike other titles, it is run, managed and edited by men, although occasionally the 'Sisters Section' of the Office of Islamic Propaganda is credited with assisting the editorial board.[48] The aims of this publication include increasing Iranian women's awareness of what the publishers regard as 'Islamic knowledge'. It seeks to consolidate family relationships and introduce authentic Islamic female role models. *Payam-e Zan* strongly opposes any kind of feminism and regularly publishes articles on women's place in the Qur'an and Islam, women from the point of view of religious thinkers (conservatives), women in families, and the importance of hejab.

Neda (Proclamation), first published in the spring of 1990, is a quarterly journal firmly in the conservative camp as the organ of the Women's Society of the Islamic Republic of Iran. Its licence holder is Zahra Mustafavi, the daughter of Ayatollah Khomeini, and its current editor is Fereshteh Arabi, his granddaughter. Indeed, much space in the early issues was devoted to the life of Khomeini as leader of the Islamic Revolution.[49] *Neda* is not specifically a women's journal, although since 1997 an increasing number of articles have dealt with women's issues. It supported Khatami in the 1997 presidential election and is certainly in favour of debating gender issues, but is broadly critical of the idea of equality between men and women. Perhaps because of its association with Khomeini, *Neda* has tried to remain uncontroversial and follow to the letter the rules of the Islamic Republic.

Another publication that is not often recognized by commentators is *Faslnameh* (Quarterly), a quarterly journal published by the Women's Socio-Cultural Council (WSCC). WSCC began its activities in June 1988 with two main objectives: to create a database on women and to contribute to the study of women's socio-cultural status in Iran. The organ of the Council was launched in 1998 and its website[50] has a large collection of data. Managed by Mehri Sueezi and edited by Akram Hosseini, WSCC's journal is not distributed widely and not well recognized. *Faslnameh* is anti-feminist and blames the 'translation movement' (translation of western books into Persian) for introducing and spreading feminism. It condemns even 'Islamic feminism' as foreign and a ploy to find a way to realize feminist ideas and goals in Iran. Identifying the enemies of Islam, criticizing their views and neutralizing their impact were listed among the major duties of this publication.[51] In 2001, however, the journal changed its name to *Ketab-e Zanan* (Women's Book), jumped on the bandwagon and turned its attention to women's demands in Iran and towards improving women's condition in society. In this way, 13 years after its formation, WSCC finally began to turn its attention to women.

Some minor secular titles should also be mentioned. The most famous and influential was *Jens-e Dovom* (Second Sex). By far the most informed and radical of women's press in Iran, it was launched in 1998 and edited by Noushin Ahmadi-Khorasani. Director of the publishing house Nashr-e Towseh, she managed to assemble a wide range of articles by Iranian feminists, including those in exile. The journal carried special reports from the Fourth World Conference on Women in Beijing in 1995 and extensive coverage of the Berlin conference of 2000. The latter issue paid special attention to Lahiji and Kar, who were neglected by *Zanan*. It reported regularly on women workers, women writers, representation of women in Iranian literature and poetry, and domestic violence, along with regional and international updates and analysis of the experience of Iranian families outside Iran. *Jens-e Dovom* was forced by the authorities to cease publication in 2001[52] but Ahmadi-Khorasani launched a new quarterly journal, *Fasl-e Zanan* (Women's Season) in May 2002.

Women, media and journalism in Iran

Clearly, all of this press activity depends on significant numbers of publishers, journalists and other media professionals, but this entire sector experiences considerable pressure. Noushin Ahmadi-Khorasani and Shahla Lahiji are among the most prolific and active women publishers in Iran. Lahiji founded the publishing house Roshangaran (The Enlighteners) in 1984, which has since published over 200 books. According to Maryam Poya there are 47 women publishers in Iran.[53] However, in an interview with *Badjens*, Lahiji herself put the number at over 400, more than half of whom are currently active and self-supporting.[54] These publishers have played a major role in introducing Iranian women to a range of ideas, issues and analysis and have been massively influential in rewriting women into Iranian history.[55]

Table 2.3

Women media proprietors and editors in Iran in 2000

Licence holders		Managing editors		Editors	
Total	Women	Total	Women	Total	Women
1512	65	1512	97	1517	50

Source: Ministry of Culture and Guidance, available from www.iranwomen.org.

A glance at the number of women journalists also indicates significant improvement. In contrast to 50 women journalists in 1972, in 1997 there were 400 women journalists working with various publications, their proportion increasing from 2.5 per cent in 1972 to 14 per cent in 25 years. They are younger than their predecessors but have a better education. Whereas the average number of working journalists with university degrees is 35 per cent, this figure rises to 50 per cent among female journalists. Nevertheless, the gains need to be put in perspective. Women publishers still face huge disadvantages and self-censorship is the rule rather than the exception. The number of women film-makers has certainly increased, but ten female directors compared with over 450 male directors is not significant. Similar problems can be seen in print journalism. Of 23 women's publications that have been allowed to publish since 1979, only nine have survived and most belong to different factions of the ruling elite.

There are few female editors or sectional editors; most female reporters are assigned to cover 'private' issues and rarely get a chance to interview high-ranking state officials. Most women journalists do their work at the base of the pyramid of the press. Many well-known reformist proprietors and editors in Iran have stated that working conditions in the media and unsocial hours prevent women journalists from attending to their 'domestic duties' properly.[56] Despite the fact that disciplines such as mass communications, humanities and social sciences are more popular among female undergraduates, and that female students in subjects such as journalism and public relations outnumber males by almost three to one, women still find it harder to secure a job. While the emergence of a number of exciting new titles in 1998 redressed the balance slightly, after their closure, many women journalists lost their jobs.

In some respects the enforced hejab in Iran may have encouraged traditional women to participate in public life and there may have been less harassment. Fascinatingly, the veil has sometimes proved an advantage for women journalists. Leili Farhadpour, recalling her experiences during the crackdown on the press in 2000, explained that, when the police arrived to seal the publications office, the women journalists could take material and documents from their offices by claiming that it was their 'personal belongings': 'In the end, the men had to leave everything there, but the women could take stuff with them. The officials couldn't touch the women, they couldn't do anything about it.'[57] This, however, hardly compensates for a lack of basic rights.

Conclusion

One certainly cannot question the gains by women in Iran or the improvement in women's condition in certain aspects of public life. What must be questioned is the idea that such changes can be understood in terms of 'Islam'. Islam is certainly an aspect of Iranian culture and has been for over 12 centuries. Yet it is only one aspect, and Islamists neither have a monopoly on Iranian culture nor are they the only influential agents in societal development. Indeed, Islamists themselves have been affected by social transformation. Contemporary Iran is also strongly influenced by nationalist sentiment as well as by a strong secular/progressive culture. The notable achievements of Iranian women under the Islamic Republic owe much more to this modern, secular tradition than to 'Islamic feminism'. As can be seen from this study of the women's press, the debate over gender and the position of women in Iran is a reflection of major dissatisfaction with the government of the Islamic Republic and opposition to its authoritarian rule. Debates over the possibility of accommodation between Islam and feminism – especially in Iran, where religion is promoted as the armoury of the state – distract attention from the economic, social and cultural conditions that have mobilized wide sections of Iranian society against a totalitarian programme to control public and private life. Islamic feminism in its different varieties is an attempt to justify 'gender sensitive' Islam as the solution. But the point is not whether Islam is more or less able than any other religion to adapt and adjust its 'codes', but the ways in which the Iranian political system gives legitimacy to an oppressive set of social relations. This is a crucial point that seems to have been neglected in debates about gender relations in Iran, and indeed within feminist debates about the relevance of 'universal values'.[58]

Equally, the difficulties facing the women's press were, at times, no different from those facing all publications at moments when the regime flexes its political muscles. In 2000 alone, over 20 publications were closed down by the regime, with journalists and editors imprisoned and even executed, driving a reorientation to the Internet as an alternative site of publication.[59] The recent history of the press in Iran, no less than in earlier periods, is of a continuing struggle to establish an open public sphere against an ailing theocracy. By questioning the 'old', the women's press has contributed to something 'new'. But this 'new' cannot be born of the current structure. What the conditions of the press, and in particular the women's press, tell us is that 'Islam' cannot be tabled as the sole signifier in gender relations or the nature of communication in the country which still remains the only one to have witnessed an 'Islamic' revolution.

3
'Till I Become a Minister': Women's Rights and Women's Journalism in pre-1952 Egypt

Sonia Dabbous

Before establishing themselves in many other fields, Egyptian women made their names as journalists and writers. The first half of the twentieth century witnessed the rise of a considerable number of publications in which women took the lead in sharing information and awareness about their rights. Most were also deeply committed to national resistance against British occupation and regarded women's emancipation and development as an integral part of national emancipation and development.

This chapter examines the evolution of women's rights and women's journalism through the journalistic activities of three women spanning a period of roughly 50 years. Malak Hifni Nassef, who wrote under the pen-name 'Bahithat el-Badiya' (Seeker in the Desert), made her contribution during a period which culminated in the demonstrations of 1919, when women and men 'poured out' onto the streets[1] to protest at the occupying power's arrest and deportation of Saad Zaghloul and other leaders of the nationalist Wafd party. Nassef herself did not see these events, having died in 1918 at the age of 32. Mounira Thabet, a Wafd supporter known as the 'young rebel', was shocked that Egypt's first elected parliament in 1924 was a men-only affair. She launched a weekly in 1925 as part of a campaign for women's political rights that she later recounted in her memoirs, published in 1945. In 1945 Doreya Shafiq, a militant advocate of equality for women, started her famous journal *Bint el-Nil* (Daughter of the Nile). When the Free Officers ousted the monarchy in 1952 and began work in 1954 on a new constitution that still failed to incorporate women's political participation, Shafiq led a hunger strike in which Mounira Thabet also took part. Shafiq's challenge to Gamal Abdel-Nasser, Egypt's president from 1954, ended in her house arrest in 1957. In 1976 she committed suicide.

Cynthia Nelson, Shafiq's biographer,[2] has suggested that the women's movement in Egypt went through two main phases during the 40 years between the nationalist upheaval of 1919 and Nasser's clampdown on all forms of independent political action in 1959.[3] She locates the beginning of the first phase between 1919 and 1923, when Hoda Shaarawi established the Egyptian Feminist Union, and sees it lasting until the start of the Second World War, characterized throughout by a 'definite separation' between social and political issues.[4] In this analysis, the second phase begins with the end of the Second World War in 1945, by which time there had been a general radicalization of Egyptian politics, with the women's movement having undergone a similar radicalization. The present chapter, by paying attention to the writing of Mounira Thabet, sheds more light on the nature and intensity of women's political demands in the first of these phases. Although perhaps a lesser known figure than either Malak Hifni Nassef or Doreya Shafiq, Thabet was a pioneer who used her own journal and the pages of the national press rather forcefully to press for women's political rights. Her contribution as an advocate of women's right to vote and stand for political office can be assessed more clearly when it is compared to that of Nassef and other activists before 1919.

Press debates before the 1919 revolt

The last decades of the nineteenth century saw many Egyptian male and female intellectuals expressing their thoughts on the matter of women's rights and duties, using all manner of outlets, such as books, magazines, newspapers and meetings. Among the best remembered publications of the time are two books by the Egyptian journalist, lawyer and politician, Qassim Amin, who published *Tahrir al-Mar'a* (Women's Emancipation) in 1899 and *Al-Mar'a al-Jadida* (The New Woman) in 1900. Yet, as Beth Baron has shown in her study of women's writing in Egypt before 1919,[5] the debate was under way well before the turn of the century, having been influenced by many factors, including the arrival in Egypt of thinkers and writers from Syria and Lebanon, many of whom were women. Indeed, one of the earliest women to sign her articles at a time when women writers often preferred anonymity or pseudonyms, was Galila Tamarhan, a female medical practitioner who contributed articles to a medical magazine called *Yaasoub el-Tib* (Leader in Medicine) in the 1860s.

Zeinab Fawwaz, the Syrian Muslim author of a biographical dictionary published in Egypt in 1894 under the title *Scattered Pearls in the Generations of Secluded Women*,[6] contributed articles to newspapers and journals, including Egypt's first woman's magazine, *Al-Fatah* (The Young Lady).

Founded in 1892 by Hind Nawfal, who was also of Syrian origin, *Al-Fatah* was dedicated to advancing the women of Egypt along the path that European women were taking.[7] Nawfal called for women to be educated but also made it clear that politics and religion were not the magazine's concerns, as it would focus on literature, education, fashion, household management, and the like.[8] However, the women's writing of this period was not restricted to journals aimed at women. It also appeared, for example, in *Al-Muqtataf* (Selections), a newspaper started in Beirut in 1876 but relaunched in Cairo's freer intellectual climate in the 1880s. The debate conducted by this means addressed all aspects of women's rights and included both conservative and non-conservative views. Proponents of each side claimed to possess the solution for improving women's conditions and achieving a civilized and modern Egyptian society.[9] The nineteenth-century Muslim reformer Mohammed Abdu wrote about women and reform in the newspaper he edited, *Al-Waqa'ea al-Misriyya* (Egyptian Events), in the 1880s and later in the weekly *Al-Manar* (The Lighthouse). According to Leila Ahmed, Abdu was 'probably the first' to argue that Islam, not the West, first recognized the 'full and equal humanity of women'.[10] Qasim Amin, a disciple of Abdu, tried in his first book to prove that his ideas were in agreement with the correct principles of Islam, even though he is said to have been influenced by western ideas.[11] In his second book he relied more heavily on secular concepts such as 'natural rights', 'evolution of society' and 'progress'.[12]

Qasim Amin faced strong opposition from both conservative religious and some nationalist leaders. Mustafa Kamel published a series of articles in his paper *Al-Liwa'* (The Standard), which first appeared in 1900, arguing that Amin's ideas were against the principles of Islam. Yet Kamel did not reject the idea that Egyptian women should be educated.[13] For many writers, education was linked to domesticity and the teaching of duties inside the home. *Anis el-Galis* (The Companion's Companion),[14] started in 1898 by the Beirut-born Alexandra Avierino, instructed women in child-rearing and home management, with an eye on homes and fashion in Europe. This magazine lasted for ten years. In the next few years a succession of women's magazines were founded, including *Al-A'ila* (The Family),[15] *Al-Mar'a fi'l-Islam* (Women in Islam), *Shagaret el-Dur*, named after a woman who briefly ruled Egypt in the thirteenth century, and *Magallat al-Sayyidat wa'l-Banat* (Ladies' and Girls' Magazine). On the whole these were concerned with domestic duties, although some also discussed how women in the West went about their tasks inside and outside the home. *Al-Sayyidat wa'l-Banat* published articles about political conditions in other countries. *Al-Jins al-Latif* (The Gentle Sex), published by Malaka Saad in 1908, avoided any political involvement; however, its coverage of women's status seemed implicitly to suggest that it had been better in pre-Islamic times.[16]

Thus the early years of the twentieth century witnessed the rise of a large number of women's magazines. They may have numbered more than 33 according to Iglal Khalifa,[17] although many ran into financial difficulties and had to cease publication after a short time. Along with the prevalence of magazines run by non-Egyptians or members of religious minorities was a tendency to stay away from politics.[18] Nevertheless the titles and illustrations characteristic of journals that started around 1907 began to demonstrate a mounting awareness in print of Egyptian national identity and the need for improvements in women's status. A factor contributing to nationalist feeling was the Dinshwai incident of 1906, when a Special Tribunal set up by the British authorities imposed death sentences, floggings and life imprisonment on villagers who had been involved in a fracas after trying to stop British officers shooting their pigeons. Mustafa Kamel said the punishments had done more to awaken people's feelings against the occupation than another ten years of occupation could have done.[19] In 1907 Gamila Hafez launched a monthly for women called *Al-Rihana* (Sweet Basil), the front page of which bore the motto 'Egypt for the Egyptians'. In 1908 Fatima Rashid founded the magazine *Tarqiyat al-Mar'a* (Women's Progress) to support the newly formed Egyptian women's association of the same name. This association was the first of its kind.

An integration of early Egyptian feminism and Egyptian nationalism developed through the pages of *Al-Jarida* (The Journal), a newspaper launched in 1907 by the founders of the nationalist Umma Party and edited from the beginning by Ahmed Lutfi al-Sayyid. By contributing to *Al-Jarida*, Malak Hifni Nassef became perhaps the first woman to write regular articles in the Egyptian national press. Under her pen name

'Bahithat al-Badiya' she wrote about all the issues that preoccupied the women of her time, including marriage, divorce, polygamy, education and the veil. Education and polygamy were subjects of which Nassef had personal experience. She had attended one of the two teacher training schools that existed for Egyptian women and taught for a few years before marrying in 1907.[20] Upon marrying and joining her husband in Fayyum she discovered that he was already married and had a daughter whom she was expected to tutor.[21] In 1911 she compiled a ten-point programme that was delivered on her behalf to the Egyptian assembly, proposing action for improving women's situation through education, increasing jobs for women and reforming personal status laws. Her demands for an end to polygamy and reform of divorce law were totally rejected.

In some respects Nassef herself appeared quite conservative. She was opposed to unveiling, although not for religious reasons. She did not believe that the veil was imposed by religion, but nor did she believe that veiled women were more ethical than unveiled women. Her argument was that 'women were accustomed to veiling and should not be abruptly ordered to remove the veil'.[22] For Nassef, the first priority was to educate women and improve the moral character of men, rather than debate the veil, in order to achieve a well-educated and well-mannered society. In her writing she bitterly attacked polygamy, which she described as women's mortal enemy. Through the pages of *Al-Jarida*, Nassef, Qasim Amin and Ahmed Lutfi al-Sayyid discussed Egypt's social problems and the need for reform. Although her choice of subjects and points of view seemed to be influenced by Amin, Nassef was conservative on the subject of men and women mixing. She believed that women should not be exposed to the 'abuse and shamelessness' of men 'such as we have at present'. She also claimed that for the 'collection of women such as we have at present, whose understanding is that of babes, … to unveil and mix with men would be an innovation that would lead to evil'.[23] As demonstrated by her ten-point programme of reform, Nassef did not envisage women's participation in politics. Indeed, her tenth point was that it was men's duty to carry out the programme.[24] Lutfi, Amin and Nassef were all clear that Egyptian women did not demand the right to vote.

Public activism and the press, 1923–45

While it is fair to characterize press material for women, by women and about women in the pre-1919 era as being focused on issues of personal and social status, it is equally reasonable to argue that it laid the groundwork for the public political activism that followed. A new period, of what Margot Badran has called 'highly visible, organized activism', began in the early 1920s, as women's initiatives 'expand[ed] their lives into public space'.[25] The process got under way with the demonstrations of 1919, during which women as well as men were killed by British bullets.[26] With the deportation of Wafdist leaders, responsibility for nationalist activism devolved to their wives, of whom Hoda Shaarawi, a leader of the women's demonstrations, was one of the most prominent. She was elected president of the first women's political body in Egypt, the Women's Central Committee of the Wafd.[27] When Wafdist leaders failed to consult with this committee over demands for independence from Britain, women began to sense that they risked being denied a role in Egypt's liberation. In the face of martial law and press censorship,[28] they redoubled their activism against the occupation, organizing a boycott of British goods and services. These efforts were consolidated when Shaarawi founded the Egyptian Feminist Union in 1923.

A new constitution promulgated that year declared, in Article 3, that 'all Egyptians' enjoy equal civil and political rights. When this article was contradicted by an electoral law granting suffrage to men only, women remained hopeful that a future Wafdist government would end the contradiction in recognition of women's contribution to the national liberation struggle. But, when the Wafd came to power in January 1924, women found themselves barred from the new parliament and were further galvanized into articulating nationalist and feminist demands.[29] In 1925, after resigning from the Wafdist women's committee, Shaarawi concentrated her efforts on the Egyptian Feminist Union, providing the financial backing for it to publish a magazine. Called L'Egyptienne and edited by Seza Nabarawi, this was a monthly, published in French, that identified itself on the cover as being concerned with 'Feminisme, Sociologie, Art'. Yet its content was highly political from the outset, discussing party politics and national independence and setting out a list of political demands about how the country should be run. These demands included the right for women to vote in legislative elections.[30]

It has been said that Egyptian women started to be accused of importing western feminism from the moment they severed their ties with the Wafdists who had not kept their promises of partnership with women.[31] The fact that *L'Egyptienne* was published in French encouraged later commentators to suggest that Shaarawi and Nabarawi, who had ceremoniously unveiled to the applause of other women in Cairo Railway Station in 1923, were westernized. They were said to have espoused a feminism that was somehow different from that of Malak Hifni Nassef, whose feminism 'did not automatically affiliate itself with westernization'.[32] Yet French was in daily use by Egypt's political elite in that era and, as Irène Fenoglio Abdel-Aal has pointed out, was actually more a mark of social class in a national context than one of subservience to the West.[33] Moreover, *L'Egyptienne* was paralleled by Arabic-language publications through which women discussed their contributions to society and the economy. The 1920s *Magallat al-Nahda al-Nisa'iyya* (Magazine of the Women's Awakening), run by Labiba Ahmad, a devout Muslim,[34] is just one example.

Another example is Mounira Thabet's newspaper *Al-Amal* (Hope), launched in 1925 with the explicit objective of educating women and helping them win their political and social rights through new laws. A caption on the paper's front page described it as 'A newspaper that defends women's rights'. It provoked strong opposition from conservatives, including government ministers and religious figures. But Thabet realized that changes in women's personal status depended on changing laws, which in turn required women's participation in the political process. She was the first Egyptian woman to graduate from the French law school in Cairo and, according to Iglal Khalifa, the first college-educated female journalist.[35] Her politics were strongly Wafdist and her launching of both *Al-Amal* and its French sister publication *L'Espoire* was supported by Saad Zaghloul, with whom her father was associated. Both papers were founded to argue the Wafdist case after Zaghloul's government fell in 1924, less than a year after it had been elected.

Thabet had begun to write in support of women's political rights in 1924 when the first elected parliament was being formed. Noticing that no seats had been reserved for female visitors, she wrote an article entitled 'Women and Politics' that was published in *Al-Ahram*.[36] In it she asked what provision had been made to invite women to the reception planned to celebrate parliament's inauguration. She addressed the question to Saad Zaghloul. Stating that Egyptian women had fought to get the parliament established and pointing out that they had not been permitted to elect its members, Thabet suggested that they should at least attend the inauguration. As a result of her letter, women visitors were allowed into the parliament for the first time on 22 March 1924. Less than three weeks later she wrote another article in the Wafdist newspaper, *Al-Balagh* (The Information), crediting Zaghloul with this achievement. Had anyone else been in charge, she wrote, her wish for women to enter parliament 'would never have been fulfilled'.[37]

Publishing articles like this was not something Thabet did without hindrance. At one point the minister of education, acting on the government's behalf, called the principal of the French law school where she had trained to ask him to try to restrain her. In her memoirs, Thabet recorded that the principal refused, on the grounds that the school in Cairo, like its counterparts in France, regarded it as part of its mission to teach lawyers to defend people's rights. Daoud Barakat, editor of *Al-Ahram* in the early 1920s, canvassed the support of other *Al-Ahram* employees to convince Thabet that she risked a jail sentence for writing so vehemently. But we learn from Thabet's memoirs that she knew editors would not turn down controversial contributions such as hers, no matter how bad the writing style, because they attracted new readers.[38]

Having established her programme through *Al-Amal* and *L'Espoire*, Thabet presented a formal petition to the prime minister in March 1927, highlighting the contradiction between the 1923 Constitution and the electoral law in respect of women's political rights. She copied the petition to the press, recommending that the electoral law be changed to allow every Egyptian 'male and female' to vote from the age of 21. In addition to quoting the Constitution, Thabet cited verses from the Qur'an asserting women's equality with men, and recalled women rulers of history, including Shagarat al-Dur. Makram Ebeid, the secretary-general of the Wafd, wrote a letter to *Al-Amal* expressing admiration for Thabet's programme and urging her not to despair if her hopes were not achieved entirely. 'Perfection', he wrote, 'does not belong to this world'.[39] In 1928 Thabet travelled to Cologne to represent the Egyptian press at an international seminar even though *Al-Amal* had closed by this time. It did not resume publication until 1952.

Thabet and the Egyptian Feminist Union did not make common cause until 1936, the year of the Anglo-Egyptian Treaty and a time when

Arab women's organizations were becoming increasingly concerned at the situation in Palestine. Many considered Thabet's early writing over-ambitious, childish and undignified. That she maintained her outspoken approach is evident from an article in *Al-Ahram* in 1938. Under the heading 'Till I become a minister', she wrote:

> Yes, I want to be a minister and till this dream comes true, I cannot help feeling disappointed at the statement by Mohammed Mahmoud Pasha to a British correspondent, saying that, as long as he is prime minister, he will not approve of giving Egyptian women the right to vote. This statement implies that Egyptian women are incompetent. But it will not stop me from nominating myself for the position of minister, because women should be represented in the legislative and executive authorities.[40]

In 1939 Thabet joined Shaarawi and Nabarawi as representatives of Egypt at the International Women's Conference in Denmark. Shaarawi, as head of the delegation, submitted an eight-point programme to the conference recommending that women's groups should cooperate internationally, should try to find the real reasons behind wars, work to end international trade barriers and the uneven distribution of wealth, and promote respect for human rights. The programme also called for governments, not private companies, to be responsible for weapons manufacture. On returning to Egypt from a stay in Paris the same year, Thabet was invited to meet the Egyptian minister of social affairs. Even during the hiatus imposed by the Second World War, with martial law re-imposed and feminist demands put on hold, Thabet's campaigning brought results. In 1944, the Kutla party, a dissident splinter from the Wafd led by Makram Ebeid, decided to advocate political equality between the sexes as one of its principles. Zuhair Sabri introduced a bill to this effect in parliament. Addressing her own petition to the prime minister, Ahmed Maher, in 1945, Thabet said the time had come to recognize that Egyptian women had performed their duties and deserved the same political rights as men. She stressed that women were tax-payers and subject to the law and should therefore take part in formulating it. Since the Egyptian government had signed the San Francisco Declaration, guaranteeing equal political participation for all citizens, Thabet said, it should either honour the agreement by giving women full rights immediately or else withdraw its signature.

Thabet recorded her journalistic and advocacy activities in her memoirs, *Thawra fi'l-Bourg al-Aagi* (Revolution in the Ivory Tower), published in 1945. She dedicated the book to the 'revolutionary women of Egypt' and declared that she had defended women's rights as a lawyer. Musing on whether Egyptian women should emulate the British suffragettes, she wrote: 'I think we will have mercy ... and postpone this revolution to give you [men] a chance to think it over'. But, she warned, this was only a 'period of reconsideration' in which men would be reminded that they needed to share legislative and executive powers.[41]

The press and the right to vote, 1945–56

Doreya Shafiq, a leading Egyptian feminist journalist, started her journal *Bint el-Nil* in 1945. The choice of name indicated patriotism and reflected aspects of Shafiq's career up to that point. She was one of the first Egyptian women to hold a doctorate from the Sorbonne in Paris, awarded in 1940 for two theses, one of which dealt with the subject of women and religious law in contemporary Egypt.[42] Despite this qualification, she was denied a teaching post at Cairo University because the dean of the faculty where she wanted to teach decided her striking good looks would jeopardize the university's reputation.[43] In 1945 Shafiq became editor-in-chief of a literary and cultural magazine in French, founded by a former wife of Egypt's King Fouad. Called *La Femme Nouvelle*, that publication continued until the early 1950s. However, Shafiq was aware of charges that editing a foreign-language journal signified that she must be in the pay of foreign powers.[44] *Bint el-Nil*, in Arabic, answered such concerns. She subsequently marked a new stage in women's activism by forming the Bint el-Nil Union in 1948, followed by a political party named Bint el-Nil in 1951. Shafiq, from a less elevated class background than the co-founders of the Egyptian Feminist Union two decades earlier, realized, like male members of her class, that the only route to power was through party politics.[45] Nevertheless, despite differences in upbringing between herself and the Egyptian Feminist Union leader Hoda Shaarawi, Shafiq felt there was a bond between them and that she had a special mission to continue Shaarawi's work.[46]

The magazine *Bint el-Nil* was such a success and received so much feedback from readers' letters that Shafiq became acutely aware, like Malak Hifni Nassef before her, of the extent of social problems in Egypt related to marriage, divorce and the custody of children. She came to the conclusion that the only way to solve such problems was for women to enter parliament to change the laws governing these issues. Shafiq thought that laws prohibiting polygamy, except in extreme cases, and limiting the right to divorce would uphold Islamic society, restore dignity to women and enhance the image of Islam in the eyes of non-Muslims.[47] She also criticized the concept of *bayt al-taa* (the house of obedience) according to which a woman can be required to remain in the marital home. In her opinion this practice, a product of Turkish rule, transformed the husband–wife relationship from one based on equality and love as advocated by Islam, to one based on humiliation and slavery. She accused many husbands of insisting their wives return to *bayt al-taa* simply as a means of forcing them to give up the alimony they are entitled to under Islamic sharia law on divorce.[48] Shafiq, whose own mother died when Doreya was 13,[49] was also convinced that custody arrangements for the children of divorced parents were contributing to delinquency and psychological problems among children, because they were being taken from their mother's care to the home of the father and stepmother at a critical age.[50]

The Bint el-Nil Union included women from all classes. In Shafiq's words, it was created to represent the demands of all Egyptian women and not to show pity on the poor or ask for luxuries. It was founded to 'question bad conditions and to help eliminate injustice and darkness'.[51] Membership of the union increased rapidly and made newspaper headlines. In an issue in May 1948, *Al-Ethnein* (Monday) magazine published a hypothetical cabinet list of women ministers. Doreya Shafiq featured in the list as minister of public relations and propaganda, having been 'appointed' by *Al-Ethnein* because of the successful way in which she had promoted the cause of Egyptian women.[52] In 1949 the Bint el-Nil Union organized a newspaper referendum on women's rights. Many leading Egyptian political figures were involved, including Ali Maher and Lutfi al-Sayed.

The Union did not want to take political initiatives before establishing itself as a body capable of leading the women's movement. This meant directing efforts to eradicate illiteracy by opening 12 schools in which thousands of women enrolled. Classes taught not only reading and writing but health education, lessons in parenting and citizenship. Shafiq saw such activity as a direct answer to the argument that illiterates should not vote. 'I have always heard that the Egyptian woman is not educated enough to enjoy political rights', she said. 'I got fed up with that excuse and I decided to change it'.[53] Writing in *Bint el-Nil* in 1951, Shafiq set out the goal of political rights for women. In an article entitled 'Our goals and means', she said:

> We will succeed soon in convincing men that the parliament, which makes laws concerning the mother, the child, divorce, and polygamy, should have female members ... Only women are able to uncover the unjust traditions which are not compatible with the spirit of Islam ... Yes, we will soon succeed as long as these are our goals and means.[54]

What Shafiq meant by 'convincing' was soon apparent. She planned a women's sit-in of parliament, at the parliamentary session convened for 19 February 1951. She did not publicize her plan for fear of police interference, but invited all women's organizations to attend a conference at Ewart Hall at the American University in Cairo. At 4 o'clock, more than 1,000 women gathered, along with hundreds of male supporters. Nobody knew what she intended. Taking the stand, Shafiq told her audience that women are half the nation and that excluding them from the legislature, judiciary and executive would deprive the country of half its productive capacity. She ended by declaring: 'This conference is our first parliament, the parliament of half the nation, which is fortunately convened at the same time and place where the parliament of the other half is held. So, let us go to them to declare that their representation of the people is incomplete unless they are joined by our representatives'.[55] When the demonstration of 1,000 women tried to break through the doors of the parliament they were surrounded by police. Shafiq entered with two colleagues and informed the president of the upper house, Ali Zaki Orabi, that they would not leave until given the right to vote. Orabi promised that he would work to meet their demands. Press coverage of this incident was a major factor in its impact. It was reported in the local and the national press and gained much public support.

That defending women's rights went hand-in-hand with defending the nation was demonstrated in September the same year when the Bint el-Nil Union organized demonstrations against the British and took part in guerrilla warfare against British forces in the Suez Canal zone. Since many families were reluctant to allow their daughters to engage in such activity, Shafiq also mounted economic warfare in the form of boycotts of British goods. In January 1952, women picketed Barclays Bank in

Cairo and were arrested. Shafiq said later that her union's idea of besieging the bank was essentially symbolic, to demonstrate that women are as capable of defending their country as men. In terms of press coverage it had the desired effect. From then on, some newspapers took a favourable stance on changing the electoral law. *Al-Ahram* ran headlines such as: 'The constitution equates men and women'; 'Discussion of a proposal to make voting obligatory and to give suffrage to women'; 'The Egyptian woman is on her way to getting her political rights'.[56] Suddenly, however, the supportive tone stopped and Shafiq knew that the king was behind the change. She began to direct her efforts to other Arab countries and spent her time in conferences and lectures on pan-Arab cooperation.

The next opportunity to make headway inside Egypt appeared to come with the 1952 revolution. Hopes were disappointed, however, when it became clear that preparations to draft a new constitution did not envisage that women would be involved in the drafting process. On 12 March 1954, Shafiq embarked on a hunger strike, staging it in the premises of the Journalists' Syndicate in order to attract as much attention as possible. As soon as the news spread, many women joined Shafiq in support. Mounira Thabet was one of them. Within hours the news of Shafiq's strike reached Alexandria and members of Bint el-Nil Union there followed Shafiq's example by starting a hunger strike at the Journalists' Syndicate in Alexandria.

At the end of an eight-day hunger strike, public opinion had been swayed and influential figures, including Mohamed Hassanein Haikal, Ali Zaki Orabi, and Fikri Abaza had joined the call for women to enjoy political rights. The government promised that political rights for women would be enshrined in the new constitution. This promise was honoured in the Egyptian Constitution of 1956. In 1957, however, Nasser closed both the *Bint el-Nil* paper and the Bint el-Nil Party in a clampdown on the press[57] and political activity that was to have lasting effects.

Conclusion

Accounts of the rise of women's activism in Egypt rightly acknowledge the high profiles of women like Malak Hifni Nassef, Hoda Shaarawi and Doreya Shafiq. Their contributions to public debate through the pages of what was – for much of the first 60 years of the twentieth century – a vibrant and diverse Egyptian press, give great depth to the historical perspective from which we can view the emergence of the Egyptian women's movement. Likewise, through the press of the period, we also see the breadth of women's involvement in attempting to shape their future and the future of their country. Publishing was something that many women aspired to and many did. This chapter, by highlighting the writing of Mounira Thabet, a contemporary of Shaarawi but one whose name is less well remembered today, has attempted to amplify our view of women's activism in the period between the mid-1920s, when *L'Egyptienne* became a flagship of the movement, and the mid-1940s, when a renewed campaign for women's rights gathered momentum under the banner of *Bint el-Nil*. Thabet, the militant advocate, was not in tune with many of her contemporaries. Nevertheless, she was explicit about the political goals women should aim at and her articles in the Arabic press carried a message that *L'Egyptienne* conveyed less vehemently in French.

The fervent patriotism of the activists discussed in this chapter cannot be disputed. Their writing in the press shows how formal political participation, through the right to vote and the right to stand for public office, came to be seen by women as a natural and logical step in their contribution to ending British occupation and promoting national development. From seclusion and a lack of access to education at the turn of the century, women either negotiated or thrust their way into public space within the next two decades. This transition from private to public space was achieved in large part through the press. While much of the early women's press was focused on household and family concerns, it provided the platform from which women writers began to make their voices heard in the organs of the country's political parties. From there they could argue the case, as Thabet did, that women should be directly involved in making the laws that govern their social and personal status. From Malak Hifni Nassef's arrival in the pages of *Al-Jarida* to winning the vote for Egyptian women took 50 years.

4
Maghrebi Women Film-makers and the Challenge of Modernity: Breaking Women's Silence

Zahia Smail Salhi

When Maghrebi women took up the movie camera at a relatively late stage in the post-colonial era, it marked an important political and symbolic breakthrough of liberation and empowerment. Liberation of the Maghreb from colonial rule did not bring liberation for women. Under French colonization, the more the image of Maghrebi women had been appropriated and distorted in French paintings, novels and film, the more the colonized men of the Maghreb sought to defend their honour by 'protecting' women from public view. Maghrebi women contributed actively on all fronts towards their countries' liberation struggles, but after national independence they were denied a voice in public, or even private, affairs. This chapter shows how the medium of film has been used to transform women's voicelessness and challenge the double repression of colonialism and patriarchy.

Colonization through art

The first iconographical representations of Maghrebi women were produced by Orientalist artists, during the end of the nineteenth and the beginning of the twentieth centuries. Although the Maghreb is only some 60 miles by sea from France, the French were content to call it 'the Orient'. The Orient they hoped to find was an imagined setting constructed out of military accounts following the conquests of Egypt by Napoleon Bonaparte in 1789, and of Algeria in 1830. Most importantly, it was inspired by images from Antoine Galland's translation of *The Thousand and One Nights*,[1] which opened to the West the wide gates of mysterious oriental palaces, where hordes of beautiful and extremely adorned odalisques roamed. In this way, images were created of the harem as the luxurious confines where the Muslim male jealously kept his wives and concubines. They portrayed Maghrebi women as rare, exotic objects of curiosity, only accessible to the lucky few artists who managed by one means or another to enter these forbidden confines. In his masterpiece, *Women of Algiers in their Apartment* (1834), Eugène Delacroix managed to transform his stolen glimpses of these closed interiors into a colourful painting, which displays a lascivious world of idle women who lie adorned as if ready for unending festivities. Although Delacroix's paintings display a striking technical realism that celebrates the colours and light of the Orient, they often symbolize western aggression directed against the East. Transforming the closed interior into a painting, exposed to the public gaze, constituted a violation of the sacred confines of this interior and rendered public what would normally be private.[2]

During the early twentieth century, the work of the Orientalist painters was succeeded by that of the colonial photographers, who rendered the remarkable photo-realism of the Orientalist painters even more real by photographing frozen instances of reality, which they made accessible to a wider audience. In *The Colonial Harem*, Malek Alloula remarks:

> History knows of no other society in which women have been photographed on such a large scale to be delivered to public view … Moreover, its fixation upon the woman's body leads the postcard to paint this body up, ready it, and eroticise it in order to offer it up to any and all comers from a clientele moved by the unambiguous desire of possession.[3]

The photographers turned their studios into fictitious harems and, in order to produce exotic picture postcards, they hired models whom they photographed in erotic poses. In this manner, the veiled became unveiled and the closed doors of the harem were thrown wide open, symbolizing a double act of appropriation of the colonized people and their land.[4]

Colonial cinema went one step beyond the simple fixated, mute and motionless image of the Oriental photographers. Through the medium of the moving, live picture, it offered its viewers fictional adventures from the Orient, embodying the encounter with the 'Other' in remote exotic lands. Dina Sherzer remarks that the oriental-tales films in the vein of *The Thousand and One Nights*, with revealing titles like *La Sultane de l'amour* (*The Sultaness of Love*, 1919), staged 'brutal, mysterious, and tragic passions with the Oriental woman as seductress'.[5] The other genre, that of colonial films, used the French colonies of North Africa as settings for such stories as Jacques Feyder's *L'Atlantide* (1921).[6] Shot in the deserts of Morocco, Algeria and Tunisia, French colonial films' main focus was exoticism, adventure and forbidden love, presenting the colonies as virgin land 'where the White man with helmet and boots regenerated himself or was destroyed by *alcoholism, malaria, or native women*'.[7] This reinforced the image of the white man as the bearer of the civilizing mission, therefore 'civilized', and that of the native as ignorant savage and therefore 'dangerous'. These opposing images were cast in the fascinating settings of the Sahara Desert, with golden sands, amazing dunes, and unique sunsets. Similar images are described at length in the colonial novel,[8] in which the main focus is the French person's journey through the desert and the presence of the native is only portrayed as part of the exotic decor. The few native subjects present in these novels are the villains, whose main purpose is to harm and destroy the central character. They are shown using a variety of harmful devices such as black magic, poisonous potions, or even destructive love, to destroy the 'innocent' white man.[9] These same images can be found in the French films of the period up to the end of the Second World War, which focused mainly on producing tales of love and adultery set in the colonies. They staged 'French characters as the main protagonists, involved in issues that placed the natives in secondary positions, as servants, traitors, or exploited sexual partners'.[10]

Giving voice to the voiceless

Such portrayals, whether in paintings, photographs, films or novels, were part of the creation and maintenance of France's cultural hegemony. The rape and sexual exploitation of the native woman is often used as an allegory for French colonial rape of the Maghreb, which in turn resulted in a complex relationship between the colonizer and the colonized. The more the former attempted to penetrate the closed confines of the colonized Maghrebi women, the more the colonized men were eager to protect 'their' women, who symbolized 'their honour', by various devices such as confinement and the veil. Native women thus underwent a double act of repression from both the colonizer and the colonized male. As to the portrayal of natives in the French colonial mediums, it could only be superficial as the French authors and artists did not know the natives well enough to be able to portray them faithfully. In 1975, Pierre Boulanger testified in his book *Le Cinéma colonial*, that 'from 1911 to 1962, 210 films were made about the colonies, mostly about North Africa, which gave spectators biased, fanciful representations that are disturbing today'.[11] Literary reactions came from Maghrebi writers in French during the 1940s, when they attempted to correct the false images produced in the colonial novel. In 1947 Taos Amrouche let out the deep cry of the alienated Algerian woman, whose sense of alienation was doubly felt in that she was 'the colonized of the colonized'. Her novel, *Jacinthe noire*, was written between 1935 and 1939 but only found its way into print in 1947. In it, Taos Amrouche's voice became definitely the first Maghrebi female voice to tell the world about the dilemma of the colonized people of the Maghreb.[12]

In 1955 another female Algerian novelist, Djamila Débèche, published her novel *Aziza*, explaining the most difficult stand of the colonized Algerian woman, who suffered from colonial as well as patriarchal alienation.[13] In an attempt to contradict the phantasmagoric image of the native woman, both Amrouche and Débèche attempted to construct, in the language of the colonizer, a true and first-hand portrait of the colonized woman. Their first motive was to debunk a succession of stereotypes of native women. The women they portrayed are ordinary characters, with feelings and anxieties like all women in the world. Most importantly, they wanted to amend the 'vulgar image' of the native woman as the fatal seductress of the harem. In this they preceded Maghrebi male writers and were able to voice their concerns from a very early stage. The same applies to another Maghrebi woman who began writing in the 1950s and whose work has portrayed the development of Arab women in general, and of Maghrebi women in particular, from that period to the present. This is Assia Djebar. Her merit is not only in her long and versatile career, through which she followed Maghrebi women's evolution from colonial to post-colonial periods, but mainly also in her consciousness and commitment to the Arab and Maghrebi feminist cause. She recorded the transition of these women from the stage of searching for personal and gender identity, to their quest for national identity both during and after the colonial period. By doing so she created an outlet for their voices to be heard.

The main purpose of Djebar's work is to confront and fight two kinds of silence. One is her own as a silenced Arab woman, while the second is the silence of those Muslim women who are denied a voice.[14] For Djebar, the act of giving a voice to muted, voiceless Arab and Muslim women means, above all, giving them the opportunity to express themselves, to tell the world who they really are, and debunk the damaging stereotypes constructed through western representations of the native woman. These were the representations that portrayed individual women as mute subjects, whose gaze speaks in so many languages to tell their fear, their helplessness and their submission. In being portrayed at a moment not of their own choosing, they were responding and satisfying the painter's, photographer's or film director's phantasm, embodying the preconceived image of the native woman as a seductive sexual object.

By taking the approach she did, Djebar engaged in an act of demystifying as well as correcting distorted images. Giving Maghrebi women a voice in literature, starting from the 1950s, and later on in film, had the effect of breaking the multi-layered silence imposed on them by patriarchy and colonial oppression. Once silence is written, it undergoes a fundamental transformation into non-silence. According to Valérie Budig-Markin: 'writing gives voice and form to the silences/signs of the temporal and spatial infinity which gives meaning to life'.[15] The novel was thus the first medium used by Maghrebi women to express their rejection of the colonial image. It was also a medium through which they asserted their existence on the Maghrebi literary scene and voiced their concerns from their own point of view, as opposed to Maghrebi male writers' point of view, which often idealized women.[16] Yet whereas Maghrebi women took an active role in the field of literature, the same cannot be said of cinema. Despite contributing to films as actresses, technicians, assistant directors and screenwriters, right from the early beginnings of Maghrebi cinema,[17] their work as film directors came rather late. For a long time cinema remained a male domain, projecting a masculine and often idealized vision of women.

In *Caméra arabe*, a documentary on Arab cinema,[18] the Tunisian film director Nejia Ben Mabrouk expresses her reservations about the image of women created by Arab male directors. She claims:

Even directors who mean well, they are either full of gloom, or they idealise the woman. A woman is a human being, with faults and contradictions. A woman is not a dream, but a reality. I would like to see that reality dealt with. She (the woman) is not just a moving picture, not a doll, a goddess, or a fairy. She is a living person with difficulties, limitations, and weaknesses. That is what I want to deal with.[19]

That Ben Mabrouk's own aim in directing films is to demystify the image of women in Arab cinema is evident in her feature film *La Trace* (*The Trace*, 1988).

Figure 4.1

Chronology of Maghrebi women's cinema

Algeria:
• *La Nouba des femmes du Mont Chenoua*/*The Nouba of the Women of Mount Chenoua*, Assia Djebar, 1978. • *La Zerda ou les chants de l'oubli*/*The Zerda or the Songs of Oblivion*, Assia Djebar, 1980. A very intimate enquiry, it questions the place of women in history and in society. Music in this film is used as a unifying factor of the Maghreb. • *Le Demon au feminin*/*The Female Demon*, Hafsa Zinai-Koudil, 1993. • *Rachida*, Yamina Bashir, 2001.
Morocco:
• *Arais min qasab*/*Reed Dolls*, Djilali Ferhati (with script by Farida Benlyazid), 1982. • *La Braise*/*The Embers*, Farida Bourquia, 1984. • *Une Porte sur le ciel*/*Gateway to Heaven*, Farida Benlyazid, 1988. • *Ruses de femmes*/*Women's Wiles*, Farida Benlyazid, 1999.
Tunisia:
• *Fatma 75*, Selma Beccar, 1978. The first feature-length work directed by a woman in Tunisia. The film was censored by the Tunisian government. Beccar set up her own production company, IMP, in 1988. • *La Trace*/*The Trace*, Nejia Ben Mabrouk, 1988. • *Les Silences du palais*/*The Silences of the Palace*, Moufida Tlatli, 1994. • *La Dance du feu*/*The Fire Dance*, Selma Beccar, 1995. • *Miel et cendres*/*Honey and Ashes*, Nadia Fares, 1996. • *Keswa: le fil perdu*/*Keswa: The Lost Thread*, Kethoum Bornaz, 1997. • *La Saison des hommes*/*The Season of Men*, Moufida Tlatli, 2000.

Maghrebi women's appropriation of the camera, though coming at a late stage in the post-colonial era, posed a challenge to both colonial and patriarchal domination. Women were active participants on all fronts during the war of liberation in Algeria and during the political struggle against the French protectorate in Morocco and Tunisia. Yet the end of foreign colonization in the Maghreb was soon followed by a deep feeling of disillusion among its women. They felt betrayed and, banished to the periphery right from the early years of independence, were utterly excluded from various domains in society and bullied into silence.[20] This is accurately summarized by Mildred Mortimer as follows:

> French colonialism once sought to stifle voice and memory, denying the colonised the right to their own language and history. Maghrebi patriarchy still attempts to restrict movement and vision, denying the Algerian woman her right to circulate freely in public space where she may see and be seen.[21]

To counter this patriarchal repression, as well as to come to terms with the colonial past, is indeed one of the main objectives of Maghrebi women's cinema. Cinema offers an opportunity to conquer the social terrain to which access has been denied and to give voice to the voiceless and muted. To investigate further how this is achieved, I have selected three Maghrebi films from Algeria, Morocco and Tunisia as follows: *La Nouba des femmes du Mont Chenoua* (*The Nouba of the Women of Mount Chenoua*) by Assia Djebar, *Arais min qasab* (*Reed Dolls*) by Djilali Ferhati,[22] and *Les Silences du palais* (*The Silences of the Palace*) by Moufida Tlatli.

La Nouba des femmes du Mont Chenoua

Assia Djebar was the first Maghrebi woman to enter the domain of film-making. She did so in 1978 with her first film, *La Nouba des femmes du Mont Chenoua*.[23] Known primarily as a writer, Djebar devoted her novels, short stories, narratives, play and poetry to the Arab women's cause. She has recorded the suppressed voices of women from various strata of society, and given her characters and her own self the opportunity to utter words they are not able or not allowed to say in real life.[24] Nevertheless, after the publication of her novel, *Les Allouettes naïves* (*The Naive Larks*), whose title refers to the name given by French legionnaires to the prostitute dancers of the Ouled Nail tribe of southern Algeria, Djebar questioned herself. She wondered whether she had succeeded in giving her female compatriots a voice, as she had hoped to at the beginning of her career.[25]

At this point, Djebar herself fell into a decade of literary silence. When she managed to break out of its confines it was by turning to cinema as another means of expression and, even more so, as another form of transgression. Djebar's appropriation of the camera, in addition to the fact that she is a female writer, constitutes a double transgression. Writing about women in a patriarchal society is a revolutionary act. It reclaims a voice for the forgotten women whose active contributions to liberation struggles were promptly obliterated by the national media, with its permanent focus on male heroes of the revolution. The only feature film made of an Algerian war heroine was Youssef Chahine's *Jamila al-Jaza'iriyya* (*Jamila, the Algerian*) in 1958. This film by an Egyptian director centres on the torture of Djamila Boubacha at the hands of the French colonial powers. It turned her heroism into the stuff of legends, as she stood firm against her oppressors and wrenched the hearts of an entire nation. Though the film was hailed throughout the Arab world and the Eastern bloc countries, it was banned in Algeria under the French and remained banned after independence.[26] Thus the voice of the Algerian 'Djamilas' remained stifled and obliterated.

Another feature film to portray the heroism of Algerian women during the revolution was Gillo Pontecorvo's *La Bataille d'Alger* (*The Battle of Algiers*) in 1965. Financed by the Algerian government, the film's focus is not Djamila or her sisters, who feature in the film, but a male hero, Ali la Pointe. The women in *La Bataille d'Alger* take important but not leading roles. They mostly respond to the instructions of male nationalist leaders, implying that Algerian women 'helped' in the revolution but 'did not make it'. Putting the film in the context of liberated Algeria, one soon realizes that political movements use women instead of working with them for liberation. Algerian women were simply used during the revolution, only to be pushed to the periphery after independence.

Djebar's transgression in getting behind the camera instead of in front of it creates a vehicle for women to be heard as well as seen, and tell the world their version of Algerian history through their own testimonies, thereby claiming their space in their society and the world at large. As the voice is recorded, the camera records the female body and its various expressions as it speaks, through gesture, posture and, most importantly, the gaze. In this way the camera becomes a voice, which speaks of the many taboos women themselves cannot speak about. By stepping into the domain of cinema, Djebar felt 'she could reach her people at last, and especially the women, in a language they can understand (i.e. through spoken Arabic) and through sounds and images'.[27] Therefore, *La Nouba* not only constitutes a record of women's testimonies in a language they would surely understand, unlike the francophone expression of Djebar's novels, but also creates a female version of Algerian history, and celebrates women's memory, through their gift of story telling.

La Nouba tells the fictional story of Lila, a young architect who returns to her ancestors' house, together with her little daughter Aisha and her temporarily paralysed husband Ali, to investigate once more the circumstances of her brother's martyrdom during the war of independence. Her itinerary mingles with the memories of six other women who lived through the war years. In brief they tell their side of the (hi)story of Algeria. The film opens with Lila, whose face is turned against the wall, saying repeatedly: '*Je parle, je parle, je parle*' ('I speak, I speak, I speak'). This opening scene bears a dual message, as on the one hand Lila affirms her existence through speech, and on the other hand she turns her back to the camera, expressing her refusal to be gazed upon. Another important feature in these opening words is that the protagonist affirms her appropriation of speech in French rather than in colloquial Arabic, which is the medium of expression given to the rest of the women portrayed in the film. As such, Lila's words are Djebar's own affirmation of her appropriation of the French language as the medium through which she has always expressed herself and has given voice to her women folk.

The film focuses on two diverse settings: scenes of the interior, portraying Lila and her family inside their small country house, and scenes of the exterior, following Lila's ventures through the countryside, visiting other women and listening to their narratives. This in itself represents Lila's double quest, both to situate herself in her married life, and to rediscover her native village. Inside the home Lila is lonely, unhappy and silent. Her relationship with her husband is marked by the absence of dialogue, betraying an unhappy relationship. At the same time she is tortured by memories of the colonial past, with images of torture, prison and the loss of members of her family conveyed through frequent flashbacks. Lila's best moments at home are spent with her daughter, to whom she tells the stories the village women narrate to her, ensuring thereby that the chain of narration is passed from one generation of women to the other. Similar scenes are repeated in the film, and at one stage the camera portrays multiple circles of children surrounding older women telling them a story.

The open-air scenes portray a happier and liberated Lila. Her journey and her coming into close contact with her village produce extensive panoramic views of Mount Chenoua and the Mediterranean sea, as well as buildings and human faces, mainly those of rural women in the fields, at work, or sitting in groups, telling their version of history, and bearing witness to yesterday's war. *La Nouba* managed to keep 'women's speech and oral history safe from the danger of extinction, from the danger of a definitive silence'.[28] Djebar's film was praised as being 'a very beautiful one, with reflections on memory and portraying the gaze'.[29] Yet it has also been severely criticized for lacking a feminist vision, confining women to brooding on their past without suggesting a way forward.

The value of *La Nouba*, however, lies in restoring oral transmission to its rightful place in a society where widespread literacy among women is a recent phenomenon. Even more important, it represents a symbolic pose for women, to restore their excised voices and memories and empower them to face the challenges of modern-day, independent Algeria. One needs to set foot on solid ground before moving to unknown destinations in the post-independence era. Djebar herself has commented:

> Women's cinema – as much in the Third World as in the 'Old World' – begins with the desire for the word. As if 'to film' means for women a mobility of voice and body, the body not gazed upon, but unsubmissive, retrieving its autonomy and innocence.[30]

Reed Dolls

Although *Reed Dolls* was directed by Djilali Ferhati, it was made from a script by his wife, Farida Benlyazid, who scripted many other Moroccan films on the condition of women.[31] The film sets up its feminist message from the outset. A sad female voice lets out a song in the Moroccan dialect:

> God my Lord, destroy these walls
> And the oppressed will then emerge …
> I will not surrender
> I will not lose hope …
> Lord, intercede that we might run from destiny.
> How can we run from destiny my Lord?

The song betrays a state of helplessness and despair, which sets the tone of the film. It indicates that the women in question are trapped by the restrictions placed upon them, which are symbolized in the song as walls. The women in *Reed Dolls* are enduring the consequences of a rigid set of family status laws, consolidated by well-established patriarchal customs. They are gradually becoming aware of their condition, and are now yearning to break free.

Reed Dolls is based on the story of a rural girl, Aisha. She is brought to the city by her aunt as a future bride for her son. A very interesting feature of the film is the way Aisha's childhood gradually gets stolen from her, as her few moments of child's play in the street are often interrupted, either by the coming home of her future husband, to whom she has to attend, or by her aunt's summons for her to carry out household chores. Aisha is portrayed as a silent and submissive girl, whose slow movement and blind obedience are, indeed, disturbing features to the viewer. The first time Aisha speaks in the film is when she has to interrupt her play, telling her friend: 'My husband is here', which is a valid excuse for her to go home. The second time we hear her speak is when she tells her aunt the news of her first period: 'I've had my period aunt' is said in whispers. This event constitutes a turning point in Aisha's life. Overjoyed, the aunt tells her niece: 'My little girl has become a woman'. She then lays bare what becoming a woman entails: 'As soon as the period ends, I will take you to the baths. Then you will start to sleep with your husband instead of me, and God willing there will be a child before the year is out'.

Obviously, Aisha is still a child entering her teens, which the viewer finds a most disturbing feature in the film, though the course of action of the story does not question it. Aisha's wedding is reported and celebrated as a normal event. Her coming of age is shortlived in the film; all too quickly she becomes a mother of three and is brutally afflicted by the death of her husband. At this stage the film's feminist message becomes more apparent, directly criticizing the patriarchal restrictions on women enforced in the Personal Status code, known in Morocco as the *Muda-wana*. This point of view becomes the axis of the film through to its end, demonstrating the destructive effects of such laws on women.

Like their sisters in Algeria, though in a different way, Moroccan women worked alongside their male compatriots in the political struggle against the French protectorate. Nevertheless, when King Mohammed V returned to Morocco, their political role was brought to an end and they were asked to return to their homes. As a 'reward', the King instructed Allal el-Fasi, the main theorist of the Istiqlal Party, to head a committee to draft a new family law code, the *Mudawana*, based on the extremely conservative Malekite interpretation of Islamic sharia law. The outcome was that, while Moroccan women had equal rights as citizens, their status within the family was defined by Islamic law on matters such as divorce and inheritance, often with additions from patriarchal customs. A good example is the institution of the matrimonial guardian (*waliy*), which does not exist in the Qur'an. Consequently, although the *Mudawana* raised the minimum age for marriage, Moroccan women remained minors from a legal point of view, being made subject to men in the family.[32]

In *Reed Dolls*, Farida Benlyazid is addressing the articles of the *Mudawana* through dramatic evidence of the heroine's ordeal. The film takes a more dramatic tangent soon after the death of Aisha's husband, when her brother-in-law, Ali, steps in as the male guardian of the household. He sits with the two women, the mother and daughter-in-law, and lays out the truth about the meagre inheritance left by his brother after his death:

> Now, about the house, a twelfth part goes to Aisha, a sixth goes to you, mother. The rest is divided by five, two parts to each of the boys and one to the girl. Then there is a small pension from the Spanish army, and finally there are his savings. This is how *God and the Law wish it to be*.[33]

The two women respond with a silence that indicates their helplessness in front of 'God and the Law'; they have no choice but to accept the deal as their destiny. In such a precarious situation they have no one to turn to but each other. Their weakness is exploited by their guardian, who proposes to marry his brother's widow in order to provide for her and the children. The law and religion allow Ali to take Aisha as his second wife and the mother-in-law tells Aisha: 'The imam told him that this would be a good course of action. Think about it. We're all alone now. *We are only women*, and there are the children to think about and their future.'[34] Outraged, Aisha responds: 'His wife is like my sister. I'd rather die.' Aisha finds the proposal rather immoral, and rejects as barbaric the custom of a man marrying his brother's widow, which remained common practice in the Maghreb until relatively recently. As the film shows the sensibility of the woman, it lays bare the crudeness of the male guardian, who not only takes advantage of the weakness of his relatives, but also wishes to engage in what the film's central female figure enunciates as an almost incestuous relationship.

Unlike the women of the previous generation, Aisha decides to go out to work. She tells her mother-in-law: 'We can count on each other. You look after the children and I work!' This sense of solidarity among women is a clear message that comes through the film. Women have to break free from their dependency on men by earning their own living. The resistance of men in the society to women gaining financial independence is exemplified in the film by the way Ali spies on Aisha, 'I see Aisha has started to go out wearing make-up now. You should talk to her', Ali says to his mother, who, to his surprise takes Aisha's side. Through working and earning, Aisha is gradually rising from the tragedy of widowhood at a young age. She not only finds her way out of poverty, but also finds a new companion, whom she thinks will stay with her for the rest of her days. Finding out that he has no intention of marrying her comes as a tremendous shock. So Aisha becomes easy prey for Ali, who emerges to get his revenge on her in the name of the law and family honour. When the mother-in-law discovers that Aisha is pregnant she tells her: 'It's no use crying. You'll have to have an abortion. Ali is capable of killing us. May God forgive us, for *we are only women*.'[35] The mother-in-law's statement surprises the viewer, as she stands with courage, defiance and open-mindedness, despite her advanced age. Her solidarity and support for Aisha give her a pivotal role in the film and in its call for women's solidarity. This call is underlined by the role of Malika, a dressmaker who fights through the courts to have her husband released from prison. She tells Aisha, whose 'bad conduct' becomes known to everyone: 'we are lost as soon as we step across the threshold … We are always inside the house, but when we have to go out we can't face the world.' Malika's statement accurately describes the condition of Moroccan women in the early post-independence period. Women were still afraid to break free because the world outside their homes was so hostile to them, and both the law and society's code of honour stifled women's movements, vision and voice. Compounding this situation was the high rate of illiteracy among women.[36] In court Aisha sits close to her mother-in-law, neither of them understanding anything of the standard Arabic spoken by the judge when he announces the verdict:

A case of bad conduct has been established. Article 98 regarding personal status and behaviour has been enforced. I decree in the name of

His Majesty the King and his court the following sentence: Aisha Kholti can no longer have charge of her children. The children are to be placed in the care of their paternal grandmother.

Aisha turns to her mother-in-law for explanation, who, in turn, turns to her son, whose face is clearly lit with joy. The impression left on the viewer by this scene is that of two helpless, illiterate female victims clinging to each other in fear and despair, with the repressive figure of the judge representing the law, flanked by Ali, who symbolizes patriarchy, as two repressive powers over women. The law, together with patriarchal customs, not only deprives Aisha of her children and them of their mother, but also offers her no alternative but the street, as she has nowhere else to go. Broken and extremely vulnerable, Aisha is temporarily rescued by Malika who finds her work as a live-in maid. In the master's home, three generations of housemaids are portrayed, indicating that Aisha's status is actually lived by the previous generation, by her own, and certainly by the next generation of women. This is made more obvious as Aisha's daughter is portrayed performing the same chores as her mother, serving food and cleaning rather than behaving like the child she is, or attending school.

In the master's house the young daughter who attends school is constantly discouraged by everyone around her from bothering about her education. When she asks to go and revise with her friend, her mother's response is: 'When will you learn to keep house? Do you think studies will honour your husband's family?' With this scene the film suggests that the path towards women's liberation in Morocco is quite difficult, and that future generations of women will not only have to fight but, more importantly, to join forces. The ending of Reed Dolls portrays Aisha as easy prey to sexual exploitation, but continuing to resist and fight the pressures to become a prostitute. Her unfortunate 'fate' leaves her a broken woman, with no one and nowhere to turn to. The last scene of the film shows her at the graveyard by the side of her husband's grave, which symbolizes the impasse in her life, with no prospect of a better future. The pessimistic ending is further emphasized by the closing song by the same voice that opened the film, voicing women's bitterness, helplessness and betrayal by the men in their society:

> Allah, Allah, if I say Allah
> My sins will be forgiven.
> I made him a friend and a brother

> But he wanted to throw me over a cliff
> I leave him to God, the real judge.

From the technical point of view, *Reed Dolls* is often criticized for its torpid pace, loaded with the sluggish hopelessness of frustrated lives. This can be explained by the reality portrayed in the film, for the condition of women in Morocco is shown as being deplorable and with no hope for the near future. The message is clear: women have to take their fate into their own hands and stand up to their oppressors by breaking out of the thick layers of silence and fear under which they take refuge but also suffer. Crucially, the film urges them to join forces and stand for each other.

Les Silences du palais

Silence becomes the main theme in Moufida Tlatli's first feature film, *Les Silences du palais,* which soon after its release was described as a rare instance of a strong female voice in Arab cinema.[37] Making a film about Arab women's silence is a direct result of a lived experience. Tlatli affirms that the first silence she wanted to speak about was that of her own mother, who was a silent woman, incapable of saying no. For the last five years of her life she barely spoke. Tlatli explained:

> Five years before my mother died she stopped speaking. I think that her decision to remain silent came out of an accumulation over the years of all those little silences. It became a form of protection while at the same time it was a signal that she did not want to prolong the fruitless dialogue. It was very painful for me, since there were so many questions I had that remained unanswered.[38]

Although *Les Silences du palais* is Tlatli's attempt to find those answers, the film is not autobiographical, nor does it concern itself with the silence of one single woman. Its concern is with the silences of her mother's whole generation. The events are cast in a twentieth-century harem, ensconced in the last Bey's castle in Tunisia, so that it becomes an evocative study of life in the castle. By choosing such a setting, Tlatli 'writes back' to the western stereotypes of eastern harems, and debunks their phantasms and preconceived ideas about the eastern woman as portrayed in Orientalist paintings, photography and especially colonial cinema. The women in the castle all live in silence, regardless of their class. Their silences, however, hide different types of stories, and 'speak' in many different languages.

Tlatli demonstrates that even the princesses are reduced to silence, unable to speak to express their unhappiness, frustrations or jealousies. Their lives are so superficial, and the way they relate to their partners is rather strange. Nevertheless, the focus of the film is on the female slaves and their sad lives in subordination. They are the princes' playthings, subject to physical as well as emotional rape and abortion.

Told mostly in extended flashbacks to the 1950s, the film begins in the early years of Tunisia's independence, casting light on the heroine, Alia. She is 25 years old and lives with her partner Lotfi, who denies her the right to become mother and wife. Pregnant once again, Alia is this time hesitant to have an abortion, as her singing career has become boring and her life empty. News of the death of Prince Sid Ali prompts her to visit the palace she left ten years ago, to offer condolences to the Bey's wife, Jneina. Importantly, however, the visit is also a visit to her childhood, which was spent in the servant's quarters as the illegitimate daughter of Khadija, who was both slave and mistress to the master, Sid Ali, whom Alia always suspected to have been her father. Through the eyes of a child growing up in the kitchens, Tlatli makes a detailed visit to Tunisia's past, both under the monarchy and colonial France. She skilfully ties the closeted rituals of the palace, which are built on silence and repression, to the political situation in Tunisia. This is achieved by framing scenes against repeated emergency radio broadcasts announcing nationalist disturbances and popular anger towards the Beys for their collaboration with the French. The suffering of Tunisia is also linked to the suffering of the wasted lives of the women slaves who live within the walls of the palace and must submit to the masters' sexual demands. When the state of emergency is declared and the news of the curfew is broadcast, the women's reaction is that it makes 'little difference' to them, as their life is a 'permanent curfew'. One of them breaks into a long soliloquy:

> We have nothing to be afraid of. I don't belong to myself. I want to go out in the street, to run unhindered, naked and barefoot, and scream and shout out loud. Only their bullets can silence me as they run through me, turning my body into a sieve.

In silence the women support the revolution, hoping that, with the liberation of Tunisia, their slavery will come to an end. Their silence thus becomes a form of resistance. This is further expressed by childhood scenes of Alia, who retreats into muteness after the shock of witnessing her mother being raped by Sid Ali's brother. Her muteness is simultaneously a sign of rebellion and despair. Conversely, Alia's coming of age and subsequent discovery of her voice as a means of expression are clearly identified with her country's struggle towards independence. This becomes even more obvious when Alia is asked to sing at the wedding of Sara, daughter of one of the princes, who was born on the same day as herself, and who helped her discover her passion for the lute. After singing songs of Egypt's famous Um Kulthum, which are clearly appreciated by the guests, Alia makes a brusque shift to the forbidden nationalist anthem. At this stage the guests leave the room in anger and Alia finds the courage to flee the palace with Lotfi, a young revolutionary teacher working for the Beys, who is hiding from the police in the servants' quarters. However, at the same time as Alia breaks free, Khadija passes away while aborting the child conceived as a result of the rape. Her death, surrounded by the silent and helpless women who have come to help her, is also a form of liberation, a liberation from her pains, her slavery and most importantly her fear that her daughter's fate will almost certainly be no different from hers. Throughout the film, Khadija fights to preserve the innocence of her daughter Alia, whom she constantly warns against the lustful rulers. Alia tells her mother in defiance: 'You leave me with them and you want me to relax? I hate them, they scare me.'

Another important feature in the film is the dialogue of silence, which often takes place between Khadija and her daughter. Their spoken dialogue is often replaced with a silent dialogue, where the gaze substitutes for many words. The eyes of both mother and daughter are so expressive that the words they cannot utter are conveyed through the gaze. The only time they engage in a long dialogue is when Alia incites her mother to flee with her. The mother replies: 'Where to? I have no one ... I saw the light of day here, spent my life here. I am afraid to leave. Where do you want me to go?' Brought up in slavery, Khadija does not succeed in transcending her condition and following in the spirit of her daughter. She makes it clear that she would not know how to become free. Tlatli's message is equally clear, that a history of repression does not easily disappear. Tormented by her daughter's persistent and embarrassing questions – 'Where do you come from? Where are your parents? You refuse to tell me', and 'Who is my father?' – as well as by the unwanted foetus growing inside her, Khadija for the first time ever shouts out her stifled rebellion in the kitchen: 'No! Leave me alone, let me go! I hate myself, everything disgusts me. I hate my body'. At this stage Tlatli skilfully incorporates a long scene of silence, as the slaves continue their chores in slow motion, their eyes filled with tears as they share Khadija's pain. They all understand her ordeal, but their only expression of solidarity is their silence.

Silence, therefore, becomes an expression for the things that are not said, or cannot be said. Silence is the language of the oppressed, humiliated and shamed women of the palace. In the end the palace becomes the embodiment of Tunisia, and the slave women represent Tunisian women under a colonial yoke, bearing the double load of oppression as 'the colonized of the colonized'. As Tlatli observes:

> The Tunisian man, as the colonised person, has his revenge by colonising the underclass that is women. They in turn put their frustrations into their daughters. In the Arab world, the woman does pay. At an unconscious level, she is responsible for keeping the status quo as regards her own position. I wanted to show how she can break from the past.[39]

The end of *Les Silences du palais* portrays Alia being reconciled with her past, and bringing her ardent quest for her identity to an end. Going through the painful episodes of her past, Alia does finally discover an identity for herself. Instead of continuing to linger in the past, she decides to become her own person and take her destiny into her hands. She now realizes that yesterday's rebellion did not help her keep its spirit right through to the present times. In other words, it is not enough to break away from colonialism; rebellion must continue in the post-independence era. Lotfi, who taught Alia nationalist principles, turns her life into a pattern of servitude almost similar to her mother's, in which she has one abortion after another and he does not recognize her as his wife. Addressing her mother, Alia claims:

> I thought Lotfi would save me. I have not been saved.
> Like you, I've suffered, I've sweated.
> Like you I've lived in sin.
> My life has been a series of abortions.
> I could never express myself. My songs were stillborn.

Looking more assertive and more empowered, Alia decides to keep her baby: 'This child, I feel it has taken root in me. I feel it bringing me back to life.' Her choice now is to challenge convention and break her silence, thereby moving inexorably towards a sense of individual liberty. The final message of *Les Silences du palais* is that Tunisian women often ignore their legal rights, which results in their failure to improve their social status.

Unlike their Maghrebi sisters from Morocco and Algeria, whose post-independence struggle for improved legal status has been protracted, they have enjoyed a relatively liberal and progressive Personal Status Law that gives them a variety of rights, including legal abortion. In Tunisia, polygamy is forbidden and women face fewer legal obstacles in suing for a divorce. Nevertheless, the grip of tradition remains strong and many women still live as prisoners of silence and patriarchy. Tlatli's film is an invitation for her generation of women to take the achievements of yesterday's revolution towards new horizons through a new social revolution.

Conclusion

Maghrebi women's cinema plays an important role in expressing the many meanings of the silences of women. But it also calls on women of the region to extract themselves from the legacy of yesterday's revolution and confront the challenge of making their own revolutions by breaking their silence. Assia Djebar confirms: 'For Arab women, I see only one single way to unblock everything: talk, talk without stopping, about yesterday and today, talk among ourselves ... And look. Look outside the walls and the prisons!'[40] Her words recall the first scene of Djebar's film, *La Nouba des femmes du Mont Chenoua*, in which Lila affirms her act of speech at the very same moment as she turns away from the camera and, by refusing to be gazed upon, refuses to be the object of the onlooker. Unlike the women in Delacroix's famous painting *Women of Algiers in their Apartment*, Lila turns away from the camera, as though what matters most is her re-appropriation of speech. In contrast to the mute women in Orientalist paintings and photography, Lila tells the viewer: 'I speak, I speak, I speak'. This confirms a change not only in the condition of Maghrebi women, but most importantly in their determination to assert their existence by speaking out.

5

The Orient and its Others: Women as Tools of Nationalism in Egyptian Political Cinema

Lina Khatib

Gender has been an essential part of the Orientalist discourse. Orientalist notions of the Arab world are invested with ideas of sensual and submissive females (the harem) and violent, yet succumbing males (the colonized). These notions have settled themselves into the European imaginary sense of the Middle East. Yet, at the same time, gender interlaces the political agendas of the East itself. This chapter analyses the construction of women as tools of nationalism in contemporary Egyptian cinema. Women have traditionally been seen as a symbol of the nation (like Marianne in France and Boadicea in England) and as 'signifiers of national difference'.[1] The chapter discusses how this woman-as-nation metaphor has meant that, in contemporary Egyptian cinema, 'women ... become the battleground of [national] group struggles'.[2] In particular, it considers the complex relationship between the representation of women and the communication of Egyptian nationalist identity in the contexts of the Arab–Israeli conflict and the politics of Islamist fundamentalism.

Floya Anthias and Nira Yuval-Davis argue that citizenship constructs men and women differently and they identify five ways in which women participate in national processes.[3] These five ways form the framework of this chapter. First, women are constructed as biological reproducers of members of an ethnic group. Second, they are constructed as reproducers of boundaries of ethnic or national groups. This has necessitated the establishment of codes determining women's acceptable sexual behaviour, limiting this behaviour within the group. Third, they are ideological reproducers of collectivity and transmitters of culture. Fourth, they signify national difference, and therefore act as symbols in ideological discourses used in the construction, reproduction and transformation of the nation. Finally, women are constructed as participants in national, economic, political and military struggles. Anthias and Yuval-Davis further argue that '[d]ifferent historical contexts will construct these roles not only in different ways but also the centrality of these roles will differ'.[4] The study of Egyptian films in this chapter shows that notions of gender and patriarchy cannot be applied universally. It therefore highlights how important it is to examine representations of the different roles of women in films in a historical context. In doing so it challenges the notion of '"Third World Woman" as a singular monolithic subject',[5] where women are seen to form 'a unified "powerless" group prior to the historical and political analysis in question'.[6]

The study explores four main themes. First is the representation of woman-as-idealized-nation. In the Middle East, the female has generally been invested with the task of being the moral gauge in society. The female's role thus goes beyond symbolizing the morals of the family and also becomes that of bearing the nation's values. In films about Egypt's former president, Gamal Abdel-Nasser, the Egyptian nation is represented as a virtuous female who does not pose a threat to patriarchy. With Egypt imagining itself in terms of honourable, subdued femininity, it is no coincidence that Egyptians informally call their nation *Umm al-Dunya* (Mother of the World). Secondly, as Deniz Kandiyoti argues, women's appropriate sexual conduct 'often constitutes the crucial distinction between the nation and its "others"'.[7] Thus, in contrast to an image of idealized femininity, films representing Israel and the United States as 'Other' nations communicate the representation of 'Other-woman-as-whore'. Other nations are symbolized by sexually permissive females who are presented as summarizing the moral depravity of the enemy. A third theme is the symbolic use of women as an oppositional tool vis-à-vis militant political Islam. Here we have two representations. The first uses women to highlight the moral depravity of Islamist militancy. The second uses the image of the silent, veiled woman to symbolize its oppressiveness. This is contrasted with the fourth theme, exploring the representation of the 'modern woman/Egypt' through women who are politically active. However, the study argues that this representation of 'active' women does not imply that they are protagonists. The films in the end construct the Egyptian nation as being patriarchal. The shift from the representation of idealized women to that of modern women indicates a historical move from private patriarchy, where women are subordinated through their relegation to the home, to public patriarchy, where 'women are no longer excluded from the public arena, but subordinated within it'.[8]

Idealized femininity

'Women bear the burden of being "mothers of the nation"'.[9] The Egyptian films analysed in this section are mainly melodramas focusing on the feminine, private sphere, where family honour and national honour are signified by idealized, wholesome women. Thus the females symbolizing the nation tend to be devoted mothers who sacrifice for their husbands and their families. One way of analysing this devotion is proposed by Ann Kaplan, who argues that the mother's passion for her children can be a '"safe" location of female desire'.[10] Kaplan also maintains that the mother who sacrifices for her husband can be 'blameless and heroic … she has ceased to be a threat in the male unconscious'.[11] Yet such a paradigm 'uncritically embodies the patriarchal unconscious and represents woman's positioning as lack, absence, signifier of passivity'.[12]

Such features are seen in the character of Tahiyya, Nasser's wife, in the film *Nasser: The Story of a Man, A Story of a Nation* (Anwar Kawadri, 1998). The film is a biographical account of the life of the late Egyptian president, and presents Tahiyya as a selfless mother and devoted wife, who not only takes care of her children and husband, but also sacrifices her own personal life with Nasser for the sake of the nation. The film ends with Nasser's death, depicting a mourning Tahiyya alone by his deathbed, saying 'it is only now that I have you for myself'. Tahiyya's sacrifice means that she is ascribed a heroic status. This status is maintained in her portrayal as an obedient wife, yielding to Nasser's wish to work long hours despite her concern over his deteriorating health. At the same time, she excels at her role as housewife and hostess. A scene depicting a meeting between Nasser and Abdel-Hakim Amer, commander-in-chief of Egypt's armed forces, starts with a panning shot revealing a long dinner table laid with food prepared by Tahiyya. As the three eat their dinner, the men praise Tahiyya's culinary skills, after which she leads them to the living-room, where she serves them tea. Yet as soon as Amer and Nasser start discussing politics, Tahiyya makes a swift exit, excusing herself as having to look after the children. She takes the sugar pot from the tea tray with her, joking that she cannot trust her husband with the sugar.

The film's depiction is closely based on the doctrines of the real-life Nasser. According to Mervat Hatem, Nasser was passively ambivalent 'regarding the impact of the roles assigned to women in modern society'.[13] Officially, he was committed to 'the integration of women in the public sphere'[14] and, despite shortcomings such as the unchanged personal status laws, Nasser's government gave women the right to vote and distributed education and health benefits equally, which women gained from. Yet Nasser quelled the public Egyptian feminist movement during most of his period in office, accusing it of being too leftist. This was in line with his suppression of all other independent political groups.[15] Nasser's revolutionary struggle relied upon 'using Islam to rally the masses for the liberation of their occupied land'.[16] Anouar Majid explains that such a 'form of Islam was obviously infused with a patriarchal spirit'.[17] As Shahnaz Khan puts it, 'these politicized, frequently anticolonial, anti-West movements exert increasing social and sexual control on the symbolic and chaste women centered at the core of an identity politics'.[18] For Valentine Moghadam, this type of revolution follows a 'Woman-in-the-Family' model.[19] The role of women in this context is more complex than that of men; whereas men and women may sacrifice themselves for the nation, it is the woman who is a symbol of the nation itself and the nation's honour.[20] As a woman's morality extends to the nation, Tahiyya becomes a symbol of the pure, nurturing, virtuous Egypt. Her political uninvolvement validates Carol Delaney's point that *women may symbolize the nation, but men represent it*.[21]

Permissive femininity

Egypt's approach to the Arab–Israeli conflict has passed through many phases. The situation has shifted from outright opposition to Israel before 1978 to acceptance after Sadat's signing of the Camp David accords in 1978. Sadat started a long process of peace talks with Israel, which culminated after his death in the return of Sinai in 1982, 15 years after Israeli occupied it, and the eventual return to Egypt of the Israeli-occupied border enclave of Taba in 1989. Yet, while the Egyptian state's stance towards Israel since this time may have been one of acceptance, the general mood in Egypt, influenced by the Israeli–Palestinian conflict, has remained hostile. Despite the country's official peace treaty with Israel, popular anti-Israeli sentiment is expressed in Egyptian cinema. All the films portraying various aspects of the Arab–Israeli conflict analysed in this chapter represent Israel as essentially an enemy. This representation may also be traceable to the fact that the Egyptian film industry is the biggest in the Middle East and caters to anti-Israel sentiment in the wider region. Gender is at the heart of this representation.

Films representing the Arab–Israeli conflict are guided by essentialist assumptions about Others and about the Egyptian/Arab self.[22] The films present a sharp opposition between Israeli women and Egyptian women acting as Israeli spies on the one hand, and nationalist Egyptian women on the other. Indeed it is possible to divide the films into two types. The first portrays Egyptian women betraying the nation by working as spies for Israel, while the second portrays Israeli women on Egyptian soil.

The first set includes *I'dam Mayyit* (*Execution of a Dead Man*, Ali Abdel-Khaleq, 1985) and *Fakh al-Jawasis* (*Trap of Spies*, Ashraf Fahmi, 1992), films that are similar in their treatment of the subject of Egyptian spies working for Israel in the 1970s. They both introduce young Egyptians enticed by the money and status that come with spying. The Egyptians in both films hide what they are doing from their families, who in turn condemn the spies when they discover what they do. The spies in the films are also similar in their 'immorality' and both films rely on females to represent this immorality. The female Egyptian spy in *Trap of Spies*, who betrays her country even after being caught by the Egyptian secret service, is blatantly representative of an Israel that relies on duplicity to achieve its aims. She symbolizes a perceived immoral Israeli state that is attacking 'us' from within and that 'we' should guard ourselves against. In *Execution of a Dead Man*, the spy Sahar also gets caught by the Egyptians yet continues to work for the enemy. Her immorality is amplified in that she gets pregnant after having an affair with another Egyptian spy. Here we see the classic use of premarital sex as a sign of moral degeneration.

The second set of films about the Arab–Israeli conflict includes *Al-Hob fi Taba* (*Love in Taba*, Hisham Abdel-Hamid, 1992) and *Fatat min Isra'il* (*Girl from Israel*, Ehab Rady, 1999), both of which contain a message about Israeli decadence infecting Egyptians' everyday lives. Both films tackle the issue of normalization between Egypt and Israel after their peace treaty. Set in the enclave of Taba in Sinai soon after its liberation from Israeli occupation, the films construct gendered self/Other dichotomies[23] that establish women as a battleground in the Arab-Israeli conflict.[24] Women are used to establish 'the boundaries of the group [Egyptian] identity, marking its difference from alien "others"'.[25] Jan Jindy Pettman argues:

> Women's use in symbolically marking the boundary of the group makes them particularly susceptible to control in strategies to maintain and defend the boundaries. Here women's movements and bodies are policed, in terms of their sexuality, fertility, and relations with 'others', especially with other men. This suggests why (some) men attach such political significance to women's 'outward attire and sexual purity', seeing women as their possessions, as those responsible for the transmission of culture and through it political identity; and also as those most vulnerable to abuse, violation or seduction by 'other' men.[26]

The films illustrate the above through constructing various binary oppositions. First are the contrasts in attire and lifestyle. The Israeli women are represented as heavily made up and bikini-clad, drinking alcohol and taking drugs as they party through the night. The Egyptian women, in contrast, dress modestly and refrain from any such activities, spending their time in Taba playing volley ball and painting.

Second is the sincerity/deception binary. While the Egyptian women are presented as not having anything to hide, the Israeli women are portrayed as deceitful. In *Love in Taba*, Israeli women hide their HIV status from the Egyptian men they sleep with. The message is that Israel, as symbolized by those women, may be attractive yet is diseased, luring 'our' men and then destroying them. In *Girl from Israel*, an Israeli woman pretends to be American in order to get through to a young Egyptian man she eventually seduces, promising him money and status if he leaves his family behind and goes to Israel. In this way, there is a focus on the contrast between the artifice of Other women and the naturalness of the moral Egyptian women. It can be said that the Other women's artifice is a symbol of the artificiality of the state of Israel itself as portrayed by the films. Established in 1948, the state of Israel had not achieved formal diplomatic recognition by the majority of Arab countries after more than 50 years of existence. An offer of recognition, made on behalf of other Arab countries by the crown prince of Saudi Arabia in 2002, was contingent on Israel's full withdrawal to its pre-June 1967 borders. Pending a land-for-peace settlement, Arab public opinion has tended to regard Israel as an impostor attempting to replace the 'real' Palestine.

Third is the films' emphasis on women's sexuality. The nation's honour is seen as an extension of the family's honour, which women are also used to signify. The greatest weight in this context is attached to pre-marital virginity, which seems to dominate any other form of expression of morality.[27] The Egyptian women in *Girl from Israel* do not have sex before marriage. In contrast, the Israeli women attract the Egyptian men by presenting the opportunity of premarital sex. Towards the end of the film, *Girl from Israel* depicts a rape of one of the Egyptian virgins (dressed in a floating white dress) by an Israeli man. The scene bears out Spike Peterson's argument that 'the rape of the body/nation not only violates frontiers but … [also] becomes a metaphor of national or state humiliation'.[28]

This self/Other essentialism has also been extended to the representation of the United States as an imperialist force threatening the sovereignty of the Egyptian nation. *Al-Akhar* (*The Other*, Youssef Chahine, 1999) represents the imperialist United States as a devouring mother. Margaret, a wealthy American businesswoman indulging in a world of fraud, serves as a classical villain. Her unholy alliance with members of armed Islamist groups, her selfishness, immorality and total immersion in a constructed cyberworld: all these detach us from any identification with her character and highlight her contrast with Egyptian purity and simplicity as seen in the character Hanan, Margaret's Egyptian daughter-in-law. Margaret sees the Egyptian people as Other: She is outraged when Adam, her son, donates blood to Egyptian victims of an explosion, saying: 'Why give blood to "them"?'.

Margaret follows the idiosyncratic character of the devouring mother who swallows her children while the father is factually or symbolically absent (a character seen, for example, in Alfred Hitchcock's 1960 film *Psycho*). In *The Other*, Margaret is obsessed with her son and tries her best to be number one in his life, casting on him the 'duty' of compensating her for the romance she never had with her husband. Unlike Hanan's devoted mother, Margaret is not satisfied with sublimating her desire though her son; she projects her unfulfilled desire on him.[29] That preludes Margaret's latent rejection of Adam's marriage to Hanan, and her consequent endeavours to undo the multi-ethnic coupling (Adam being a

Christian Egyptian-American and Hanan being an Egyptian Muslim). The inevitable and classical outcome of this drama is that Margaret ends up destroying her child. Throughout the film, Adam and Hanan's anti-essentialism is caught up between the poles of imperialism and fundamentalism. This entrapment is epitomized in the film's tragic ending. In front of Margaret's eyes and amidst a shoot-out between religious insurgents and government military troops, the loving couple die holding hands.

In the final third of the film, we learn that Margaret is an alcoholic. She is also portrayed as having a derogatory view of other women, whose purpose, in her eyes, is merely that of (sexual) pleasure. Margaret's role is ultimately as a symbol for the supposed degeneracy of the United States. This symbolism is stressed towards the end of the film in a conversation between Margaret and her Egyptian husband. We hear Margaret reminding him that he would be nothing without her. At the same time she declares 'he who leans on me, I bust him', while throwing her whisky bottle at a television set. Using the only distinguished avant-garde technique in the film, the scene is then cut to that of missiles being launched – obviously a sign of destruction.

Oppressed femininity (and masculinity)

Appearing as if out of nowhere, a sultry woman in a revealing red dress, with big hair, lots of jewellery and lots of make-up, appears on the screen. She taps her feet gleefully in a short dance routine. Then, to the background of cabaret music, sashays slowly down a flight of stairs, smiling at the people in front of her and swaying the frills of her dress, like a diva who knows she is making a big entrance. Jaws drop at the sight of her, as her colourful aura contrasts with the greyish-yellow background of the place and the dull outfits of the crowd. She explains that she was being interrogated by the police, accused of prostitution. This scene featuring the Egyptian actress Yousra in *Al-Irhab wa'l-Kabab* (*Terrorism and Barbecue*, Sherif Arafa, 1993) is one of many in which her nameless call-girl character is juxtaposed with that of the fundamentalist Islamist Rashad (whose jaw also drops in the staircase scene). The call-girl is a classic example of cinema's seductive, 'immoral' whore, who epitomizes men's suppressed desires and is an object of men's gaze, both in the film and in the audience. In this film the call-girl literally walks into an armed protest against the government, led by a man named Ahmad, inside a 13-storey complex of government ministries. She joins the protesters and, when asked by Ahmad to give her reasons, she answers that she is too shy to say. To this his response is: 'Do you feel shy like we do?'

Ahmad's spontaneous response epitomizes the call-girl's 'essential otherness',[30] and the expectation that she – being an 'immoral' call-girl – is inherently evil and emotionless. The film thus demarcates the simple, innocent, moral Egyptian people who, in a comedy of errors find themselves labelled as terrorists, from the call-girl, who is presented as different, both in the way she looks and in her immorality. The call-girl plays a key role in the film, being used to point out the moral dissolution of the character Rashad. Gazing hard at the call-girl's breasts, his eyes almost popping out, Rashad – a civil servant caught up in the protest – 'advises' her in religious terms to 'return to the right path', declaring that if she wears a 'long dress and a veil' she will be 'virtuous'. Rashad is thus portrayed as regarding the veil as the passport that will legitimize action prompted by his desire. Without it his desire remains forbidden and all he can do is stare, causing the call-girl to wonder out loud: 'Is this look on your face that of an "adviser"? And how come you are not "advising" the rest of the people?'

The scenes containing the call-girl in *Terrorism and Barbecue* provide what Mulvey refers to as 'scopophilia', defined as 'pleasure in looking'.[31] The way the camera traces her footsteps as she walks down the stairs; the way it caresses her face while she looks empathically at a desperate suicidal man who falls for her; the soft music that we hear every time she moves; her husky voice; the slow pace of her speech; her bright red dress and the way she uses her bosom to store her make-up and accessories: all work to emphasize her sex appeal and therefore intensify the gaze of both the male audience and the male characters in the film, especially Rashad.[32] Ahmad, on the other hand, is presented as being uncomfortable with her overt sexuality, stammering and diverting his gaze away from the girl. The call-girl is therefore used to underline the morality of ordinary Egyptians, as opposed to the corruption of Islamist fundamentalist groups.

A similar example is the lawyer Fat'hi's sexy neighbour in *Touyour el-Zalam* (*Birds of Darkness*, Sherif Arafa, 1995). All we know about her is the way, squeezed into a tight dress that emphasizes her ample breasts, she enters his house, submitting her chest to Fat'hi to pat as a form of greeting, in front of his fundamentalist friend Ali. She then goes straight to Fat'hi's bedroom and starts undressing on his bed, all the way laughing and calling Fat'hi to join her, disregarding the presence of a stranger. Thus the anonymous woman is shown to know her place, which she accepts and submits to robotically and without protest. After Ali asks Fat'hi about her, we find that Fat'hi used to be her lawyer and saved her from prosecution for murdering her husband. The woman has apparently made a deal with Fat'hi: he proves her innocence, in return for which she gives him sexual favours. This immoral woman is later used in the film to juxtapose Ali's suppressed desires with Fat'hi's gratified ones. Ali enters Fat'hi's bedroom only to find the woman's red bra left on the bed.

A comparable ambivalence is found in *Al-Akhar* (*The Other*, Youssef Chahine, 1999) where a cyber-meeting set in a virtual Paris finds the fundamentalist Fat'hallah, who chose the location, in the presence of Parisian prostitutes in the Eiffel Tower. Because this is the realm of virtual reality, we know that the presence of the prostitutes is the product of Fat'hallah's fantasy. However, his overt reaction is to say how he wishes to eliminate the presence of these women, whom, in such a realistic fantasy, he can only gaze at. This representation of women as objects to be desired and controlled[33] ascribes an Orientalist status to fundamentalist Islam, which is represented as constructing women as Other.[34] But desire on the part of the fundamentalist is shown to oscillate between being forbidden and being permissible. The fundamentalist Ali in *Al-Irhabi* (*The Terrorist*, Nader Galal, 1994) is a man with sexual desires like everybody else. Ali is convinced by his leader that 'possession' of 'infidel' (in this case 'non-fundamentalist') women is permissible. After he gets run over by a woman whose non-fundamentalist Muslim family welcomes him into their home while he recovers, Ali does not hesitate to follow his leader's suggestion: he makes a sexual move on the woman's sister, which she blatantly rejects. Ali is also torn between his religious commitment and his voyeurism. In one scene he walks down the street behind a woman wearing a tight dress. The camera displays Ali gazing at her bottom, which the camera then zooms in on to give us Ali's perspective. At home, Ali peeps from his window at the woman, now wearing a low-cut red dress and on a lower floor in the building opposite his. Ali fantasizes about having sex with the woman, but this disturbs him and drives him to seek refuge in vigorous exercise and prayer.

Tseelon analyses such gendered acts of looking/being looked at by saying that in such a distinction 'there is an assumption that one position, that of the onlooker, is inherently more powerful than the other'.[35] In the case of the woman he harasses, the woman is visible as the object of Ali's gaze. Tseelon argues that being visible does not mean possessing power: 'visible as objectified is powerless, but visible as prominent and dominant [here, Ali] is powerful'.[36] In the case of Ali's neighbour, both the woman and Ali are invisible to each other. In the same way, Tseelon argues, '[i]nvisible as ignored and trivialised is powerless, but invisible as the source of gaze ... is powerful'.[37] Hence, invisible or not, the fundamentalist man constructs the woman as an object of his gaze and she is therefore always powerless. In this way, the films dealing with fundamentalism discussed in this chapter represent it as commodifying women. In *The Terrorist*, the fundamentalist leader Ahmad promises Ali a wife if he performs a terrorist activity. In *The Other*, the fundamentalist Fat'hallah promises to let his friend marry Fat'hallah's sister (Hanan) if the friend helps him to get her divorced from her husband. In neither case does the woman have any say; she is used as a mere commodity that can be exchanged for services. To summarize, women are used in the films as indicators of the corruption of fundamentalist Islamists. This serves to devalidate the latter's political agenda while at the same time strengthening the Egyptian nationalist agenda that sees Islamic fundamentalism as Other. This discourse of difference is an illustration of how the nation 'utters different narratives for its different inhabitants'.[38]

Moreover, the films portray fundamentalist oppression through the image of the silent, veiled woman.[39] It is important to note that, in these films, veiling in a fundamentalist context is seen to involve the long, loose black chadoor, perhaps because of its dramatic look. This form of veiling is implicitly contrasted with the headscarves adopted by the majority of ordinary urban Egyptian women in recent years or the colourful head-covering typically associated with traditional *baladi* (countryside) women in Egyptian cinema. The image of the chadoor-wearing woman brings to mind the images of colonized women reproduced in Malek Alloula's book *The Colonial Harem*.[40] As Khan puts it, 'both poles [Islamism and Orientalism] essentialize the ideal Muslim Woman and reduce her to the same symbols and icons'.[41] Almost always, with the exception of religious historical films, any woman in Egyptian cinema who wears this type of veil is connected with Islamist fundamentalism. The epitome of fundamentalist oppression can be seen in *The Terrorist*, where such women are shown to be blindly obedient to men. This film contains a scene in which Ali, the eponymous terrorist, knocks on the door of his fundamentalist leader, Ahmad. The first shot is that of Ahmad eating with his four chadoor-wearing wives. We hear knocking on the door and Ahmad quickly dismisses his wives with a wave of his hand. Words are not necessary for the women to understand their place in the hierarchy. In *Birds of Darkness*, the oppressed, veiled woman steps out of the house. But that does not take her beyond the limits of any 'expected' female roles: she is either secretary to the lawyer Ali, or a messenger who gives Ali a letter from his opponents. These submissive women are contrasted with other female characters in the film. For example, the character Raga' is a successful businesswoman. Success in these cases is portrayed as such even if the business has been literally or metaphorically 'inherited' from a male partner or father. The film implies that, despite their 'involvement' in the movement, fundamentalist women are still oppressed.

There are multiple assessments of the meanings behind the 'uses' of the veil; a prominent one is to see the veil as a sign of resistance.[42] Yet Egyptian films seem to concentrate on only one assessment, in which the veil signifies backwardness and oppression. In all these films, if we hear the veiled women speak, their relative passivity sends the message that, in essence, they are silent. In contrast, the films' depiction of businesswomen implies that it is unveiling and 'liberation' that gives woman a say in society and makes them 'advanced'. This view resonates with Nawal El Saadawi's argument that 'Islamic fundamentalist groups are trying to push women *back* to the veil, *back* home, *back* under the domination of their husbands'.[43] The veil becomes a sign of the sexual and psychological repression of the fundamentalist identity – an identity deemed foreign to the Egyptian national one. The veil then is a tool of nationalism 'through which social difference is both invented and performed'.[44] The demarcation between Islamic fundamentalism and the construction of the Egyptian national identity as modern and oppositional emphasizes how 'definitions of the "modern" take place in a political field where certain identities are privileged and become dominant, while others are submerged or subordinated … [and where] secular notions of modern nationhood subordinate and sometimes seek to destroy alternative bases for solidarity and identity'.[45]

Resistant femininity?

Women participating in national struggles form another category that constructs the Egyptian modern national identity. When the woman, expected to be weak and powerless, becomes a fighter, she becomes a symbol of the ability of the powerless to fight.[46] However, as Kandiyoti argues, activities of women participating in nationalist movements

> could most easily be legitimised as natural extensions of their womanly nature and as a duty rather than a right. Modernity was invested with different meanings for men, who were relatively free to adopt new styles of conduct, and women, who, in Najmabadi's terms, had to be 'modern-yet-modest'.[47]

Franco argues that, even 'when a woman managed to become a militant, she was often forced into a traditional gender role and classified as either butch or seductress.'[48] Kandiyoti's and Franco's arguments are illustrated in three films depicting politically active women: *Al-Tariq ila Eilat* (*Road to Eilat*, Inaam Mohamed Ali, 1986), *48 Sa'aa fi Israel* (*48 Hours in Israel*, Nader Galal, 1998) and *Naji al-Ali* (Atef at-Tayyeb, 1991). Both *Road to Eilat* and *48 Hours in Israel* present female fighters going undercover to Israel in order to accomplish missions that would aid in preparations for the October 1973 war against Israel. Both women use seduction to achieve their aim of entering Israel and gathering intelligence, the first by luring Israeli men (*Road to Eilat*), the second by working as a showgirl (*48 Hours in Israel*). Both films use elaborate shots of the women's bodies in action, with a whole dance sequence in *48 Hours in Israel* and a scene of Maryam's body being caressed by an Israeli man in *Road to Eilat*.

Mulvey argues that women's sexuality is the condition that makes them visible in a male-dominated world.[49] It is this sexuality that makes the women in these films visible in a male-dominated resistance movement. The display of the women's bodies means that they no longer become sex objects for foreign men only;[50] in this 'nationalist movement', 'the native continues to retain the same essential characteristics depicted in Orientalism, but nevertheless imagines himself [sic] as autonomous, active and sovereign'.[51] As Meyda Yegenoglu argues, this nationalist movement sustains the legacy of Orientalism and its view of Oriental women as objects of men's gaze.[52] But Maryam's role in *Road to Eilat* is not confined to seduction. The film explains her participation in the struggle by reciting her story. The time-line of the film starts in 1969, when Palestinians were seeking refuge in Jordan as a result of the harsh conditions of being under occupation. These conditions resulted in several traumas ranging from illiteracy to lack of hygiene, and consequently 'heightened political consciousness among [Palestinian] women'.[53] Some of these women broke through traditional prejudices to become fighters.[54] *Road to Eilat* accords with Rosemary Sayigh's account of how, at the end of the 1960s, a 'revolutionary tide' was generated by the defeat of the Arab armies in 1967.[55] Maryam is a fictional example of the real phenomenon noted by Sayigh, in which Palestinian women underwent training as members of the Resistance Movement. She is shown carrying a gun, wearing military uniform just like her male counterparts and actively participating in missions for the Egyptian marines (her mission is to go undercover to Eilat as an Israeli).

Sayigh explains that a number of women joined the Resistance Movement having been encouraged to do so by male kin.[56] In the film, however, Maryam explains rather romantically that she joined after her brother died for the Resistance. This invocation of equality resonates with Majid's point that 'it was the national struggle ... that brought women out of their confined, privatized social spaces into the public sphere'.[57] Palestinian resistance generated the slogan *al-ard qabl al-ird*, meaning 'land [the Palestinian homeland] before honour'.[58] However, as Rick Wilford argues, 'fighting alongside men to achieve independence does not provide a guarantee of women's inclusion as equal citizens'.[59] The film's presentation of the brother's death as the incident that caused Maryam to become a fighter serves as a justification of her actions (as if one were needed), and a reassertion of her femininity as well.[60] Moreover, the film ensures that Maryam does not stray 'too far from socially acceptable roles for women'.[61] Maryam's role in the Egyptian marines' operation, for most of the film, tends to be complementary to that of her male colleagues. She spends most of the time encouraging her male colleagues and taking care of them in a sisterly way. For example, she pulls out a photograph of her deceased brother and shows it to one of the men, emphasizing the resemblance between him and her brother, whereupon they strike up a quasi-sibling relationship. Moreover, when Maryam is in a military uniform she does not fight, and when she is carrying a gun she does not shoot. This exemplifies Anthias's and Yuval-Davis's assertion that 'in national liberation struggles ... generally [women] are seen to be in a supportive and nurturing relation to men even where they take most risks'.[62] Moreover, Maryam's display of emotions serves to tone down her toughness and to 'reassure the audience that ... [she] is a "normal" woman'.[63] Looking at how Maryam's character is portrayed, we find that she generally acts in reaction to men's schemes: we do not see her planning, but executing her male leaders' strategies.[64] Thus she can be said to be a sidekick, and not a central character, despite the length of time she spends on screen.

The journalist Suad in *Naji al-Ali*, a biographical film about the Palestinian cartoonist of the same name, is another woman 'fighter'. Perhaps Suad brings us the closest we can get in recent Egyptian cinema to what Doane calls a 'woman's film',[65] whereby the woman is a central protagonist instead of an object to be looked at. Resisting the proposals of her ex-fiancé, who offers to 'protect' her from the perils of her job as a journalist during the Lebanese civil war, and dedicating herself to the cause of Palestinian/Lebanese/Syrian resistance against Israeli occupation, she runs fearlessly along battlefields and engages actively in political debate, epitomizing female power and confidence. Stacey explains that such a character serves to '[offer] women fantasies of resistance'.[66] However, after an assassination attempt on Naji's life, we see Suad helpless in the hospital, staring at Naji who is lying in a coma. Yvonne Tasker argues that the woman's role in a representation like this one is merely to provide 'an audience for the hero's suffering, his powerlessness emphasised by her gaze'.[67]

Both Maryam and Suad are single women, which might be seen as a rejection of 'the responsibilities of adult womanhood',[68] or as strengthening their tough image.[69] This is emphasized in the character Suad, who is not only single, but has left her fiancé for her political involvement. She is also sometimes a 'tomboy' in the way she acts (and sometimes dresses).[70] Maryam also fluctuates between being 'feminine' in her swimsuit and 'masculine' in her military uniform. Such cross-dressing can be seen as a negotiation of the portrayal of women's fighting bodies – as atypical, even deviant – in relation to women's traditional non-fighting role.[71] It can also be seen as emphasizing their toughness yet reaffirming their femininity. Suad and Maryam are both the only central female characters in otherwise all-male environments. While this can be seen as highlighting their strength, their contrast with the other women in the films, who assume more traditional roles, emphasizes their portrayal as being exceptional women. Hence 'their toughness is understood not to be a common trait of women'.[72]

Thus, despite Suad and Maryam being strong characters when taken at face value, they are a 'revised stereotype'[73] of women in cinema, being strong but with their toughness undermined.[74] Perhaps because *Naji al-Ali* does not want to transgress patriarchy totally, in a scene where a party is held to celebrate Naji's safety, it is Suad, the only woman present, who makes the cake. This not only reaffirms Suad's femininity, but also undermines her toughness. The same can be said about Nadia El-Guindi's character in *48 Hours in Israel*, where she disguises herself as a dancer. Sherrie Inness explains the use of disguise by saying that a woman's 'toughness can be seen as only another example of her play with disguises; we need not fear her if we can believe that underneath the tough exterior a "true" woman resides'.[75] As Cynthia Enloe argues, this depiction of women in nationalist movements derives from conceptions of nationalism being primarily masculine and patriarchal.[76] Kirsten Schulze points out that nationalist movements do not erase the view of women as inferior to men: 'When they are needed they may carry arms and fight, but ultimately they are still seen as "other"'.[77]

Conclusion

'Nations are contested systems of cultural representation'.[78] Through an analysis of the different roles that women play in Egyptian films about Middle Eastern politics, this chapter has shown how women are presented as tools of nationalism. Women are used in the cultural construction of the Egyptian nation, and as instruments of demarcation between the self and the Other. As demonstrated by the representation of Tahiyya and the Egyptian virgins in *Girl from Israel*, 'idealized images and real bodies of women serve as national boundaries'.[79] This is contrasted with the image of the whore who epitomizes the Otherness of the enemy, in these cases Israel and the United States. Situated between the virgin and the whore is the silent, veiled woman who signifies the oppression of fundamentalist Islam, and the politically active female who embodies the modern face of Egypt.

In all those representations, we find that women are embedded in struggles around the authenticity of the Egyptian national identity.[80] The face of this struggle has changed throughout history, moving from representing Egypt as a virtuous mother to a modern woman. However, the films send conflicting messages about tough, modern women. On one

6
Multiple Literacies, Multiple Identities: Egyptian Rural Women's Readings of Televised Literacy Campaigns

Sahar Khamis

This chapter is based on in-depth ethnographic audience research conducted in an Egyptian village. It analyses how two generations of Egyptian rural women struggled to reconstruct and redefine their cultural identities in order to make sense of the messages in televised governmental literacy campaigns. In investigating why and how these women came up with differential readings of these televised texts, and how they positioned themselves differently in relation to them, the study highlights the changes in these women's complex productive and reproductive roles, their shifting maternal and feminine identities, and their competing knowledge systems.

The study explores how the complexity of these multiple social and cultural factors influenced the internalization, negotiation, acceptance or rejection of the hegemonic dominant ideology put forward by the Egyptian government through its televised messages. In doing so, it investigates how this complex media reception process links everyday 'micro' issues to broader 'macro' issues and contexts, and how it could play both a divisive and an integrative role, reflecting the divisions and commonalities of these women across the traditional–modern dichotomy. By describing the background to the changing roles and identities of the women of the village of Kafr Masoud, the study sheds light on the shared socio-cultural context that contributes to the formation of their common cultural identity as Egyptian rural women. But it also compares and contrasts their 'traditional' and 'modern' identities, and investigates how these changing cultural identities affected these women's patterns of television exposure and shaped their complex media reception process.

New audience, new genre

The fact that the study was conducted in the Egyptian countryside has special significance in terms of audience research. It examines media reception in a culturally specific, non-western context, thereby exploring the impact of different values, traditions and beliefs on media reception. Studies conducted within western cultural settings do not necessarily offer a generalizable model. When talking about women's consumption of the media, we must always ask ourselves: 'Which women exactly are we talking about?', since it is only by keeping in mind ethnic and cultural differences, in addition to differences in age, generation, religion and class, that we can fully address these issues.[1] A prevailing neglect of Third World rural women in audience research at the international level also extends to the local Egyptian context. In a bibliography of audience research dealing with women in Egypt, Laila Abdel-Migeed notes that most of this literature has focused on middle-class, urban women.[2] This clearly indicates that the marginalization of Third World rural women in the priorities of governments, development planners and media coverage is matched by their marginalization in the area of academic writing and research. It could be argued that Egyptian rural women are not only 'invisible', in terms of a lack of recognition of their social existence, but are also largely 'unknown', since little is written about their lifestyles, needs and social relations.

It is also noteworthy that, despite a growing recent trend to extend media research to non-western contexts, only a few non-western studies have been conducted by women researchers on women audiences in a way that tackles the transformation of gendered identities and media reception within the context of social change.[3] The present study therefore sets out to shed light on a neglected aspect of a neglected group. But it is also unusual in focusing on the reception of a largely overlooked media genre: one the Egyptian government describes as 'public awareness messages'. Women's reception of media content is more usually explored in relation to soap operas, romantic novels, girls' and women's magazines, music video and film.[4] This applies equally to studies of women in Egypt, which have concentrated on soap operas and film.[5] In fact, television soap opera and film melodrama are often seen as 'women's genres', being assumed to be aimed primarily at female audiences.[6] Issues falling within the public sphere, such as news and current affairs, have tended to be neglected in research among female audiences. Most studies on this aspect of media in Egypt have focused on the representation and portrayal of women or on the media's role in integrating women into development projects through delivering messages to them about health issues and family planning.[7] In other words, they focused on media images of women and the effects of the media on women, rather than on women's responses to media messages and their role as active receivers in analysing and making sense of the media messages which are targeted at them. By focusing on women's reactions to textualized dominant governmental ideologies about issues such as literacy, the present study extends analysis of media reception beyond the private sphere.

The shared socio-cultural context

The study was conducted on a sample of 30 rural women in the village of Kafr Masoud in Egypt, who were all wives and mothers. Despite the many aspects of social change that have taken place in the village in recent years, which are discussed below, we could still highlight many aspects of similarity among the women in this sample that contribute to the formation of their shared cultural identity. The first is the great value they attach to motherhood. These women see themselves, first and foremost, as 'mothers'. Motherhood is considered the main target of their lives, their prime responsibility, and the most important characteristic defining their identity. My research participants were all married women and mothers, and motherhood emerged as a dominant theme in my discussions with them.

The great value that these women assigned to motherhood was clearly manifested in the amount of time and effort that they devoted to their children, as well as the tone of pride with which they spoke about their children and about their experience of motherhood. They also defended themselves against any attacks on their identities and capacities as mothers. This was clear in some of the conflicting views and debates that emerged between these women, during which they came up with very strong, but very different, arguments for legitimizing themselves as 'good mothers'. That is to say: although motherhood is a shared experience among these women, they relate to it in different ways. This is reflected in the different arrangements of their needs and priorities, and their degree of willingness to sacrifice their own interests for those of their families and children.

Beside their familial and maternal responsibilities, the women of Kafr Masoud also play a number of multi-faceted roles within the village community, which cover three main aspects: the domestic, economic and social roles, or what could be described as 'women's triple role'.[8] All of these multiple roles are considered vital for their families' survival and well-being, and they take up most of these women's waking hours, leaving very little room for them to relax or to enjoy any leisure time. Additionally, all women in the village tend to abide by certain conservative moral codes of behaviour. These include modest and conservative dress codes (although the form and type of dress is starting to vary among the new generation), as well as generally observing the conservative, sex-segregated social environment in the village. This is also starting to change gradually among the new generation of women who have entered the public sphere of formal education and formal employment.

The village of Kafr Masoud, like most rural communities in Egypt, has a strong oral tradition. Therefore, despite the presence of modern mass media, such as radio and television, face-to-face interpersonal communication has always been, and remains, the most effective and powerful form of communication in the village community. The impact of interpersonal communication is clearly manifested in the effect of rumour, gossip, peer-group pressure and the influence of informal opinion leaders such as family members, neighbours and friends. This is particularly obvious when it comes to shaping women's ideas, attitudes and behaviours towards sensitive and controversial issues, like family-planning practices and contraceptive use, for example.

Interestingly enough, my study revealed that modern mass media, especially television, are firmly embedded in these women's traditional oral culture, since all my respondents reported watching television with the rest of their families, and engaging in discussions with them about themes and programmes. This collective pattern of television-viewing provided an excellent forum for influencing and shaping women's views and ideas, especially towards sensitive issues like family-planning, sometimes in ways that challenged the propagated dominant ideologies put forward by the government through its televised campaigns.

Shifting identities: from 'traditional' to 'modern' roles and spheres

The village of Kafr Masoud has witnessed a number of shifts in recent years, which, in turn, led to a number of parallel shifts in women's lives and identities. The first and most important shift has been from agricultural to non-agricultural modes of production. The decline in agricultural activities in recent years led to two interrelated shifts: from informal to formal female employment and from informal to formal female education. These aspects of social change, which influenced women's access to education and employment, subsequently affected young women's perceptions of the social and economic value of formal education, and the prestige and status attached to it. This could be attributed to the exposure of formally educated women to a different set of social relations, experiences and contacts, which, by relocating them in different spaces, contributed to the formation and assertion of their 'translated' identity. The new social spheres of formal education and formal employment enabled women in the new generation to build new social networks. Here it is important to take account of peer group pressure, including the impact of similar experiences of friends, relatives and neighbours, as well as the respondent's personal experience, as influences on the complex process of media reception and interpretation, as will be discussed later.

The new shift towards formal female employment and education certainly increased the status and prestige attached to formal education and consequently changed the perceptions, needs and ambitions of young women in the new generation. Older women did not share the same positions and perceptions, since for them illiteracy was the norm rather than the exception. It would seem that generational changes helped to relocate the women in new socio-cultural contexts and new temporal and spatial locations. These in turn reshaped their needs and motives for seeking literacy, and their multiple definitions of its meanings. Additionally, the shift to formal education and employment provided women in the new generation with other sources of self-satisfaction and self-esteem in addition to their traditional roles as mothers and wives. Among women in the older age groups the traditional maternal role was characterized by total 'self-denial' and 'self-sacrifice', through constantly prioritizing their children's needs and interests above their own. In contrast, women in the new generation adopted a more 'individualistic' approach, which enabled them to recognize both their personal needs and interests, as well as their families' and children's needs and interests, in parallel.

Another important aspect of social change to have a strong impact on women's changing roles and identities has been a shift from the 'extended' to the 'nuclear' family arrangement, which now prevails among the young educated couples in the new generation. This shift had strong implications for the degree of autonomy and independence that could be enjoyed by women in the new generation. Most felt that they were 'lucky' to escape from the direct control of dominant family figures in their husbands' families, especially their mothers-in-law. This in turn allowed them to enjoy much more autonomy in their private lives, away from the interference of authoritative members of extended households.

All of these social changes allowed women in the new generation a better chance to assert their status, independence, autonomy and individualism, which culminated in the formation of their new 'translated' identities. In the rest of this study, we will try to examine how women's reconstruction of their identities affected their multiple readings and interpretations of the key themes in four televised literacy messages that were displayed to them on videotape through organized focus group discussions.

These four government messages focused on the following four themes. First, the theme that 'a literate mother is a better mother' was conveyed through a clip featuring an illiterate mother who gives her sick child the wrong medicine because she cannot read the labels on the medicine bottles. Second, the theme that 'literacy helps people to live better lives' was highlighted in a message featuring an illiterate woman who always relies on her neighbour to read her letters for her and consequently falls victim to her greedy neighbour's exploitation and blackmailing. Third, the theme that 'educated children should help in educating their illiterate parents' was presented through a scene showing children teaching their father how to read and write. The fourth theme was that 'it is possible for illiterate married women and mothers to overcome illiteracy if they have the strong will and determination'. This theme was highlighted in a message portraying an actual rural woman who was able, despite her many maternal and familial responsibilities, to attend literacy classes and overcome her illiteracy.

Using Stuart Hall's 'encoding/decoding' model,[9] we will attempt to analyse women's different readings and interpretations of these four themes in the governmental literacy campaign. This model divides the interpretative positions of readers of media texts into three main categories. First are dominant readings, which are perfectly in line with the original meaning of the media message and its objectives, and which internalize the 'dominant ideology' embedded in the text. Second are oppositional readings, which are totally different from the originally intended meaning of the media message, and which reject the 'dominant ideology' in media texts and diverge from it. Third is a negotiated reading, which falls mid-way between the two other readings, representing some form of compromise or reconciliation of both positions.

Dominant readings

Most of the dominant readings of the televised literacy messages, which were perfectly in line with the originally intended message and the government's hegemonic ideology embedded in it, came from the formally educated women of the new generation. The majority of these women held intermediate secondary diplomas; two were university educated, and some had finished primary school. Most lived in nuclear family households, and some had full-time or part-time jobs, either inside or outside the village. Taking into consideration the fact that the televised literacy campaign propagates the dominant literacy ideology, it is not surprising that those who belong to this dominant 'literacy club'[10] are, indeed, the ones who came up with the dominant readings of the messages in question. This reminds us that the 'preferred readings have the power of the institutional/political/ideological order imprinted in them and have themselves become institutionalized'.[11]

The most obvious example of the internalization of the dominant literacy ideology was these women's description of illiteracy as a 'problem' that inevitably leads to committing 'mistakes'. This was clear in their readings of some of the messages, such as the one showing an illiterate mother giving her son the wrong medication. Similarly, in the case of the woman exploited by a neighbour who is called on to read her letters, most women of the new generation read into the message that the illiterate woman had made a double 'mistake'. The first was to remain illiterate and the second was to be dependent on a neighbour who could find out her secrets and exploit her.

By putting the blame on the illiterate woman in every case, mainly because of her illiteracy, this group of women indicated that they considered literacy to be the only form of education and overlooked other options and alternatives. They perceived reading and writing as 'the be-all and end-all',[12] forgetting the strengths, talents and forms of expression available to people without literacy. It could also be said that, in asserting their own distinct identity as formally 'educated' women, they excluded women who did not belong to the dominant 'literacy club' as the 'Other' – someone who is prone to make all types of mistakes as a result of 'illiteracy'. This position was also clearly reflected in their acceptance of the concept of children educating their father, as portrayed in one of the literacy messages. Most respondents in this group praised the children in the message for being 'good children, who care for their father and are eager to help him'. They also described them as 'grateful children, who are keen to pay their father back for all the sacrifices he must have made for them'. In other words, in valuing formal education more highly than other forms of learning, these women could be said to have accepted reversals in the traditional hierarchies of age, seniority and social positioning, which are still strongly adhered to in the conservative village community. Although these women unanimously praised all the characters in the televised messages who decided to seek literacy, they particularly admired the mother who went back to study because of her 'strong will and determination, as well as her multiple motives for seeking literacy'. These included helping her children with their studies, reading newspapers and magazines and getting better chances in terms of future job opportunities.

Taking into account the fact that identities are gender-specific, the above comments tells us a number of important things about these women's shifting and changing identities, as well as their own reconstructions of the ideal image of femininity. It reminds us that 'we can begin to explore the constitution of femininity and masculinity as not fixed or appropriated, but struggled over in a complex relational dynamic.'[13] Here, it could be said that in their struggle to redefine the image of the 'ideal woman', these women have constructed new criteria and new attributes, which are directly related to their own changing identities and the changes in their social positioning. Bearing in mind that literacy needs are not gender-neutral or gender-impartial, but are actually 'gender-engendered needs',[14] these women's modified social roles and identities also affected their perception of literacy and literacy needs. This was evident in their admiration for literacy as an empowering strategy, as well as their admiration for perseverance in seeking literacy. This point was particularly clear in their criticisms of the illiterate women in their own village for lacking these attributes.

These respondents' admiration of the married woman's motives for seeking literacy also indicate their attempt to create a link and a synthesis between 'private' and 'public' worlds of literacy.[15] In bridging this gap, they acknowledged both the importance of literacy for performing a woman's traditional role as mother and carer within the 'private' sphere and its importance in terms of gaining access to 'public' knowledge and general information, through reading newspapers and magazines. Arguably, these women did not abandon an 'old' identity in favour of a 'new' one. Rather, they adapted and modified 'traditional' identities and 'translated' them into new ones.[16] Additionally, their acknowledgement that it is legitimate for a woman to have some spare time to pursue her own personal interests, reflects a modified outlook on their own identities as 'individuals', rather than 'just housewives'. This modified view of the concept of leisure and women's legitimate right to it[17] is perfectly in line with their prevailing individualistic orientation, and new arrangement of their personal values and priorities.

Their esteem for the literacy-seeking woman as a 'good time manager', also indicates a new sense of time, or a new temporality, which was particularly evident in the case of those women holding full- or part-time jobs. Most of these criticized illiterate women in the village for wasting time and thereby denying themselves the chance to do more useful and important things, such as attending literacy classes. This clearly indicates a shift from the 'traditional' to the 'modern' in the social construction of time, from what could be described as 'task/event-based' time to 'clock-based' time.[18] Such a shift could be attributed to these women's mobility and their relocation in a different historical, temporal and spatial context, facilitating their adoption of an 'urban', rather than a 'rural', concept of time.

All the educated women who came up with dominant readings of the literacy messages were particularly pleased with the portrayal of real rural women in these messages. As one woman put it, they felt that 'it sends a clear and strong message to other rural women about the possibility of overcoming their illiteracy, and encourages them to do the same'. In other words, it is clear that, in supporting the dominant ideology of literacy, these women also endorsed the power of the televised text to spread this ideology to others who do not endorse it. It could be said that acquiring literacy skills helped these women to acquire a new form of mobility, dynamism and empathy,[19] which contributed to the formation of new and modified identities. This was clearly reflected in their new hopes, ambitions and dreams in terms of pursuing their careers and proving themselves in the public domain of formal education and formal employment.

The impact of social change, especially the shift from the extended to the nuclear family arrangement, was also evident in changing these women's perception of the importance of literacy and changing their literacy needs. Unlike respondents who live in extended family households and who, as one woman put it, 'can always find someone around to help', those who live in nuclear family households may feel a more pressing need to acquire literacy skills. This could be mainly attributed to the decline in traditional networks of support and 'collective' forms of literacy, which are usually available in extended family households. A shift would seem to be under way from the view of literacy as a 'shared experience', which is available within the family or wider community, to a view of literacy as an 'individual' experience.[20]

Oppositional readings

While the dominant readings of literacy messages came mainly from formally educated women, all the oppositional readings came from women who had no formal education and were 'outsiders to the dominant literacy club'.[21] In addition, whereas most of the dominant readings came from young women who had part-time or full-time jobs and an urban sphere of contacts and social relations, the oppositional readings mostly came from older women who were not formally employed and were locally based. Here it could be said that the formation of these women's differing identities, reflected in their differing perceptions of themselves and others, and their 're-creative' readings of the televised messages, could be directly attributed to their differing temporalities, social positionings and spatial locations. This point reminds us that 'all identities are located in symbolic space and time'.[22]

The strongest example of these women's oppositional position was evident in the fact that they never regarded the illiterate women's actions in any of the messages as 'mistakes'. Instead they consistently saw the main characters as 'victims'. When discussing the mother who mixed up the medicines, they made comments like the following:

> She is a very poor woman ... she was going to lose her son because of something which is certainly not her 'fault'. It is, of course, her parents' fault, because they did not educate her or send her to school. What can she do?

These women's tendency to exonerate the illiterate woman and shift the blame to her parents could be considered a perfect example of their high degree of emotional empathy and identification with this televised character and their implication in her mistake.[23] However, it is also clearly an indirect attempt on their part to free themselves of any blame associated with, or resulting from, their own illiteracy, in order to legitimize themselves as good and competent mothers. This was clear in the fact that some of these women strongly defended the illiterate mother with the sick child as a 'good' and 'concerned' mother. Such clear counter-hegemonic and asymmetrical readings of this televised text[24] provide strong evidence that these women have denounced the dominant ideology that proposed the image of the 'literate mother as a better mother'. The older women saw this image as an attack on the most important aspect of their identity, namely their motherhood, which is their main source of pride and fulfilment. They cited multiple arguments and examples to prove that illiteracy does not undermine their capacity or competence as good mothers.

Similarly, the theme of 'victimization' came up again in reading the character of the woman who could not read the letter on her own. The blame in this case, instead of attaching to the illiterate person, was transferred to her neighbour for trying to 'exploit her and take advantage of her illiteracy'. Remarks like these consistently portrayed the women in the televised messages as 'victims' of other people's faults, while also revealing a prevailing fatalistic orientation in which all bad happenings are attributed to misfortune and bad luck. Such approaches not only reflect the reading positions of these women but also point up both the importance of the text itself as productive of meanings and 'the central importance of cultural practices in producing forms of thought and positions for women'.[25] Here it could be argued that women are inserted into positions which serve to produce and reproduce femininity, through the privileging and favouring of certain qualities and attributes that became largely perceived and stereotyped as 'feminine' qualities, such as helpfulness, selflessness, silent suffering, passivity and fatalism.

To understand the complex process whereby readers are constructed in the text, while at the same time they construct readings of the text, we have to look at readers as '... pre-existing, classed, gendered and racial subjects who are formed through certain material relations of production, who have a "lived reality", a material base, which stories help or hinder'.[26] In the light of this understanding, we can revise our outlook on the readings and interpretations that these women produced. These cannot be perceived as oppositional readings, misunderstandings, or distortions of practices that do not exist in the 'real world'. Rather, we have to realize that:

> ... those practices are real, and in their construction of meanings create places for identification, construct subject-positions in the text itself ... those practices within the text itself have relational effects that define who and where we are ... the positions and relations created in the text both relate to existing social and psychic struggle and provide a fantasy vehicle which inserts the reader into the text.[27]

The previous oppositional readings provide evidence that these women have, in fact, rejected the proposed image of the illiterate woman as an incompetent woman who is unable to cope with everyday problems in the proper way. The women actually used their comments on the televised texts as a site through which they expressed their rejection of media misrepresentations of themselves and their dissatisfaction with their own images as presented on the television screen. This is a clear example of how 'the discourses of the programme attempt to control and confine its potential meanings, while the discourses of the reader may resist this control'.[28] This group also used their readings of the television texts as a place where they highlighted the value of their own informal education, derived from everyday, real-life experiences, compared to the value of formal education. They expressed pride in themselves as hardworking, prudent and wise people, who were capable of managing their lives and overcoming their problems without recourse to reading and writing. In other words, it could be said that in their struggle to define the meaning of literacy, these women were actually struggling to defend and assert their own distinct identities. Indeed, 'different literacy practices position us differently in social space'[29] and, therefore, we tend to take on the particular identities associated with them.

In line with these women's pride in their informal literacy practices, which encompass many aspects of their traditional wisdom and indigenous knowledge, they strongly resisted any reversals in the traditional hierarchies of age, seniority and social positioning. That they rejected the possibility of children educating their father was reflected in their oppositional reading of that message. Most respondents in this group read into the message that the father was studying for his children, instead of the other way around. This is a good example of how members of the audience, who are constructive, knowledgeable and resourceful viewers, bring their own social knowledge and 'extra-textual' everyday resources and experiences to bear on interpreting textual codes.[30] Other women who came up with oppositional resistant readings admitted that they resisted their own children's offer to teach them reading and writing, because they felt that they were 'too old to learn'. In other words, they felt that acquiring new literacy skills would not be of real benefit, especially since they had been able to manage without them for many years. In asserting their own distinct identities, the women appeared to have restored the former purity and certainty of 'tradition' in their effort to secure a distinguished position for themselves in the face of significant 'Others', in this case their own children.

Although these women granted legitimacy to the concept of a single woman attending the literacy class, or a divorced woman seeking education for her children's sake, they fiercely objected to the idea of a married woman and mother doing the same thing. They thus came up with a totally oppositional reading of the message portraying the married woman who decided to attend literacy classes; for them she was by far the most controversial character in the televised texts. These women strongly believed that a good mother is the one who always puts her children first in everything. They perceived what this woman did as undermining her ability to be a good mother and considered her an 'irresponsible mother' and 'negligent woman'. This point seems to highlight a strong tendency among these women towards collectivism and familism, evident in the prioritizing of family and children's needs over their personal, individual needs. This could be also attributed to the production and reproduction of femininity through cultural practices and 'regimes of meaning', which advocate stereotypical gender images whereby 'selflessness becomes a virtue and doing anything for oneself is by implication bad and selfish'.[31] These women's remarks are a direct reflection of their internalization of prevailing gender socialization patterns and socially accepted codes of behaviour, which characterize any woman's tendency towards fulfilling self-interests as totally 'undesirable', and which advocate 'a view of the self as existing only for and through others'.[32]

Additionally, some members of this generation felt it would not be socially appropriate or acceptable to leave their homes and families behind in order to attend a mixed literacy class in the evening. This is closely related to the strong impact of interpersonal, face-to-face communication that made these women reluctant to attend the literacy class in the village, mainly because of their fear of becoming victims of gossip, sarcasm and criticism. As active social subjects and active media receivers, these women projected their own personal experiences and real-life situations into their readings of the texts.[33] As resourceful viewers, they came up with divergent decodings through 'the use of everyday social knowledge for "slot-filling" in the televised text'.[34] Nevertheless, their starkly oppositional readings of the literacy messages chosen for this study also clearly highlight the 'asymmetry' and 'lack of equivalence' between the producers and receivers of such texts.[35] They demonstrated the receivers' refusal to occupy, or even to perceive, the positions marked out for them by those who produced the texts.[36] Interestingly, some of the women who came up with oppositional readings even doubted the realism of the scenes pictured in the messages. They accepted that the women on screen were not actresses but actual rural women, but doubted that the scenes were shot in a real village setting. This is a clear example of how members of the audience could (re)define and (re)construct their own sense of realism in the televised text, depending on their own perceptions of reality and the multiple discourses which come to bear on them.

Negotiated readings

While most of the dominant readings came from women who defended their identities as 'formally educated' women, and most of the oppositional readings came from women who defended their 'informal education' and traditional wisdom, there were others who oscillated between these two poles. In exploring the dynamic and complex process of 'meaning negotiation' and 'identity negotiation', it is important to highlight how 'these concerns interlock, conflict and coalesce'[37] in these women's everyday lives, and how they are, in turn, reflected in their sense-making process. Most of the women who came up with negotiated reading positions were 'outsiders to the dominant literacy club'.[38] That is to say, they either had no formal education or had left school early before fully mastering basic literacy skills. Most of those who had left school early, however, expressed some regret for not finishing their education. They expressed a verbal desire, which was not always translated into effective action, to have a chance to resume their studies. In most cases, these women were influenced in some way by the experiences of others around them, notably friends, relatives or neighbours who were either educated or had tried to resume their education. This was especially true of the younger women in this group. In (re)defining and negotiating the meaning(s) of literacy, the women in this study came up with nuances and delicate shades of meaning, representing different positions on a spectrum between the two poles of dominant and oppositional readings. At one end of this spectrum, women with no formal education strongly defended their 'informal' education and upheld the value of their every-day experience. At the other end, formally educated women defended the dominant ideology on literacy without making compromises or nego-tiations. In between, women with limited education and/or a desire or willingness to study, acknowledged the value of 'formal' education and acquiring new literacy skills, while still upholding the value of their dis-tinct forms of literacy.

In reading the message of the mother who mixed up the medicines, the women with limited experience of education read into the message that the woman made a mistake, but they did not attribute that mistake to her illiteracy. Rather, they saw it in her failure to seek help from educated relatives or neighbours. These respondents, who always talked proudly about their alternative informal, oral, literacy practices, did not see their inability to read and write as an obstacle to competent performance of their maternal duties, or their many other chores and responsibilities. They felt they could always find successful ways to cope in their everyday lives without acquiring formal literacy skills. According to these women, the illiterate mother's fault was in not finding a successful coping strat-egy. Some recalled incidents similar to the mixed-up medicines happening to their relatives and commented proudly on their ability to avoid such problems, thereby asserting their traditional wisdom and alternative knowledge systems. A further interpretation among this group attributed the mistake over the medicine bottles to inexperience. They inferred from the television message that the woman had no other children and therefore did not know what to do.

This view was shared by other women, who put a higher value on everyday experience and informal advice coming from 'voices of experience' in childcare matters, such as mothers, aunts and mothers-in-law, than on formal education and medical expertise. They cited a popular saying in Arabic: 'Asking an experienced person is better than asking a doctor'. Once again, we should be careful to avoid 'ignoring the positivity of the subaltern as the possessor of other knowledges and traditions; as having their own history in which there are power relations defined within the ranks of the subordinated'.[39] Likewise, in the case of the character who was unable to read her own letters, most of the women with limited education read into the message that she made a mistake. For them, however, the mistake was not her illiteracy but that she relied on the wrong person, instead of relying on very close relatives who could be trusted.

These women were proud of the successful coping strategies that they were always capable of inventing and deploying in their everyday lives, in order to avoid the difficulties posed by their inability to read and write. This kind of strategy has been described as one of 'familiarizing one's "otherness" in terms of other "Others"'.[40] Taking into account that 'the self is a product of a differentiating machine',[41] it seems that these women were defending their legitimate alternative knowledge systems by a technique of isolating and excluding other women. These 'others' were people who fell outside the mainstream literacy position like themselves, but who were not, in their view, equally successful in utilizing other forms of literacy to avoid or minimize any potential damage due to their illiteracy.

Interestingly, most of the women who shared the above views felt that it was quite realistic for the literacy messages to show an urban woman unable to read letters or medicine labels. While most women who came up with dominant readings said that it would have been more realistic to feature rural women in these messages, since 'they are the ones who suffer the most from the "problem" of illiteracy', most women who came up with negotiated readings gave comments like the following:

Of course, it is more realistic to show an urban woman in this situation … it is very unlikely that something like that could happen to a rural woman in a village like ours, for example. Everyone is very helpful and friendly over here. If a woman is stuck and can't find one of her immediate family members to help her in something like reading a letter or reading a label on a bottle of medicine, she can always seek the help of some neighbour or friend. No one will exploit her or ask for money in return.

Comments like this show how the women brought their own everyday resources and 'extra-textual' social knowledge to bear in reading the message, reminding us to 'recognize both the structuring role of the text and the constructive role of the viewer in negotiating meaning'.[42] It is also clear that these women used their comments on the televised text to express pride in some positive aspects of their social life in the village community, such as social solidarity and cooperation, as well as the absence of negative aspects like materialism and exploitation. Most importantly, however, they were also upholding and defending the value of the 'collective' form of literacy, which is available in their community, and which makes reading and writing a 'shared experience' and a 'social activity', rather than an individual asset. They showed how 'communities develop networks of exchange and interdependence in which literacy is just one skill among many being bartered'. In this situation, the acquisition of literacy skills is not a first order priority at the individual level, so long as it is available at the community level.[43]

Overall, it could be said that these women detected a high degree of 'urban otherness' in the government's literacy texts and the characters featured in them, who were felt to be quite alien and out of touch with their own real-life situation. This high degree of alienation, and low degree of self-involvement and emotional connectedness with these characters,[44] was evident in some of their divergent readings. For example, some women read into the message about the woman whose neighbour reads her letters that the illiterate woman was paying her neighbour 'in return for confidentiality, not just in return for reading a letter'. They saw the illiterate woman's fault as 'keeping some bad, and potentially scandalous, secrets, which she was certainly ashamed to let any close relative or friend find out about, and that's how she easily became a victim of exploitation and blackmailing'. This view was also shared by most women who came up with oppositional readings. This example reminds us of the relationship between real and textualized identities, and how identities can be simultaneously (re)constructed and reflected back in the mutual engagement between readers and texts. It shows how television may reinforce, legitimize or challenge viewers' prior beliefs, values and experiences, through showing characters in similar situations being rewarded or punished.[45]

Some of the older women who had no formal education and who had unsuccessful or nonexistent experiences in terms of learning from their own children, adopted a negotiated code in reading the message of the children who educated their father. They granted legitimacy to the general concept of educated children educating their parents, but adopted a situationally defined or modified code at the level of concrete practice[46] by doubting its applicability to their everyday lives. Some read into the message that 'the father and the children were studying together and helping each other'. These women highlighted the value of illiterate parents' real-life experience, and they sometimes prioritized it over the value of their children's education. They attributed this to the fact that these parents usually have many first-hand experiences and multiple sources of learning, which are 'usually not available to their educated children, who depend mainly on the school as their prime source of learning'. However, unlike the women who totally resisted the principle of children educating their parents, these women recognized the value of their children's formal education, and did not rule out the possibility of learning from them.

The fact that these women acknowledged two parallel forms of literacy, regarding them as equally valid knowledge systems, provides us with an image of 'border-crossing' or 'between-ness' between the two poles of 'traditional' and 'modern' identities.[47] Thus the formation of identity is always a shifting, movable and mixed phenomenon that exists in an area of negotiation between the dominant and the subordinate or oppositional cultural and ideological values. Overlaps and crossovers may take place between the three categories in the classic typology of viewer clusters, namely the dominant, negotiated and oppositional readings of media texts.

Conclusion

We can infer from the foregoing discussion that, in oscillating between the two poles of 'dominant' and 'oppositional' readings, women in this study were also oscillating between the two poles of 'tradition' and 'modernity', accommodating some aspects of both positions in the process. Yet there is no simple or straightforward answer to the question of how they moved into this new terrain of negotiation of meaning and identity. It is obvious that this process was influenced by a complex of subtle factors, which were not equally or similarly shared by all respondents. These factors included the respondent's personal motivation, individual experience and social and generational changes. Younger women, for instance, appeared to be influenced by the experiences of some of their educated peers as well as by the acquisition of basic literacy skills in the case of early school leavers. This complex dynamic between meaning negotiation and identity negotiation involves a view of the audience not as 'biological individuals', but as 'subjects' who are never 'fixed', but who are always shifting and changing, and who always 'partially', rather than fully, identify with what is viewed.[48] So we can conclude that:

> ... 'the meaning' of the image cannot be seen as fixed, stable or univocal across time or cultures. Also, the subject itself is not a completed entity but something which is produced, through complex and unfinished processes which are both social and psychic – a subject-in-process.[49]

It also emerges from the study that literacy learning is not simply a neutral technical skill but one that is 'connected with much deeper cultural values about identity, personhood and relationships',[50] and that 'different literacy practices position us differently in social space'.[51] Most importantly, the controversial and contrasting opinions and views that emerged between the women in this study clearly reveal that they belong to different 'worlds of literacy', each of which is shaped and patterned by wider social practices and values in society'.[52] However, in analysing these women's competing and conflicting forms of literacy and their different knowledge systems, I am aware that they do not all carry the same weight or have the same power. Rather, we have to realize that the formal, institutional educational system remains the most powerful world of literacy, which dictates what counts as real knowledge or proper language.[53] Other forms of literacy continue to be devalued, excluded, isolated or unrecognized, which requires a struggle to redefine and negotiate the existing worlds of literacy and to press for the validity and recognition of the devalued forms. This process involves resistances and challenges to the dominant ideology of literacy and posing several alternatives to it.[54]

7
Echoes: Gender and Media Challenges in Palestine

Benaz Somiry-Batrawi

Palestinian women have played a central role in Palestinian political history as part of the national resistance movement. Displaced from their homes by the creation of Israel, they led the way in relief work, joined political parties, entered professions in health, education and the media and struggled to bring up families, often in humiliating and difficult circumstances.[1] With the national liberation struggle paramount, Palestinian society has not given priority to gender issues. For many years, women's struggle for fairness and equality was widely regarded as a separate issue and one that was secondary or subordinate. When women in the resistance movement drew attention to obstacles affecting their participation, as some did in the 1970s and early 1980s, a common rhetorical response was to ask which of the two objectives – 'liberating Palestine' or 'liberating women' – was more important.[2]

As the Madrid peace talks started between the Palestine Liberation Organization (PLO) and the Israeli government in 1991, the media began to show the role of Palestinian women more clearly. In particular, Dr Hanan Ashrawi was appointed as a spokeswoman for the Palestinian delegation to the peace talks. Behind the scenes, however, efforts to bring gender awareness to the media faced many challenges. Given the all-pervading, everyday impact of Israeli occupation on Palestinian lives, the Palestinian media have remained focused first and foremost on fighting the occupation, paying little attention to gender issues. Although some sections of the Palestinian media are ready to develop gender awareness, they have been held back by adverse factors. One is a lack of resources, including a lack of journalists who understand gender issues or are able to promote women's rights and gender equality through the media. In 2002, this was compounded by the debilitating effect of Israeli military attacks on media installations.

This chapter considers some of the challenges facing the Palestinian media institutions that have sought to promote women not only as the subject of discussion but as part of media production teams. In particular, it examines the example of a gender and media project initiated by the private Palestinian station, Al-Quds Educational TV (AETV). In order to view this project in context, the chapter starts by outlining phases of development relating to women's representation in and through the Palestinian media.

Before the Oslo Accords

Although the history of Palestinian media goes back to the years before the British Mandate in Palestine, Palestinian women's opportunities in media were less than men's, because of social restrictions on mixing of the sexes. The disruption and upheaval experienced by Palestinian society also had a major effect. For example, women began to work in radio stations in the 1930s and 1940s but were dispersed to neighbouring Arab states after the establishment of Israel in 1948.[3] The General Union of Palestinian Women, established in 1965, generated committees focusing on culture and media, which in turn issued publications for women.[4] Scarcely had these begun, however, than the Six-Day War in June 1967 ended with Israel's occupation of the Gaza Strip and West Bank, causing new waves of Palestinian refugees. The Union's publishing activities resumed from outside Palestine. Media activity inside the Occupied Territories was subject to strict control by the Israeli occupying authorities. Israeli military orders banned broadcasting, allowing only newspapers to function under tight Israeli censorship.[5]

Women began to establish themselves more firmly in the media sector inside the Occupied Territories as a result of the first Palestinian uprising (intifada), which started in December 1987. The intifada attracted the attention of the international media, so that journalists and television crews started arriving from all over the world. They found it very difficult to work in the Occupied Territories without the help of local Palestinians, whom they hired as guides and 'fixers' in places that were troublesome from a security point of view.[6] When Israeli undercover intelligence units began to pose as journalists, making the Occupied Territories potentially dangerous for bona fide foreign reporters, western media teams began to insist on being accompanied by Palestinians.[7] In this way the Palestinian fixers acquired the equipment, confidence and expertise to start compiling their own video footage. As the situation became more difficult on the ground, the opportunities for indigenous Palestinian audiovisual workers increased. News agencies started hiring Palestinian cameramen inside Palestinian towns, villages and refugee camps to capture footage of areas under curfew or deemed too risky for foreign crews to enter. Some foreign journalists found they could over-come social restrictions and interview Palestinians in their homes if they relied on university-educated female guides with foreign language skills, who could accompany them into households. Among the Palestinian women journalists who learned their reporting skills at this time were the CNN reporter Rula Amin, photojournalist Rula Halawani, film director Buthaina Khoury, camerawoman Suheir Isma'il and two reporters, Majida al-Batsh and Ruba al-Husari.

Another side effect of the first intifada was an erosion of restrictive boundaries between the public and private spheres, brought about by the methods of resistance adopted. For example, communiqués from the Unified National Command and leaflets distributed by women's organi-zations expressly called upon women to take part in demonstrations, strikes and political rallies.[8] So, when women's groups found themselves sidelined again in the aftermath of the intifada, they were ready to do something about it. It became clear that women were being marginalized when technical committees were formed to negotiate under the frame-work of the multilateral Arab–Israeli peace talks that started in October 1991. In these committees the ratio of men to women was 410:5.[9] Women activists looked around at liberation struggles in other countries and discovered, for example, that Algerian women had been subjected to a discriminatory Family Code in 1984, two decades after Algerian men and women fought side-by-side to achieve independence from French colonial rule. So they called for the formation of a dedicated women's technical committee to address women's political, social and civil rights and to work for better representation of women within the other male-dominated technical committees.[10]

This was how the Women's Affairs Technical Committee (WATC) was born. It was formed in August 1992 by 16 volunteers, who all had other jobs as well as political and family obligations. Later, after Israel and the PLO agreed the Declaration of Principles (DOP) in Oslo in August 1993 and the fledgling Palestinian National Authority (PNA) was formed, the other technical committees were merged into ministries. The WATC developed instead into a coalition of non-governmental organizations and became instrumental in bringing gender issues to public attention through the media. Meanwhile, other initiatives were also putting women in the media spotlight. In July 1993, before the DOP, a group of Palestinian journalists, led by Daoud Kuttab of the Jerusalem Film Institute, compiled an experimental television news broadcast to develop an idea about what Palestinian television might be like. Three Palestinian women and one man appeared in that very first Palestinian news broadcast.[11]

From 1993 to the second intifada

The DOP was hammered out in Oslo and signed in Washington on 13 September 1993. It paved the way for agreements on the withdrawal of Israeli occupation forces from major cities in the West Bank and Gaza Strip and the creation of the PNA. The first Annex to the DOP also provided for the 'possibility' of licensing a radio and television station. These were to be the first Palestinian-run broadcasting operations on Palestinian territory. The Palestinian Broadcasting Corporation (PBC) was established by the PNA and stayed under its total control. As an alternative to the PBC, a number of Palestinian journalists, businessmen and non-governmental organizations (NGOs) initiated the idea of establishing their own private television and radio stations.[12] The ensuing growth of media outlets created new opportunities for women to be part of the broadcast industry in Palestine. In the West Bank alone, by 2001 there were 31 private television stations.[13] Most of these were very small operations, often run by a family or group of two or three young colleagues working from a single room. Nevertheless, many women found work as presenters, reporters, camerawomen, sound technicians, administrators and sometimes in decision-making positions.

Women achieved some advances through media activity. The WATC established regular slots in the press and on radio and television for coverage of issues that women wanted to see discussed in public. *Al-Ayyam* (The Days) was launched by a group of Palestinian entrepreneurs in 1995. *Sawt al-Nissa'* (Women's Voice) was started as a bi-weekly supplement in *Al-Ayyam* newspaper, along with other supplements on education and the environment that *Al-Ayyam* also carried, likewise prepared by local NGOs. The Palestinian Working Women's Society for

Development started a magazine called *Al-Yanabeea* (Springs), a radio programme called *Bi Ayyun al-Nissa'* (Through Women's Eyes), and a television programme called *Shababik* (Windows) in collaboration with AETV. WATC, which organized training for women in communication, gender awareness and human rights, took a particularly proactive approach to the media in the run-up to elections to the Palestinian Legislative Council in January 1996. In this period it produced a newsletter calling for women to have a quota of 30 per cent of the Council's 88 seats. In the event, 28 women ran for election and five won seats. When the subsequent plan to elect municipal councils was cancelled in favour of appointing representatives, the WATC organized its own local elections in villages to enable women to choose their own representatives. The Committee then demanded that the women chosen be included on municipal councils, with the result that 30 women were appointed.[14]

As Palestinian public and private media were getting established during the 1990s, so were pan-Arab satellite channels. In fact there was often a close relationship between the two, as some of the private Palestinian stations chose to rebroadcast programmes screened by the satellite channels, whether or not they had legal authorization to do so.[15] Most Arab channels took a lenient view of Palestinian piracy. In consequence, a much larger number of Palestinians were familiar with the material shown on the satellite channels than would be guessed from the number actually owning satellite dishes.[16] This close link opened the satellite sector to Palestinian women journalists working as correspondents in the West Bank and Gaza. When the second Palestinian intifada started on 28 September 2000, Arab and foreign satellite channels gave more airtime to Palestinian affairs and more Palestinian women reporters appeared on screen. Their success can be gauged from the number of Arab journalism prizes they received. Out of 22 awards made to individuals and publishers in 2001, of which ten were for women, five were won by Palestinians. Four of these were working for satellite television, namely: Daniela Khalaf, correspondent for the Saudi-owned MBC, Shuruq al-Assaad (Egypt's Nile TV), Laila Awda (Abu Dhabi TV) and Shirin Abu Aqla (Al-Jazeera). The fifth was Omaya Joha, cartoonist for the Palestinian daily newspaper, *Al-Quds*.[17]

Not all developments were so positive, however. A statistical survey by Heba Assaf for the Palestinian Ministry of Information in 2001 showed that, although 313 women graduated with media qualifications from five

Palestinian universities in one year, women accounted for only 20 per cent of Palestinian media professionals.[18] Assaf's study showed a higher proportion of women doing administrative work than were actually reporting or editing and few of these held managerial posts. The ratio was 41 administrators to 25 practitioners.[19] A study by the United Nations Children's Fund (Unicef) in 2000 found that 71.4 per cent of media specialists questioned considered Palestinian media coverage of issues related to women to be unsatisfactory, while only 3.6 per cent considered it good. The remainder thought it was average.[20] One reason for this low satisfaction rate is thought to be a deliberate policy among Palestinian media institutions of avoiding controversy or causing offence in a conservative society. Another is the limited resources and professionalism of the private Palestinian television stations. The majority of their programmes are for entertainment; only certain stations have followed a clear policy of showing programmes that include local production aimed at building civil society, promoting democracy and pluralism and encouraging positive social behaviour. Only a few stations have paid attention to gender issues and put women behind the camera as well as in front of it. One of these is AETV, working under the umbrella of the Institute of Modern Media at Al-Quds University.

Case study: the Institute of Modern Media

The Institute of Modern Media (IMM) was established in 1996 as an independent non-profit Palestinian institution at Al-Quds University. (Al-Quds is the Arabic name for Jerusalem). It was founded by Daoud Kuttab, who was also behind initiatives such as the experimental news broadcast in 1993 (mentioned above) and the *Palestinian Diaries* television programme shown on Swedish, Dutch and British television in 1992.[21] The rationale behind the Institute was that, by mastering modern media technology, Palestinian media practitioners could 'level the field' between themselves and practitioners in the 'first world' by 'knowing what is required to make it in the world media'.[22] To serve this objective, the Institute established AETV as its community relations wing, obtaining a licence for AETV from the Palestinian Ministry of Information in 1996. Its aim was to increase awareness of the audiovisual media and raise the technical level of Palestinian television productions. It supports cooperation among local independent television stations in areas such as programme exchange and training. Its commitment to community involvement means focusing on local needs and issues such as nation-building, pluralism, democracy, human rights and freedom of speech. AETV put its plans into practice in early 1997 by airing sessions of the Palestinian Legislative Council. The Palestinian security authorities jammed these programmes and imprisoned Kuttab for eight days without charge.

Because of its orientation towards education and community development, AETV puts programmes on literacy, healthcare, social attitudes, the environment and consumer awareness at the top of its agenda. For this it needs journalists who can specialize in fields like education, culture, gender concepts, reproductive health and human rights.[23] That was why the IMM and AETV together established a number of departments, including the Gender and Media Department. This was set up in April 2001 with funding from the Ford Foundation. The idea of the department came about when interest in gender-related programmes increased after a one-month series of screenings of documentary films the previous year, dealing with topics like social segregation and domestic violence. Another project that predated the Department's creation was a co-production between AETV and the Palestinian Working Women's Society for Development. This involved an eight-episode series of television programmes examining issues related to women and work, women as political prisoners, women as role models, women and international conferences, women and family law, distinguished women, women and the school curriculum and women and human rights. These programmes, shown in 1999–2000, hosted expert guests in the fields of economy, law, politics, education, public relations and art. Since the IMM/AETV aims to increase the involvement of other civil society institutions, it also airs programmes it has not produced. The regular, 55-minute social affairs programme *Bisaraha* (Frankly), a WATC-PBC co-production, was aired by AETV.

A major project the IMM did produce itself was a series of documentary films and television shows aimed at promoting a balanced and non-stereotypical image of women in the Palestinian media.[24] The project comprised six documentaries, of 12–17 minutes each, each profiling a different role model figure, including women and men, educated or not, well known or not well known. The aim of the profiles was to examine normal life in a way that would expose gender issues in the Palestinian community. Some of the issues handled in these films were equal rights for education, micro-credit for small businesses run by women, oral political history and the role of Palestinian women in the period 1930–50, and stories of women political activists. AETV aired the six documentaries over five days and distributed copies to other television stations. Beyond that, the films were also shown at a regional conference in Amman and an international meeting in the US. Some women's organizations are still using them as tools to promote women's participation in social and political life and to gain recognition for their contribution to the life of their country.

A second project was funded by the British Council. This revolved around a training workshop for professional journalists in mid-career to increase their gender sensitivity and to promote positive images of women in Palestinian and Arab media. Taking the UN Convention on the Elimination of All Forms of Discrimination Against Women (CEDAW) as a framework, the training programme centred on the topics of gender and human rights, gender and media, and gender and TV production. The project as a whole comprised three stages: preparation, training and production. Participants came from two women's organizations and eight private TV stations. The preparation process included compiling the training material and communicating with trainers and trainees. Training then took place in two stages. Human rights were discussed in relation to domestic violence and disability. The image of women in the media involved analysis of talkshows, cartoons and films. As for the production component, at the end of the workshop the trainees produced their own TV talkshow under the title *Palestinian Women and Media Coverage*. It included four field reports on the portrayal of Palestinian women in advertising, TV series, local TV programmes, and the role of Palestinian women journalists in news coverage. This programme was also distributed to seven TV stations in the West Bank and Gaza Strip, including the PBC's terrestrial and satellite channels. All stations aired the programme on 8 March 2001, International Women's Day.

The success of such ventures encouraged the IMM administration to establish their specialized Gender and Media Department to build on the experience and carry it forward. However, as the political situation in the area deteriorated, seeing projects through to a successful conclusion also became more difficult. One project undertaken aimed to include two activities: producing 12 talkshows, including drama scenes and field reports, and organizing a guest lecture series hosting gender experts from Arab countries, Europe and the US. The drama scenes were produced to a length of six minutes each and field reports of five minutes each were also produced, despite many delays and obstacles. The final output was thus a series of 12 talkshows, complete with drama scenes and field reports, tackling gender and education, environment, reproductive health, domestic violence, information technology, globalization, reproductive rights, ageing, sexual harassment, promoting positive portrayals in broadcast media, anti-poverty initiatives and micro enterprises, and women in armed conflict. The significance of this production lay in the amount of research conducted for it and the methods used. It was very rare in Arabic-language television for a series tackling gender issues to integrate studio discussion, drama scenes and field reports. The use of drama scenes with Palestinian actresses and actors was a great advantage.

The next phase of the project, consisting of guest lectures, did not take place. Continuous Israeli military incursions, reoccupation of Palestinian towns and long hours of curfew made it impossible. Many of the gender experts who had previously been enthusiastic to participate became hesitant to travel to Palestine and were warned against it by their governments. In fact, since its establishment the Gender and Media Department faced many challenges. It came into being soon after the start of the second intifada, at a time when the priorities of local media outlets changed. Although the IMM and AETV tried to stick to their agenda, it was impossible to ignore political issues. The Department continued to work with minimal staff, equipment and resources, but, increasingly, Israeli roadblocks and other restrictions on movement prevented staff – even those with Israeli press accreditation – from getting to work. When the Israeli government Press Office decided not to renew press cards for Palestinian journalists, AETV crews faced more obstacles. As individuals had more and more reason to worry about their own safety and security and that of their families, the process of arranging meetings and filming could not proceed.

At the end of March 2002, Israeli troops launched their most far-reaching military operation in the West Bank, reoccupying every major Palestinian town. During their incursion into Ramallah and Al-Bireh in April 2002, Israeli forces occupied the IMM headquarters for 18 days, from 2 to 20 April. When the IMM regained access it found a scene of vandalism and devastation. The eyewitness accounts of its staff were corroborated by independent international observers.[25] A senior Israeli military officer told the Israeli daily *Ha'aretz* on 30 April that there had indeed been a 'wide-scale, ugly phenomenon of vandalism' by Israeli soldiers entering Palestinian buildings.[26] The IMM/AETV was one of several television and radio stations where soldiers 'literally used sledgehammers' to smash microphones, tapes, CDs, monitors, mixers, players/recorders.[27] In its own report on events, the IMM stated:

> As the Israeli forces entered the compound, two employees of the IMM were attempting to continue transmission of AETV. They were broadcasting entertainment programmes for children; public and medical service information, including addresses and telephone numbers; informative films to help parents deal with the trauma, fear and stress experienced by their children; and short first aid films. The two employees were found by the Israeli forces and held for four hours of questioning before being released and warned not to return. They witnessed the Israeli forces throwing cameras and video archives out of the fourth floor, where the Institute and AETV are located. Tanks and armoured personnel carriers proceeded to occupy the faculty compound.[28]

Losses incurred by IMM as a result of the soldiers' actions were estimated at over $200,000. The damage was mainly to equipment that had been donated by international agencies and western governments, including the US government, American foundations, European countries and a number of American Jewish organizations. Estimates by several station owners suggested that the total damage sustained by Palestinian broadcast media during Israel's six-week military offensive amounted to at least $700,000.[29] The UN and World Bank put the total cost of destruction caused by the offensive at $350 million, taking account of all damage to Palestinian infrastructure, buildings, homes, roads, equipment, cultural sites and offices.[30] Reporting on the devastation suffered by several private radio and television stations in the Ramallah area just after it happened, Wasim Abdullah, AETV's technical director, said the stations affected had been helping to build a civil society, through 'better reporting, more local programming, more experience and more innovation'. Now, he said, they lay 'in ruins'.[31]

Conclusion

The process of raising gender awareness in the Palestinian media has been subject to interruption and disruption over the years. It could not begin in the audiovisual media until Palestinian-run broadcasting was permitted in the West Bank and Gaza Strip in the mid-1990s. The many small radio and television stations that sprang up had both advantages and disadvantages. They created job opportunities for women and men, but could not always support the level of professionalism and local programme production required. For that reason, cooperation among small stations in promoting gender awareness was particularly valued. Such cooperation was part of wider attempts to create networks of local stations that would share programmes and collaborate in training.

Despite serious social and political obstacles since late 2000, and particularly in the early months of 2002, the IMM/AETV and a few other media outlets have attempted to lay the foundations for progressive media in Palestine. The echoes of the voices of Palestinian women raised in AETV programmes can still be heard. Other media institutions in Palestine must be encouraged to take a similar initiative before these echoes fade.

8

Engagement in the Public Sphere: Women and the Press in Kuwait

Haya al-Mughni and Mary Ann Tétreault

This chapter considers the role of newspapers in debates on women's rights in Kuwait. Looking back over 40 years of print-press coverage, and based on field research and interviews with female activists, we argue that, with respect to women's rights, Kuwaiti newspapers are neither reflexively conservative supporters of the status quo nor reliably progressive supporters of liberalization. Press coverage and activists' perceptions of that coverage are more complex. Overall, coverage appears to be even-handed with respect to women's political activism. Advocates and opponents of women's rights seem to enjoy more or less equal access to the media, both as subjects of news stories and as authors of op-ed style advocacy articles. At the same time, individual media outlets tend to favour advocacy pieces that reflect their respective publishers' points of view. Thus, a reader must consult more than one newspaper and construct her or his own version of 'balanced coverage', rather than relying on any one source to do this. However, the task is complicated by the growing diversity of the women's movement and the resulting complexity of women's goals and strategies. In the face of such diversity there has been a contrary tendency in the media to reduce women's activism to contention between two 'sides'. Despite these deficiencies, Kuwaiti female activists themselves believe that they have been covered fairly by the print press.

The media and politics

Many contemporary theories about the political role of the news media are based on analyses of large states and focus primarily on electronic media.[1] However, in what is perhaps the most influential study of the role of mass media in the formation of national identity, Benedict

Anderson[2] examined the historical role of newspapers and popular novels in creating a sense of community and filling it with the specific content that enables its members to imagine themselves part of a larger whole, separate from non-national others.[3] Anderson emphasized the commercial character of the press to explain its important role. 'Print-capitalism', he said, displays a 'revolutionary vernacularizing thrust' that, in the process of seeking markets for its products, creates 'unified fields of exchange and communication'.[4] As a by-product of this process, language is standardized across population groups, not only improving communication within the nation but also becoming a more effective medium for the exercise of political power by the state. At the same time, the market orientation of the printer-journalist, a modern political actor originating in the eighteenth-century 'New World' and epitomized by Benjamin Franklin, democratizes mass communication by providing news in response to market demand. Thus news is not simply top-down communication from the state to 'the nation' but also a way for the neighbourhood, the region, the market and, ultimately, those who occupy different ethical and ideological positions, to define themselves and speak to one another as members of a national community.

The plurality of commercial news media, theoretically at least, is the basis for John Stuart Mill's 'marketplace of ideas', where readers, listeners and viewers can find variety in coverage, stories and perspectives to suit their individual needs. However, the commercial character of the press is not without its problems. Publishers can use their proprietorship to block information and perspectives they oppose, and shape coverage to suit their ideological positions. Where there is competition for readers and viewers, studies have shown that the news 'product' tends to become standardized. This is potentially more serious for electronic than print media because of the more nearly exclusive pattern of consumption of electronic media; although a 'consumer' can see or hear programmes on more than one station by taping them, this pattern is rare as compared to the consumption of multiple newspapers or news magazines. Even so, in both print and broadcast media, fewer stories are covered overall and, within those that are, fewer pieces of information and contextual cues (historical background, analysis, commentary) are provided.[5] Long-running or repeat stories quickly become stereotypical and may pander to what the media entrepreneur perceives as the prejudices and expectations of his target market.[6] When Daniel Hallin examined US coverage of antiwar protesters during the Vietnam conflict, he found that, where groups and ideas outside the mainstream were covered at all, the coverage tended to marginalize them and belittle the policies they advocated.[7] Since all these observations would seem to be applicable to news coverage of women's groups and women's rights, this chapter examines such coverage in the Kuwaiti context with these findings in mind.

Media access, censorship and power struggles

Kuwait has long been renowned for its free press and lively public debates. This small country, home to 2.5 million inhabitants – of whom two-thirds are non-native – produces far more newspapers and magazines than any of its neighbours. Kuwait has five Arabic and two English-language dailies. The first daily newspaper, *Al-Ra'i al-Aam*, was established in 1961 by a wealthy merchant, Abdel-Aziz al-Masa'ed. This was followed the next year by *Al-Watan* and *Akhbar al-Kuwait* and, in subsequent years, by *Al-Siyassah* (1968) and *Al-Qabas* (1972). *Akhbar al-Kuwait* was later purchased by the Al Marzouk, a wealthy merchant family, and renamed *Al-Anba'*. The English-language dailies are *Arab Times*, owned by the Al-Siyassah publishing house, and *Kuwait Times*, owned by Yousef Alyan. In addition to daily newspapers, Kuwaitis publish many magazines. Almost every political group in the country has its own publication. The Islamic Reform Society, (Jamiyat al-Islah al-Ijtimaiyya), representing the Muslim Brotherhood movement, has a weekly political magazine, *Al-Mujtamaa*, which has been in circulation since 1971. The Arab nationalist group also has its own political weekly, *Al-Talia*. Other influential magazines during the period reviewed in this chapter included *Al-Zaman*, a notably open and critical political forum owned by a member of the ruling family, Sheikh Nasser Sabah al-Ahmad Al Sabah, and *Al-Dostour*, a magazine published weekly by the parliament. The print press, on the whole, reflects merchant views in advocating political reforms, principal of which are a constitutional government, a fair distribution of oil revenues, and national autonomy.

Until the Iraqi invasion of Kuwait in 1990, Kuwaitis relied almost entirely on locally produced newspapers and magazines for the bulk of their news. Before the advent of satellite dishes, radio and television news broadcasts came primarily from state-owned and operated stations and concentrated on ceremonial events such as state visits. Campaign and election coverage on electronic media was so limited as to be virtually non-existent, a situation that continued well into the 1990s.[8] The invasion highlighted the inadequacy of the state-controlled media. Even though the government had been given access to US satellite photographs of Iraqi troop movements on the border, most Kuwaitis remained ignorant of the magnitude of the looming danger. Apart from those who regularly monitored foreign radio, people knew little about the crisis because censorship had 'banned any mention of it' in local news outlets.[9] After the invasion had begun and before state radio and television stations were closed down by enemy forces, 'there was nothing on the news whatsoever' other than slogans.[10] In contrast to the orchestrated majesty of state-controlled broadcast news, the privately owned print press offered extensive local news and commentary during normal times. However, as shown below, their ability to report and comment on events was highly constrained during periods when civil liberties were suspended.

Freedom of the press is guaranteed under Kuwait's constitution (Article 37), a guarantee that was reiterated on 21 May 1996, when Kuwait acceded to the International Covenant on Civil and Political Rights.[11] Yet freedom of expression has often been curtailed through various forms of political pressure, and was violated absolutely during two periods when the National Assembly (parliament) was dismissed and portions of the Constitution suspended. The first occurred in 1976, when the government dismissed the National Assembly, closed down *Al-Talia* and imposed restrictions on what the press could publish. This lasted until 1981, when new parliamentary elections were held in vastly redrawn constituencies.[12] A second round of suspensions was imposed in 1986. In addition to closing the parliament, the government instituted press censorship so tight that it was impossible for the leader of the pro-democracy movement, which had formed in response to the suspensions, to use the press to change the programme of what originally had been scheduled as a protest meeting.

> Two days before this meeting, the amir had made a televised speech calling for a dialogue with the opposition. Ahmad al-Sa'doun insists that he had responded in the same spirit of conciliation, sending a press release to the newspapers. ... announc[ing] that the meeting would not include speeches by the opposition, but that the organizers planned to present information about the amir's address and report

how the Group of Forty-five had responded to it. ... [G]overnment censors refused to allow the newspapers to publish the press release. When crowds of citizens and opposition leaders [came to the meeting] ... they faced regular police, the Kuwait National Guard, riot police, and tanks shooting chemical foam.[13]

After Kuwait was liberated from Iraqi occupation, parliamentary elections were resumed in 1992. However, press restrictions were not formally lifted. Journalists, writers, and academics continued to face censorship and prosecutions. Under the Press and Publications Law it is a criminal offence to criticize the emir, or publish materials offensive to Islam, or those that might incite violence, hatred, or dissent. Suspension of publication of newspapers charged with violating this law has occurred several times since 1992. Examples include a five-day suspension of *Al-Anba'* in 1995 for publishing interviews with members of the political opposition that advocated separating the position of crown prince from the position of prime minister, and a five-day suspension of *Al-Siyassah* in 1999, after it published an article considered damaging to the emir and the country's interests.

Government efforts to restrict the press were reinforced throughout the 1990s by a parallel campaign waged by Islamist groups advocating pre-publication censorship and the institution of some form of *raqaba* (control), not only over the news media but all fields of cultural production such as books, films, and social entertainment. This campaign resulted in attacks on publishers, the banning of hundreds of books from Kuwait's annual book fair and a series of trials against liberal writers and academics. In 1998, Mohammed al-Saqr, then the chief editor of *Al-Qabas*, was sentenced to six months' imprisonment for publishing a joke about Adam and Eve. The verdict was overturned on appeal. In October 1999, Islamists brought charges of blasphemy against Dr Ahmad Baghdadi, chair of the Political Science Department at Kuwait University, regarding an article he had written for the university's student magazine, *Al-Shoula*. The article stated that the Prophet Mohammed had failed to convert non-believers during his time in Makkah.

Convictions of Kuwaitis under the blasphemy regulations are common but so are suspended sentences and early release. When Baghdadi was sent to jail, he promptly began a hunger strike. Islamist leaders lauded his imprisonment as a victory for their religious crusade. But the danger to Baghdadi's health – he has a heart condition – and the vigour with which colleagues and neighbours responded to his plight by holding public meetings and calling for his release, moved the emir to have him discharged after two weeks.[14] Women convicted of blasphemy have had similar experiences. A battle extending over several years was initiated by Islamists against two female writers, Layla al-Uthman and Alia Shuaib, for novels that allegedly contained improper and immoral language. These efforts finally resulted in blasphemy convictions for both women in January 2000. Shuaib was sentenced to two months' imprisonment but the sentence was overturned on appeal and a fine was substituted. Al-Uthman's sentence also was reduced to a fine.[15]

Islamists claimed that their *raqaba* was undertaken as part of their quest to Islamicize society and ensure public adherence to Islamic mores and values. But what really is at stake is their desire to control society and marginalize the liberal forces which have dominated the print media for decades. The impact of their campaigns was revealed following the resolution of the case of Alia Shuaib, who was interviewed by *Christian Science Monitor* reporter Ilene Prusher. Shortly after the trial, Prusher wrote that, despite the conclusion of her long ordeal, 'in the court of public opinion … the trial [of Alia Shuaib] continues'. Strangers approached her on the street and, after verifying her identity, spat on her. Alia was nominally free as a result of the appeal court's decision, but she shared with the reporter her realization that, if she were to continue to teach and write what she thinks, she would have to do it somewhere other than Kuwait.[16]

The press and political reform

Kuwaiti merchants pioneered the production of newspapers and weekly magazines to bring about political reforms. The reformist position of the merchants was clear even before Kuwait had its own print press. In 1938, the opposition group known as the National Bloc, which had substantial support among the leading merchants, used the Iraqi press to publish its reform programme. The 1940s saw the launch of magazines such as *Al-Baatha* (1946), *Al-Kazima* (1948), *Al-Iman* (1953), *Al-Fajir* (1955) and *Al-Shaab* (1957), which published articles on a wide range of political, economic and cultural issues pertaining to Kuwaiti society. These outlets promoted the cause of modernism and sought to spread the influence of the new reforming trends taking place in the Arab world.[17] The lack of political coverage in the broadcast media left the Kuwaiti political arena to the newspapers and magazines whose role expanded in importance after the adoption of the constitution in 1962. This became evident during the first parliamentary election in 1963. The print press was the premier institution of Kuwait's new 'political space', offering candidates and critics a forum for initiating and carrying on discussions of the major issues of the day. As compared to western media outlets, Kuwaiti dailies and magazines carry large numbers of analyses and opinion pieces, most by columnists who write for them regularly.

Until the early 1990s, apart from the prominent weekly Islamist magazine *Al-Mujtamaa*, few newspapers invited Islamists to contribute opinion pieces. In Kuwait, daily newspapers occasionally feature articles and editorials opposed to the political views of their owners but, although such alternative views do appear, the featured spots go to regular columnists and contributors. Many of them see their privileged access to the print media as a stepping-stone to larger political ambitions: aspiring and already successful parliamentarians write regularly for the daily papers. Contemporary examples include Ali al-Baghli, Ahmad al-Rubaei, Mubarak al-Duwailah and Khaled al-Adwa. Their media exposure enhances their reputations and influence, and also helps them to reach voters.

As we have noted, the Kuwaiti dailies were established by liberal merchant families and individuals. In the mid-1990s, acting through a syndicate, a ruling family member, Sheikh Ali al-Khalifa Al Sabah, bought the daily *Al-Watan*. Sheikh Ali had long been criticized in parliament and the press for his handling of government finances, including transactions of the state oil company, during the many years he had served as minister of finance and minister of oil.[18] Acquiring his own newspaper gave him a widely accessible public forum in which to mobilize constituencies and undermine his enemies, many of them from or affiliated with the merchant class. His purchase of *Al-Watan* opened up a new space in which the growing number of Kuwaiti Islamist and tribalist writers could openly express their anti-liberal political views. Having such a prominent forum adds to the public visibility of these writers, and to their viability as parliamentary candidates.

Women, the media and social change

Control of the print media by the liberal merchant class offered access to Kuwait's premier public space to another formerly silenced group, Kuwaiti women, who used it to voice their concerns and call for their rights. On the surface, this seems paradoxical. The merchant class had practised strict female seclusion in pre-oil Kuwait. However, merchants were also the first to educate their daughters. They saw that women could extend their families' power, thereby maintaining traditional power relations between merchants and the ruling family in the transition to the new oil economy.[19] Thus the merchants' movement from strict observance of female seclusion to encouraging full participation by their women in society can be seen as a strategy for cementing their influence over a modernizing Kuwait. In consequence, liberal-owned media played a central role in the lives of Kuwaiti women. There was an almost symbiotic relationship between women and all forms of media: radio, television and newspapers. The media supported women's issues and women sought the support of the media to change society's perception of women's roles. Women also found in the media important tools to change their life situations and promote new roles for themselves.

From the early days of the print media, women wrote about their condition not simply to 'voice' their concerns but even more to transform, or at least to affect, the social traditions pertaining to gender relations. At first, several magazines had a section designated the 'Women's Corner'. It was headed by a picture of a western woman, embodying the aspirations of modernity and civilization inherent in the ideal model of womanhood for the rising generation of educated Kuwaiti women. Women were encouraged to write and express their views in the 'Women's Corner', and many young merchant-class women who were eager to emerge from seclusion contributed short articles about their needs and what kind of 'liberation' (*tahrir*) they wanted. Some wrote under pseudonyms; significantly, during an era when any publicity about a specific woman was a social anathema, others wrote under their own names. The 'Women's Corner' soon became the focal point of debate and analysis of issues such as lifting the veil (*sufur*), conceptions of women's honour, and the desirability of education and paid work for women. For almost a decade, these writings served to initiate and then to frame a public discourse on the traditional practices of female seclusion and the constraints that such practices would have on modern Kuwait. The 'Women's Corner' thereby changed public perceptions of women's role in society. It made women's issues an integral part of the national debate, ending their marginalization as belonging only to the private sphere.

By the 1960s, women's relationship to and representation in the media began to change. Women's writing escaped confinement to the 'Women's Corner'. Articles written by women appeared alongside those written by men. Women were interviewed about their views on society and women's rights. Pictures of merchant-class women dressed in western clothes appeared on the covers of magazines and in newspapers. The women depicted in those photographs represented a new generation of Kuwaiti women: modern, educated and salaried. As one reporter observed during this period, 'The new woman has arrived. She is educated. She earns. She wants the vote ... The new woman is lobbying MPs, getting a lot of press coverage'.[20] Women were indeed receiving a lot of media attention. Much of their increased public visibility was the result of advocacy by both individual women and women's organizations. The new generation of educated Kuwaiti women were professionally engaged in media work: writing, editing, publishing, appearing on television and acting. Peter Mansfield, a British writer on Arab affairs, had the following recollection of a visit to Kuwait in 1980:

> I watched with astonishment on television a beautiful young Kuwaiti woman who had her own theatre troupe in a series of sketches on such subjects as drunkenness, the problems of bureaucracy and of Kuwaitis who marry foreigners. At the end of each sketch she would come before the curtain and discuss it with the audience.[21]

It should be noted that, during the 1960s, few families in Kuwait allowed their daughters to appear on television or take up acting as a career. Such activities would have put them in direct contact with unrelated men and were therefore perceived as less respectable than working in an office.[22] But in spite of the prevalence of social taboos, a few women did take on work as broadcasters and actresses, forcing public acceptance of these professions for women. Fatma al-Hussein, from a wealthy merchant-class family, directed and presented a women's programme on television. Suad Abdallah chose acting as a career and is today one of the most respected and renowned Kuwaiti performers. As a consequence of the normalization of such public roles for women, many more women today work as actresses, broadcasters and host their own television shows. In addition, professional Kuwaiti women are regularly invited to participate in televised public debates on a variety of issues.

Women's media activities included editing women's magazines. The first women's magazine was started in 1965 by Ghanima al-Marzouk, who came from a wealthy merchant-class family. She set the course other women subsequently followed in publishing their own magazines. The most influential is *Samra*, launched in 1991. Edited by Fatma al-Hussein, it is intended, as she put it, 'to enlighten the life of women in the Arabian Peninsula and the Gulf' on a wide range of issues.[23] *Samra* was one of the first women's magazines in the Gulf region to deal with controversial subjects such as domestic violence, arranged marriages and marital infidelity.[24] By 1994, *Samra* had a print run of 35,000 with 200 pages per issue. In 1996, a group of Islamist women began publishing a women's magazine called *Nissa'* (Women) which looks at women's issues from an Islamist feminist perspective.

Criticizing certain aspects of society can incur serious repercussions for women. In March 2001, Hidaya Sultan al-Salem, an outspoken feminist editor of a weekly political magazine, *Al-Majalis*, was assassinated, apparently by Lieutenant-Colonel Khaled Diab al-Azmi, a high-ranking police officer. The killing occurred on a public thoroughfare while the victim was travelling to her office. Speculation about the reasons for the attack settled quickly on accusations that Hidaya had insulted the tribe of the accused, in an article published nearly a year before the killing. In it she had described female dancers from the tribe as 'all temptation and sexual suggestion'. Such an explanation cast the murder as both private and motivated by a concern for family honour.[25] Indeed, after it was first floated, this explanation pushed out others, including that the murder was connected to alleged 'financial problems',[26] or to avenge a professional insult.[27] Only a week before the killing, Hidaya had published an open letter to the emir, claiming that the police had refused to act on her complaints about criminal acts she said had been committed by some of her employees.[28] Identified in much of the press coverage as a suffrage activist, the notion was conveyed that Hidaya was somehow at fault for her own murder because she had transgressed decorum in her writings. The theme of dishonour was highlighted by reports of the crowds of Awazem tribesmen who sought to attend court hearings[29] and it permeated coverage of the crime throughout the investigation and court action.

As noted above, women also suffered psychological damage as result of their writings. Alia Shuaib, whose writings had been strongly criticized by Islamist groups and individuals, was especially affected. Alia had pub-licly claimed that Islam did not order women to be veiled but rather to dress modestly. Paradoxically, within a year of her trial, she had put on the veil and covered her red-coloured hair. She also became a supporter of Islamist groups. Had Alia succumbed to Islamist pressure or did she find a new 'self' as she claims? It is hard to know. Nonetheless, it seems clear that the hostile public reaction to her writings from both liberals and Islamists forced her to question herself and, perhaps in self-defence, to adopt a new lifestyle.

Islamist women and changing norms in public space

Islamist women activists are also aware of the print media's importance in the production of social values. In the late 1970s they began their own media efforts by generating publications within the university. The first was a newsletter called *The Voice of Keifan* (referring to one the campuses of Kuwait University). This publication was renamed *Manbar al-Taleba* (Woman Student's Forum) in 1981, when it became a monthly magazine. The new venture was intended, as the editors stated in the first issue, to create 'a forum around which all the female students would gather to voice their opinions, call for their rights and take part in directing the stu-dents' movement as well as in changing society and directing it towards the right path'.[30] Like the first generation of educated women, Islamist female activists also hoped their publications would transform society and its perceptions of women's roles. However, the images of women they projected differed, sometimes sharply, from the prevailing model of the westernized professional woman featured in liberal publications.

Before the Iranian revolution and continuing through the early 1980s, the proportion of female students at Kuwait University who wore the hejab was lower than the proportion of women dressed in western clothes. Yet the photographs that filled the pages of *Manbar al-Taleba* from the beginning were almost exclusively of veiled Islamist women, who were shown attending conferences, studying, and working in the library. Pictures and captions conveyed the impression that these women represented the majority of female students at the university. Even if pic-tures speak louder than words, *Manbar al-Taleba* also paid attention to texts, publishing interviews with Islamist women students in which they discussed their views on women's political and social roles. This brought into the print media voices and images that were new and different from those of the female role models promoted in the daily newspapers. *Manbar al-Taleba* enabled Islamist women activists to increase their visibility and assert their presence in the public sphere. But they did not confine themselves to student publications for long. Many now write for the daily newspapers and express their views on a variety of issues. Articles by a Shia Islamist activist, Khadeeja al-Mahmeed, a fervent advocate of women's suffrage, are published in the liberal newspaper *Al-Qabas*, whose publishers also support women's suffrage. In general, however, Islamist women activists are more likely to be published in *Al-Watan* and *Al-Ra'i al-Aam*.

As with the media prominence of earlier feminists such as Fatma al-Hussein and Suad Abdallah, the growing number and variety of media representations of Islamist women – not only as veiled and devout female students but also as writers and political activists – are changing popular perceptions of women's identities. The 'norm' of westernization has been challenged and even rolled back by a counter-normalization of Islamist women. As photographs of veiled women increasingly dominate media that were formerly populated primarily by images of women in western dress, what Kuwaitis perceive as 'normal' and therefore acceptable behaviour and demeanour for women is shifting. The consequences of this shift are wide-ranging, especially for young women. The depiction of veiled students eases concerns in traditional Bedouin families about sending their daughters to the university. The prominence of Islamist women in media representations supports the mobilization of young women into the Islamist movement. As we discuss below, however, media stereotyping of women as westernized or Islamist polarizes not only women but Kuwaitis generally with regard to political issues bearing on gender.

Like individual women of different persuasions, women's groups have also enjoyed more or less equal access to the media, both as subjects of news stories and as authors of op-ed style advocacy articles. Individual media outlets tend to favour advocacy pieces that reflect their respective publishers' points of view. Consequently, articles about liberal women's groups are featured more extensively in liberal newspapers such *Al-Qabas* and *Al-Siyassah*, and in the weekly political magazine, *Al-Talia*. The latter concentrates on the activities of the Women's Cultural and Social Society (WCSS), and rarely mentions other women's groups. *Arab Times* likewise devotes considerable space to the activities of liberal women's groups, including their efforts to win political rights. It publishes reports on all their conferences and regularly interviews their leaders. Islamist women's groups are covered more extensively in *Al-Watan* and *Al-Anba'*. In putting forward a new model of womanhood, Islamist women reshaped public discourse on women, doing so for the most part by positioning themselves in opposition to the liberal women's groups. This often entailed questioning and criticizing liberal positions on women's issues. Such oppositional standpoints helped to depict an Islamist version of the ideal woman as a selfless creature, a caring mother, and a virtuous civil servant who subordinates her sex's interests to social order.[31]

The leaders of women's groups have meanwhile become recognized as public figures. Fatma al-Abdali, a liberal activist who campaigned throughout the 1990s for women's suffrage, told us that 'the media made me interactive with people, especially *Al-Qabas* newspaper, which never deleted one word from my articles'.[32] A similar comment was made by Khawla al-Attiqi, an Islamist activist who spoke of the 'openness' of the media. Khawla writes a regular Friday column for *Al-Watan* on issues related to women and the family.[33] Both women also reported that they thought the newspapers generally were fair in their coverage of women's political activities. Fatma noted wryly that women needed to be sure that, when they sent out a press release about an upcoming event, the event would be well-run and well-attended since accurate coverage can cut two ways.

Media coverage and women's political rights

The campaign for Kuwaiti women to be accorded their right to formal political participation has lasted decades. At the same time, as we have outlined here, they have not been denied access to public space. Indeed, issues related to women's rights, particularly women's political rights, have been widely reported in newspapers and, more recently, on national television. The first campaign to win political rights began in the early 1970s. It was spearheaded by the Arab Women's Development Society (AWDS), which put forward a series of demands to the National Assembly.[34] Early rights activists gave press conferences and made other efforts to publicize their campaigns as a way to mobilize public support. Nouria al-Sadani, the leader of AWDS, wrote in *Al-Siyassah* newspaper under the pseudonym 'Daughter of the Sun'. Not all Kuwaiti women supported the equal rights campaign. Opponents also expressed their views in the daily press, dismissing the movement as 'political chaos' and advising women to keep quiet and wait until the time was right. These views were echoed by an Islamist group, the Social Reform Society, which invited prominent Islamists, including the well-known Egyptian female activist Zeinab al-Ghazali, to speak about women's rights and duties in Islam.[35]

The fact that women were themselves divided on equal rights issues at first had little effect on the campaign. Women activists successfully publicized their cause through various media, presenting themselves as a united front by disdaining to notice the claims of their female opponents. The mostly liberal press showed support for the suffragists. Cartoons appeared in newspapers making fun of the male deputies who were opposed to granting suffrage to women. Most belittled men, showing them as sexist and concerned about losing their masculinity.

Later, after the Iranian revolution of 1978–9 and the 1981 reorganization of Kuwaiti electoral politics, which added to the number and prominence of Islamist and tribalist deputies in the National Assembly, the press started to pick up on divisions between women's groups. By the mid-1980s, activist women were increasingly presented as fragmented, pursuing competing agendas, and unable to unite to push for their rights. Divisions among women were cited by liberal Kuwaiti men as the main reason why the 1981 parliament had refused to pass a bill granting women's political rights. During the 1992 parliamentary elections, candidates presenting themselves as generally favourable to women's rights – but 'not right now' – attributed at least part of their desire to defer women's suffrage to alleged divisions among women and to their perceptions that the majority of women did not want political rights.[36] This trope became even more apparent following the controversial decree, issued by the Emir of Kuwait on 16 May 1999, granting women the right to run for office and vote in parliamentary and municipal elections. Liberal as well as Islamist men criticized the decree. The print press, including the liberal *Al-Qabas*, ran headlines emphasizing disunity among women's leaders and groups. Islamist critiques concentrated on discrediting the suffragists personally, depicting them as a 'minority of bourgeois women' and as 'idle spinsters who have no work or children'. Had they been married, this refrain ran, they would not have called for political rights since they would be too preoccupied with domestic duties.[37]

Ironically, in response to the emir's decree, women activists were more united than ever before. Once the decree had been issued, several groups emerged as active suffrage organizations. The conservative Federation of Kuwaiti Women's Associations (FKWA) re-activated its Women's Political Committee. Liberal activist Nouria al-Sadani established a grassroots organization called The Kuwaiti Women of the Twenty-First Century. Also campaigning for women's political rights were the WCSS and the Women's Issues Committee (WIC) headed by Fatma al-Abdali. There was so much activity across the spectrum of women's organizations that a Voluntary Working Group was formed by Khawla al-Attiqi and Khadija al-Mahmeed, both Islamist activists, and Badriya al-Awadi, an attorney and liberal activist, to coordinate the efforts of the different women's groups campaigning for the passage of the decree in the National Assembly.

These different women's groups worked together to gain public support for women's political rights. Compared to the early days of female activism in the 1960s, by 1999 Kuwaiti women had grown in political maturity and experience. Their organizational capacities expanded dramatically as a result of their myriad and often heroic roles during the Iraqi occupation. After liberation, they had campaigned hard to win their political rights, petitioning the National Assembly, lobbying members of the parliament for support and attempting numerous times to place their names on the electoral rolls. They held public conferences on women's rights, organized protest marches, gave interviews to the press and appeared on television to discuss women's suffrage. The suffragists were visible, vocal and organized. They refused to surrender to what might have been paralysing political reversals, as the National Assembly repeatedly rejected suffrage bills, both in committee and on the floor. In spite of these discouraging setbacks, the suffragists kept the debate on women's political rights alive.

Given the number of women involved in the suffragist movement from the Islamist and liberal camps, it seems odd that the opponents of women's suffrage, both inside and outside the National Assembly, could blame the defeat of the emiri decree on differences of opinion among women. Yet despite the new-found solidarity among Kuwaiti women on this issue, when the votes in parliament were tallied to record yet another defeat, opponents of suffrage for women spoke with presumed authority about how frictions and competing agendas among women's groups were responsible for bringing the measure down. Portrayals of the women's movement across Kuwaiti media outlets supported anti-suffragist assertions that the suffragists themselves were responsible for the defeat of the emiri decree. For example, *Al-Qabas* featured a series of interviews with suffragists situated in contexts implying that the women's groups had been unable to work strategically together. A telling example was an interview with the liberal Sarah al-Duaij. This ran under the head-line, 'We were very late in raising the awareness of women who are opposed to political rights'.

As Pierre Bourdieu wrote, 'The simple report, the very fact of report-ing, of *putting on record* as a reporter, always implies a social construction of reality that can mobilize (or demobilize) individuals or groups.' Bourdieu calls this a '*reality effect*. They show things and make people believe in what they show.'[38] 'They', of course, are the media who, when they speak from a unified perspective, can impose on the public their own interpretation of events. In Bourdieu's words: 'Journalists can impose on the whole society their vision of the world, their conception of problems, and their point of view.'[39] What is so unexpected given the history we have recounted here is that the liberal and the Islamist media converged at the turn of the century to oppose women's political rights. What caused the old liberal reality to change?

The community of interests bridging the ideological gulf between lib-eral and Islamist men and the media they own and control continues to centre on the role of women. However, the internal structure of this community has changed. During the era of early modernization, liberal encouragement of women's rights, including political rights, was strongly class based. Upper-class women were educated and sent out to hold stra-tegic positions in the economy to prevent their take-over by the rising numbers of 'new men' produced by mass public education and ruling family cultivation of alliances with men outside the old merchant elite.[40] Liberal advocacy of women's rights, like liberal advocacy of democracy, was predicated on a patriarchal vision of Kuwaiti society. Upper-class women served as extensions of their families' power and, like their broth-ers, were deployed under the direction of family patriarchs. Prior to 1981, women's suffrage could be seen as a strategy for maintaining the status quo.

When members of the rising middle classes sought to break the stran-glehold of the merchant class on the best positions in the public and private sectors, their status was achieved via multiple pathways. Not able to rely so extensively on family resources as merchant-class youth, they rose to prominence through patronage, superior education and professional performance, electoral politics, the mosque – and usually more than one of these. The importance of the mosque as a stepping-stone to social and political prominence led to a politics that masked class divisions behind conflicts dividing liberal modernists and traditional Islamists. This ideological polarization transcended gender and distributed women along and across the same lines dividing men. What has changed is that this ideological division is no longer so effective at separating women as it was before, leaving gender politics less useful as a proxy for other political conflicts. The result is that masculinist opposition to women's rights can no longer can be concealed behind a veil of Islamist-versus-liberal politics. Liberal men could no longer justify their opposition to women's political participation as necessary to prevent Islamists from reducing liberal representation in the parliament. Islamist men could no longer can justify theirs as protecting their women from dishonour and, in any case, as divinely ordained.

A few pro-suffragist analyses of the 30 November 1999 parliamentary vote concentrate on this point. Political scientist Abdullah al-Shayeji argues that the liberals voted strategically.[41] They wanted to defeat the bill but still allow liberal and Shia Islamist parliamentarians to appear to be supporters of women's rights. The strategy required that two of them abstain, which maintained the appearance of a nearly even split that could be hailed as progress in the foreign and domestic press, but still produce the outcome that most men on both sides preferred. Ahmad al-Saadoun, a liberal, and Hassan Ali al-Qallaf, an Islamist, supplied those abstentions, leaving observers with the impression that parliamentarians who otherwise would have had to vote against the measure to prevent its passage actually supported extending political rights to women.

Conclusion

Who would have thought in the early 1980s that liberals would one day have to disguise their opposition to women's rights? That they did so demonstrates the complexity, analysed in this chapter, of the underlying political and social context and the rapidity of change on gender issues in Kuwait. As might be predicted from wider studies of the reductionist coverage of activist groups by competitive commercial media, our research found that the Kuwaiti media downplayed the complexity of Kuwaiti women's groups. Yet, despite the media's disingenuous role during recent campaigns for women's suffrage, our research also indicates that it is probably too soon to dismiss the print or broadcast media as being unlikely instruments of women's advancement. The number of Kuwaiti women working in different media institutions as journalists, reporters and editors continues to grow. By 2000, the 99 Kuwaiti women working for the official Kuwait News Agency represented 24 per cent of its workforce. The number of Kuwaiti women working in the Ministry of Information increased fourfold in 15 years, from 106 in 1980 to 427 in 1995. Many women occupy managerial positions. Individually and collectively, as recounted in this chapter, none has so far been able to correct the distorted views and stereotypes that continue to create 'reality' with regard to Kuwaiti perceptions of women's status. But as we have also shown, the media continue to be filled with stories and images of female achievers, contributing however unwittingly and unwillingly to the normalization of an ever-broadening range of public roles for women.

Other forms of media also present opportunities for liberation from the gender rules that currently shape Kuwaiti society. Kuwaiti women today seek to transform their lives through non-traditional media channels such as the Internet. Field research conducted by Deborah Wheeler shows that Internet usage has given young Kuwaiti women new paths towards autonomy in running their lives and making friends, even though some transgress conventional social norms and traditional rituals of sociability.[42] Like their counterparts throughout the world, Kuwaiti women activists are pursuing autonomy through self-help, extending their autonomy by asserting it. As this chapter has revealed, the greater the solidarity among the rich diversity of Kuwaiti women's groups, the more they have been presented as fragmented and disunited by the mainstream media. Whether media depictions of women impose a 'reality effect'[43] that is 'traditional' or 'modern', these depictions – in Kuwait as elsewhere – are nearly always shaped by the instrumental values of media owners and confected from their wishes about how the world should be.[44] '*Main*stream' outlets are usually '*male*stream' outlets. Mastering (mistressing?) the media requires change not only of the media but, even more, of the society that they reflect.

Missing features in measuring Internet use

Estimates in 2001 suggested that only 4–6 per cent of all Middle Eastern Internet users were women.[3] Table 9.1, drawn from 2002 figures compiled by the Women's Learning Partnership, shows how much higher the percentage for female Internet use was in countries such as China and South Africa than it was in Arab states. Besides having the lowest figures on this count, the Arab world is also seeing Internet connectivity for society as a whole grow more slowly than elsewhere. Slow uptake has been a cause for concern, since Internet access is becoming an indicator of human development and knowledge capacity, as well as a key economic indicator. Of a total 5 million Internet users in the Middle East in 2001–2 (excluding North Africa), nearly half were in Israel. Of the 7 million Internet users in the continent of Africa, 5 million resided in South Africa. As Table 9.2 shows, the total number of users for all Arab countries and Iran was 4.9 million in 2002. This was well below 1 per cent of the 600 million Internet users worldwide.

Table 9.1
Women's Internet usage by country/region, 2002

Region/country	% of all users
Arab states	6
China	37
European Union	25
Japan	18
Latin America	38
Russia	19
South Africa	17
United States	50

Source: Women's Learning Partnership, Technology Facts and Figures, online at www.learningpartnership.org/facts.

Table 9.2

Internet use in Arab countries and Iran, 2001–2

(*End-2001 estimates, unless otherwise stated*)

Country	Number of users ('000)	% of population
Algeria (*March 2001*)	180.0	0.57
Bahrain	140.2	21.36
Egypt	600.0	0.86
Iraq (*December 2000*)	12.5	0.05
Iran	420.0	0.63
Jordan	212.0	3.99
Kuwait	205.0	8.91
Lebanon (*August 2002*)	300.0	11.22
Libya (*March 2001*)	20.0	0.24
Morocco	400.0	1.28
Oman	120.0	4.42
Palestinian Authority	103.0	3.03
Qatar	60.0	7.59
Saudi Arabia	570.0	2.50
Sudan	70.0	0.21
Syria	60.0	0.35
Tunisia	400.0	4.08
UAE	900.0	36.79
Yemen	10.0	0.09
Total (*August 2002*)	4902.2	2.45

Source: Madar Research, 'PC penetration vs. Internet user penetration in GCC countries', *Madar Research Journal: Knowledge Economy and Research on the Middle East*, 1/0 (October 2002), p 10.

Among Arab countries, the highest per capita concentrations of Internet users are found in the United Arab Emirates, Bahrain, Lebanon and Kuwait. The level of 37 per cent recorded in the UAE compares with levels of 72 per cent, 62 per cent and 55 per cent in the US, Canada and South Korea respectively.[4] Some have argued that the amount of data transferred in and out of a country is a more robust indicator of Internet use and impact than the number of users. Measured in bits and bytes, Egypt comes top of the list of Arab states in terms of the amounts of data transferred in and out.[5] Abdel-Latif al-Hamad, chair of the Arab Fund for Economic and Social Development, estimated in 2000 that IT investment in Europe is around 1,000 times higher than in the Arab world.[6]

Internet use per capita is generally calculated by multiplying the number of Internet subscribers by the number of users per machine, which is usually a factor of 2–4. Yet a comparison of Tables 9.2 and 9.3 suggests that, where per capita use appears to be low, the number of Internet cafés is often relatively high. For example, Internet penetration in Algeria, based on the number of Internet accounts, is estimated at 0.57 per cent. But a high availability of Internet cafés yields a ratio of 9.52 cafés per 100,000 inhabitants. In Libya the corresponding figures are 0.24 per cent penetration and an estimated 13.21 Internet cafés per 100,000 inhabitants.

Because it is difficult to determine what percentage of the population has access to the Internet via Internet cafés, judging the Internet's true importance to the majority of people in the region is also difficult. Limitations in terms of PC ownership, telephone access or affordable connections do not signify a lack of demand for the Internet. If public demand is sufficient to support 2,000–3,000 Internet cafés in Algeria and Morocco, then the Internet must be more important than indicated by conventional estimates. Access to the Internet in cafés could parallel access to newspapers in coffee houses during the late nineteenth century. It was difficult then to determine the public influence of newspapers in cases where sales were low but copies were shared among readers in coffee houses, making them more of a mass medium than official circulation figures indicated. The same may be true for the Internet, with cafés and computers becoming like coffee houses and newspapers of the past.

Table 9.3

Internet cafés in Arab countries (*number*)

Algeria	3000
Bahrain	90
Egypt	400

Iraq	50
Jordan	500
Kuwait	300
Lebanon	200
Libya	700
Morocco	2150
Oman	80
Palestinian Authority	60
Qatar	80
Saudi Arabia	200
Sudan	150
Syria	600
Tunisia	300
UAE	191
Yemen	120

Source: Adapted from Madar Research: 'PC penetration vs. Internet user penetration', p 5.

The dynamics of marginalization

Building an information society in the Arab world is viewed as a cure for two kinds of poverty that plague the region: a poverty of capabilities and a poverty of opportunities.[7] In the *Arab Human Development Report 2002*, the United Nations Development Programme (UNDP) argued that failing to provide women with easy and equal access to information and communication technologies (ICT) can slow the development and progress of society as a whole. For this reason, the UNDP ranks access to ICT as the third most pressing concern facing women worldwide, second only to the alleviation of poverty and violence. Similarly, the International Telecommunication Union (ITU) observes that society as a whole will benefit from ensuring that women have equal access to the ICT sector, since it is one of the fastest growing areas of the world economy.[8] Many high profile women have drawn attention to the same issue, Dale Spender wrote in 1995: 'the computer is not a toy; it is the site of wealth, power, and influence, now and in the future. Women – and indigenous people, and those with few resources – cannot afford to be marginalized or excluded from this new medium'.[9] At the World Bank's Global Knowledge '97 meeting, Lourdes Arizpe, UNESCO's assistant director-general for culture, observed that women in the Arab world and beyond can use the Internet to present their autonomous voices in the service of their own culturally diverse and regionally specific forms of liberation. Queen Rania of Jordan, addressing the Second Arab Women's Summit in 2002, noted that 'it is important for Arab women to make use of the latest technology, particularly the Internet, to reshape their lives'.[10]

Najat Rochdi, president of Morocco's Internet Society, explains that the Internet can be used to expand women's leadership skills, provided that what she calls the 'culture of machismo in Muslim countries' is also changed, so that women are valued as 'clever and accomplished people' in their own right, 'outside the tutelage of a father or husband' and not only as 'mothers and caretakers'.[11] In January 2003, the Dubai-based information consulting firm i3me organized a conference in Beirut called 'Women on the Web'. Speaking for the company, Shirin Moatamed explained that it was restricted to women to avoid conflicting with social taboos. Of its purpose she said:

> We want to start a 'web' family by connecting women from different countries through the Internet. Imagine all these women from Iran, Lebanon, Jordan or Egypt, being able to exchange information and communicate … The group could bring a new face to Middle Eastern feminism. Or on a smaller scale, simply help keep families, which are so often spread out, in touch.[12]

Observations like these raise doubts about Manuel Castells's assertion that access to IT largely shapes a country's destiny.[13] Rather, it seems the opposite might be true, in the sense that a country and its operating systems, so to speak – its political culture, social values, public discourse, national identity, level of human development, gender practices – shape the life and maturation of the Internet within that context. Certainly there are a number of specific factors affecting women's uptake of the Internet in the Arab world and the extent to which they remain marginalized in using this resource. For example, nearly half the women in the region over the age of 15 cannot read and write. Women occupy only a tiny fraction of the seats in most Arab parliaments, ranging from 0.7 per cent in Yemen to 11.5 per cent (the highest) in Tunisia.[14] Universal suffrage is still not established in parts of the Gulf. In terms of access to the economy, men in the Arab world have around 3.5 times the earned income of women; and the female economic activity rate in all Arab states combined is less than 33 per cent.[15] Women also face significant legal challenges, especially in rules regarding freedom of movement, since women in many countries still require a male family member's permission to obtain a passport or travel abroad. Thus, unequal access to information technology is just one of many facets of uneven development facing women in the region.

The question, then, is how far the Internet can enable women to increase their power and influence in both public and private spheres and how far that process is obstructed by local constraints. In the public sphere, Internet access can allow women to project their voices across the globe. It can unlock information about women's rights in other countries and offer connections to professional networks. Internet literacy, being a marketable skill, makes women more competitive in the job market, or more indispensable in the jobs they already hold. In the private sphere it provides a way to stay in touch with friends and family members located abroad. The present study probes beneath the surface of the picture drawn above. By interviewing women from the region who are Internet active, it explores how women become Internet users, what they find most useful about the technology once they are regular users, why they think more women are not active Internet users, and finally, what they think will be the major impact of the Internet on women's lives in the region. The narratives on these issues come from women in Egypt, Morocco, Kuwait, Saudi Arabia and Bahrain. Interviews, conducted both face-to-face and online, took place between 2000 and 2003.[16] The conclusion reviews the main patterns and findings produced by the narratives, thus giving us a comparative perspective on gender and the Internet in the Arab world.

Egypt

Writing about women and the Internet in Egypt is a daunting task. Contrasts between information-rich and information-poor within the country make simple descriptions and explanations challenging to sustain. The cluster of female policy-makers and IT professionals linked with the cabinet's Information Decision and Support Centre (IDSC) and dispersed throughout the upper echelons of Egypt's private sector, non-profit organizations and government ministries – especially the relatively new Ministry of Communication and Information Technology – are all highly skilled knowledge workers. At the same time, Egypt is a poor country, where nearly 70 per cent of the population of Upper Egypt lives on less than US$1 a day. There are only 600,000 Internet users out of a possible 68 million countrywide. Although this figure is expected to grow to 2.6 million users by 2006, the increase will leave more than 96 per cent of Egyptians without Internet access.

UNDP data show that only 10.4 per cent of Egyptians had access to a telephone in 2001 and 0.93 per cent were Internet users. The same source puts adult literacy at 56 per cent, with female literacy at 44.8 per cent.[17] Only a fraction of those who are literate can also read and write English, the dominant language of the Internet. Access to computers is rare in schools. Yet interviews with Egypt's female 'e-heroes' yield mostly encouraging visions of an information-rich and economically prosperous Egypt in the twenty-first century. Many women have learned to use the Internet at work and one interviewee, who works in the library of a foreign diplomatic mission, asserted: 'If you want to keep your job, you have to be computer literate'. She added: 'the focus [in Egypt] has changed from food security to a focus on computerization and privatization ... [T]he language has changed now and we have no choice but to be a part of it.'[18] The connection between work and computer use becomes apparent in Hanan's narrative. Hanan, who works for the Regional Information Technology and Software Engineering Centre (RITSEC) in Cairo, became aware of the Internet in the late 1980s. She remembers the difference that browsers like Netscape made. Now she uses the Internet every day, mostly for work. Hanan's experience reflects a common pattern, whereby the Internet rapidly becomes an ordinary part of life once the hurdles of getting training and obtaining regular, reliable and cost-effective access have been overcome. Being motivated to overcome them depends on whether there are obvious rewards. Hanan believes the Internet can help the poor:

> The Internet and IT provide a way out for the less fortunate. If I give them bread and clean water then I've helped them for a day and they expect more from me tomorrow. But if I teach them to fish for information and to think beyond their poverty, then they can provide long-term solutions to their unfortunate life circumstances. Thus the Internet is a way out of the trap of poverty.[19]

Asked whether the Internet has any special significance for Egyptian women, Hanan replied:

Personally, I have never experienced any discrimination in terms of my career because of my gender. I have more trouble with my youthful appearance and happy countenance, which seems to enable some first impressions that lead people to take me less seriously. The Internet masks appearances, thus all are taken as equals to a degree. The Internet has been a real tool of empowerment for me. I have networked and built relationships with colleagues that might not have emerged otherwise.

In other cases, 'lastminute.com' was started by two women in their basement who were mothers and wanted to have a career too, so they developed a web site and recently sold it for $40 million. In Egypt there are no women dot.com entrepreneurs yet, but there's no reason not to expect some in the near future. I do know women who have used the Internet to telecommute after having had a baby. I think more women in Egypt, where family is so important, will find this helpful.

Hanan's comments reaffirm the Internet's importance as a professional networking tool, enabling women to advance and interact on the basis of other criteria than those that may influence face-to-face communication. Again, like multi-tasking female professionals worldwide, Hanan argues that the challenges of being a parent and a professional can be managed more easily with telecommuting. However, Marwa, a graduate of Cairo University, in her early twenties and employed by a Cairo-based network solutions company, reminds us that Internet access is still limited in Egypt.

I learned to play with computers while growing up. We had a computer in our home. Most of my friends also grew up with computers at home. But many students at Cairo University did not. I did my degree in the Commerce Department in the English Language Division, and the Commerce Department had its own computer lab, with computers connected to the Internet. This was very useful for the students without access to the Internet and/or a computer at home. I didn't use it because I didn't need to. I use the Internet for research, for work and for e-mail mostly. I find that the most serious impediment to the spread of the Internet in both business and Egyptian society is that Egyptians don't like change, thus it's hard to convince people, especially in business, that saving time or doing something more efficiently is a good thing. Thus transitions to the information age are slower here than in many parts of the world, because demand for the technology is low.[20]

Marwa's explanation for lack of connectivity and interest in the Internet goes beyond infrastructure, to the realm of culture. Her explanation is not unusual. It has been suggested that innovation as an end in itself is a concept foreign to some societies, who may not accept the value of 'technique', in the sense of a more efficient way of operating.[21] But Laila, an employee of the US Agency for International Development (USAID) in Egypt, sees more tangible causes.

> I think there are several significant constraints on the spread of the Internet in Egypt. For example the educational system does not encourage creativity and analytic thinking. If it did, there might be more demands placed on government. Without this, the entrepreneurialism required by the knowledge economy is not present in Egypt, so demand is low for information technologies, like the Internet, which support the new economy and the information society. Banking in Egypt does not promote e-commerce. It inhibits it by forbidding credit card sales that are transacted online. Content in Arabic online of interest to most Egyptians is lacking. Most Egyptians don't understand the utility of the Internet, so they are not demanding access. Moreover, Egyptians are resistant to change, and have not as of yet been presented with clear incentives to change the ways business, education and social interactions are done, thus transitions to an information society lag. The government is working hard to change this, but so far, efforts have been ineffective.[22]

Laila indicates that, while some government agencies are working hard to speed up Internet access, other aspects of the country's political economy have the opposite effect. Many strategies have been publicized, including educational reform, the drafting of e-commerce legislation, transformations of banking and finance, free websites and free Internet access to small and medium-size enterprises, and the creation of community telecentres in poor urban neighbourhoods and rural areas.[23] Yet Ghada, a Cairo University professor in her late thirties, is clear that access to the Internet depends on practical basics such as telephone lines and household budgets. Her analysis implies that difficulties of access and a lack of demand may be mutually reinforcing.

> I learned to use the Internet through work, in order to send e-mails and do research. I learned to use it before Netscape and Eudora, using

Gopher instead. I use the Internet every day. I use it in my teaching. It's hard to use it from home, however, because we only have one phone line. We tried to get a second line, but got tired of waiting [it can take up to five years, even more to get a land line at home in Egypt]. It's almost impossible to get one. That's why I got a mobile, so our phone line could be free while on the Internet.

Our students don't have easy access to computers, even at the University level. How can I teach them or expect them to use a computer if I can't provide access. Still I 'require' Internet assignments and they have to go to Internet cafés to do it. We have departmental meetings to discuss what technologies are needed for the classroom and we ask for overhead projectors, but we don't get them. How can we expect to get Internet connectivity, and a laptop, if we can't even get an overhead projector?

Because of the slow growth in public demand for the Internet and the difficulties in access, especially at home and at school, it will take 10 or more years before the Internet really has any effect on Egypt in a big way.[24]

Morocco

As early as 1996, Morocco already had 20 Internet Service Providers (ISPs), 'some 50 cybercafés, an estimated 10,000 Internet subscribers, some 50 websites, 1.4 million fixed telephone lines and an estimated 100,000 mobile phones. The average cost of an Internet subscription was US $50/month'.[25] Access has more than doubled each year since then. Morocco has the second highest per capita Internet use in North Africa and the highest percentage of female Internet users in the region, at 25 per cent of all Internet users in Morocco. Only around 29 per cent of Moroccan Internet users have a dial-up connection at home. But 58 per cent of users go online in cybercafés and 53 per cent do so at work.[26] Najat Rochdi, president of Morocco's Internet Society, says the government is 'seeking to use the Internet to compete more effectively in the global economy, grow employment opportunities and slow down the drain of skilled workers to Europe'.[27] This has led to a national action plan called 'e-Maroc', issued by the Prime Minister's Office in May 1999, following the passage of a telecommunications law in 1997 and creation of a national agency (ANRT) to regulate telecommunications and ICT in 1998.

Two of the e-Maroc initiatives are targeted specifically at women. One aims to support women 'in rural areas either in ICT businesses or using ICTs, with online mentoring and financing; building links between women-owned businesses and corporations for business-to-business markets'. A second initiative aims to help women entrepreneurs build their businesses through e-cooperatives, with the government and private companies sponsoring an e-commerce platform to commercialize women's agricultural and handicrafts production.[28]

The number of women in Morocco's parliament increased from four to 35 after a quota of seats were reserved for women in the elections of September 2002. For many, however, a wide variety of social and legal reforms are still required. One project under way is to reduce female illiteracy in rural areas, which is sometimes as high as 90 per cent. Female literacy in Morocco as a whole is 37 per cent.[29] In spite of this, women are well represented among the professional class. One-third of doctors and one-quarter of university professors in Morocco are women. Professional women, as explained in the following narratives, tend to be Internet users. Aida, for example, is a professor of Media Studies and Communications from Rabat, Morocco. In her late thirties, Aida considers herself 'totally disconnected' unless she has regular and easy access to the Internet. She learned to use it with friends whose father is a telecom engineer and says she now feels dependent on the Internet for work and maintaining personal and professional relationships.[30] Aida says women's Internet use in Morocco generally is 'extremely limited' for all the same reasons as in other poor countries, including illiteracy, unfamiliarity with computers and the high cost of connections. Although she regards primary education as more urgent than Internet access at this stage, she is sure of the advantages for women who do have access, citing the possibility of communicating across regions, dialoguing with like-minded women and gathering information unavailable inside the country. Aida sees the Internet holding out the promise of change in Arab politics and society:

> The change would take place in society because the Internet offers interesting opportunities for circumventing the numerous restrictions and censorship acts imposed by culture, society and often the political system. Men and women (separately or together) can create new spaces for bonding, communicating and establishing communities because they have chosen to be part of them. This is in a way how the

change in politics can take place: the new spaces allow for a greater flow of information of all types and across social classes and distances (ideological and geographical) which often disturb authoritarian regimes. I also see the change coming from citizens and civil society organizations using the technology to counter the hegemonic rule of the establishment (political or religious).

The censorship Aida refers to includes restrictions that the government places on the press. For example, in 2001, the government resurrected the infamous Article 77 of the Press Law, under which it is authorized to suppress publications deemed to threaten Morocco's political or religious foundations.[31] Newspapers have been confiscated, editors jailed and foreign correspondents forcefully expelled. The opposition group Al-Adl wa'l-Ihsan launched two websites to circumvent an official ban on its activities and publications,[32] thereby demonstrating Aida's point about the Internet subverting censorship. Beyond its use as a means to counter authoritarianism, Aida's narrative also suggests that the Internet allows subtle transgressions of traditional boundaries of class, gender and geography which keep society compartmentalized.

Samia's narrative confirms the importance of Internet cafés in Morocco since, even among the relative elite, home-based Internet access is patchy at best. Internet cafés provide locations in which training is possible, as most staff have an IT background themselves and are often responsible for maintaining machines. Explaining why she is not a regular Internet user, Samia, a university professor, cites cost as a major deterrent.[33] Free Internet accounts do not seem to be available at her university. She finds cybercafés offer slow connections but, for her purposes as an e-mail user, they are 'better than nothing'. Asked about the effect on women, Samia said:

> I believe that women will benefit a lot from the new technology for many reasons. They can access all the information they want and need … that is they can choose what to read and know they can find lots of information on it … also, they are free [*enfin libre*] to access and choose the information: nobody controls them and nobody tells them it is right or wrong … I also think this helps them to open up more to the world [*s'ouvrir sur le monde de manière plus large*]: they can correspond with people and find centres of interest …

Even so, Samia sees the Internet as a 'double-edged sword'. Freedom to access information is good, but 'what information are they exposed to?'

she asked. Samia worries that they will be open to manipulation by extremist groups or pornography. Like Samia, Khulud also uses the Internet mainly for e-mail and has used it on an 'almost daily basis' since starting a year and a half before the interview. This is despite the fact the she describes herself as 'not really an Internet person'. Khulud says she prefers the phone or person-to-person contact but uses the Internet because of her job. As a programme coordinator in a cultural centre in Rabat, Khulud needs to correspond with people in other countries. Having no Internet access at home or at her centre, she uses cybercafés. She is sceptical about the Internet's impact on a society with high illiteracy:

> I think it concerns just a small minority anyway [*une stricte minorité*] … I don't think we can yet generalize from this … I don't know how many Moroccans in general use the Internet, in any case women are left out … remember the number of illiterate women … I think we have other priorities and concerns and the Internet cannot have much of an impact on our society … Ha, Ha, Ha [laughs] of course, I hear stories about girls who go online to find a husband … there are a lot of covered girls [*mutahajibat*] who go to the cybercafés for this reason … they chat and chat and chat … I think it's great …

Khulud's narrative provides more evidence that only a select group of women have access to the Internet in Morocco, because of the cost of access and issues of illiteracy. For those who do have access, Khulud celebrates the ability of young women, even religiously conservative ones, to use the powers of the Internet to cyberdate, thus giving young women more control over their selection of a spouse. Khulud's comments are in fact highly relevant to the Gulf, where one of the Internet's main attractions for young women is that it enables them to transgress gender norms, as we shall see in the case of Kuwait.

Kuwait

Internet services were first made available in Kuwait in 1992, with Gulfnet as the sole provider of access. Kuwait University was Gulfnet's first customer, becoming the first university in the Arab world to provide free Internet access to its students, with the result that scientists, scholars and students were the first general Internet users in Kuwait, soon followed by business and government. Today the Internet is an important part of the country's youth subculture and many young people choose to surf the Internet at one of the numerous Internet cafés. The most popular net-based activity among young people is visiting chat rooms. While the sexes do not mix freely in public, the picture is different in cyberspace, where communication across gender lines carries little social risk, making the Internet an important place for getting to know members of the opposite sex. The ability to cyberdate is one of the main appeals of the Internet to young Kuwaiti women. In fact, the desire to join chat rooms is one of the main forces drawing women online.

In Kuwait, the Internet is mostly a tool for entertainment and socializing among the young.[34] Other applications such as e-commerce, e-banking and e-governance are also present, but young people constitute the majority of users and, within that group, studies suggest that women constitute the majority.[35] It is not uncommon to find professional women in Kuwait over the age of 30 who have no familiarity with computers, because they are not required to use computers for their jobs. Many do not know how to type and have administrative staff who use the computer for them. Perhaps over time, as more young female Internet users enter the workplace, this will change. In present circumstances, given that young women are the predominant users of the Internet in Kuwait, this section focuses upon their Internet practices.

Buthaina, a 20-year-old college student completing a BA degree, draws attention to the importance of reputation in Kuwaiti society.[36] A woman's reputation is something to be carefully guarded and interacting too freely and openly with the opposite sex is a sure way to blemish one's social standing as a respectable woman. Men are not subject to the same rules. If they talk with women, it is the women who are at risk, not the men. The Internet, as Buthaina observes, is a place where young Kuwaiti women can overcome this double standard.

> I have been told that you have lived for a while in Kuwait, so I would gather you are familiar with the way in which the Kuwaiti society is built. There is a somewhat double standard, and there are many grey areas in terms of the two sexes mingling with each other. Therefore I think the most common place for both sexes to mix with each other is through the Internet. Girls especially cannot form relationships with boys, even as friends in many families in Kuwait, so the Internet is a 'safe' place, I guess, for them to do so. And the fact that the two sides don't know each other – they feel safer to voice their concerns, ideas,

etc. without having their reputations ruined or without it affecting their social life.

Asked whether the Internet has any special significance for Kuwaiti women, Buthaina's response resonates with those of other women in the region, especially in Morocco, as she celebrates the Internet's ability to provide women with access to information that may be considered socially or politically sensitive. She replied:

> The Internet makes it easier for a woman to experience much of what she might not be able to experience in real life, even though this may just be virtual. In terms of research, it is also different, for there are many subjects in our society that are considered taboo, whether they are sexual or not, so the Internet makes it easier to delve into many worlds, sometimes answering questions that cannot be asked, or just opening new horizons.

Sabiha, aged 19, is also finishing a BA degree. Her testimony is similar in character to Buthaina's. Illustrating the conservative nature of Kuwaiti society, Sabiha finds that there is a difference between chatting online (which is relatively harmless) and having a 'relationship' with someone online.[37] This, she observes, is 'impossible' as well as inadvisable, for reasons explored below.

> The main reason the Internet is so popular with the Kuwaiti youth is because it's the most effective way for boys and girls to communicate with each other. Mostly they use the Internet to chat with people from the opposite sex because, to them, it is easier to communicate with a name and not a face. Very rarely if ever do they use the Internet to do any research.

Sabiha is concerned about cyberdating but sees some possibility of online chatting helping women to breach the mysteries and 'otherness' of the opposite sex in advance of marriage:

> In some ways there is a positive effect on women because they are more able to communicate with guys and it's a way for them to know that guys are not so bad. The bad thing is that some girls try to have relationships with someone online and that isn't possible. Many guys think this is possible and wind up having something like three or four if not more girlfriends online. Then there are the girls who try and do the same thing. Of course this causes the problem that girls wind up not wanting to trust guys and vice versa. So this is a major problem.

Sabiha is one of the few women interviewed who saw an overt political importance associated with women's Internet use.

> One thing that I see changing is that women try to do research on women's suffrage which is a major issue in Kuwait at the moment. So women try and find a way to convince the government to let women vote, and the Internet is helping them do this.

Yet Sabiha's own Internet use is limited to 'research for school' or chatting with friends. Like Khulud in Morocco and many others, she is more comfortable in face-to-face communication with people who are already part of her social network. As she stated very clearly: 'I'm not really into talking with a bunch of strangers'.

Saudi Arabia

Internet services became available to the Saudi public in 1999. All connections to the Internet are routed through a state server located at King Abdul-Aziz City for Science and Technology, where the Internet Services Unit (ISU) handles the traffic. The ISU does not service end-users. Instead, connectivity is provided to universities and licensed commercial ISPs. The Ministry of Information lists 28 licensed ISPs on its website. These serviced more than 112,000 users in 1999, and 490,000 users by 2001. Ministry of Information surveys reveal that Internet access in Saudi Arabia has grown by at least 20 per cent annually, that an estimated 83 per cent of Internet users are between the ages of 20 and 35 and that males account for over 78 per cent of all Internet use in the kingdom. In other words, females account for just 22 per cent. The average Internet user is online for approximately 3.5 hours a day. Some users, an estimated 6 per cent, go online from one of the 200 Internet cafés in the kingdom, while as many as 78 per cent of Saudi Internet users have access to the Internet at home. As of May 2001, Saudi authorities at the ISU were censoring on average 200,000 websites, most of which were pornographic or contained materials critical of Saudi or Gulf regimes. Nearly half (45 per cent) of all Internet use takes place from the capital, Riyadh, and over half (56 per cent) of all users have bachelor degrees. In terms of use, 93 per cent of Internet users surf the web, 72 per cent use e-mail and 32 per cent engage in Internet chatting.

The narrative here is provided by Feda, a 20-year-old college student from a prominent Saudi family, whose patterns of use and remarks about the Internet parallel those observed in Kuwait.

> I learned to use the Internet in the early 1990s [1993–4]. I got a computer a few years earlier by winning a bet with my father – I was able to grow my hair half way down my back. A representative from the company who did technical support from my father's work came to my house after strenuous nagging on my part and explained how to connect (via Bahrain, there was not yet Internet access in Saudi Arabia, so the phone bill was ridiculous!) and use e-mail.[38]

Here we see that a very feminine act brought this young woman online: she grew her hair! Long hair is an important manifestation of female beauty; concealing this beauty is one reason for veiling. Most importantly, connectivity came with parental consent and access to technical support was provided from the parent's business. Moreover, this family could afford expensive long-distance phone calls to Bahrain, which used to be required when the Internet was officially banned in Saudi Arabia. Feda asserts that most women Internet users in the kingdom are members of the elite, or those who have encountered the Internet in private schools. These aspects of the narrative separate Feda's experience from the masses of women in the region who are poor, uneducated, and lack access to centres of business and political power.

Asked about her use, Feda gives a hint as to the Internet's magnetic qualities in terms of chatting, shopping and obtaining information. She is keenly aware of pitfalls associated with chatting and of advantages in relation to information.

> When I first began using it I frequented chat rooms and met as many people as I could online. I now use it for much of my research papers, to keep connected with my friends and family, and the various consumer products available online.
>
> Because of the nature of the Saudi society, I feel that people have abused the openness of chat rooms. I think that it has done wonders for some, where they have even met their husbands online, and for others, like a friend of mine I was talking to earlier today, it has ruined their lives. This girl got in a fight with a colleague, and apparently the colleague spread the girl's phone number in chat rooms. She claims she had gotten phone calls and obscene messages from all around the world, which led her to get in trouble with her family, and she eventually changed all of her phone numbers. I also think that many women

are also discovering the amount of useful information that is available online, and many women are using it for medical information, as well as shopping.

Feda's narrative once again highlights a common theme – that the Internet can both help and hinder women. Despite censorship, Feda notes in other conversations that it is really impossible to filter everything, and software to break through the protective firewalls is commonly available in the kingdom.[39] In addition to overcoming censorship, the Internet promotes young people's interaction across gender lines. But it can also be used to harm a young woman's reputation. Feda's explanation for why some people in Saudi Arabia abuse the freedoms offered by chat rooms and the Internet is based on the restrictiveness of Saudi culture. Like a starving child who has no time for table etiquette when confronted with a lavish buffet, Internet freedoms can bring out unaccustomed behaviours, including what would be considered misuse of the Internet given Saudi social codes. Joshua Teitelbaum, who has analysed uses of the Internet in Saudi Arabia, quotes the minister of the interior, Prince Nayef bin Abdel-Aziz, to summarize local attitudes towards the technology. The prince told a gathering of imams that 'the Internet, while containing much negative material, could be used as a tool to inform the world about Islam in Saudi Arabia'.[40] Feda herself is optimistic about the Internet's impact in the long term:

> I believe that having a portal to the world is extremely necessary in the world we live in today. I do believe that being able to access information from all around the world does help build tolerance and understanding. I also believe that it can be harmful, not only because of the instance I mentioned earlier, but because it is still very difficult to control the information that is available online, and any charismatic psychos are able to mislead the weak into flying airplanes into buildings.
>
> I hope that by seeing that an open society online functions on a normal level, which hopefully it can prove to do, Saudis will begin to consider transforming their closed and very limited social activities. I think that interaction between the sexes especially in the workplace is inevitable in the future, and I think that the Internet may be the only means to proving that decent and respectable interaction is possible. Hopefully the good will overcome the evil that is spread online, and people can see that the glass really is half full.

Feda's reference to the Al-Qaeda network resonates with the efforts of liberal-minded Saudis to illustrate to the world that extremism is not the norm in their country. She celebrates the Internet's ability to encourage Saudi society to be less insulated from the world and sees it as a platform for promoting global understanding.

Bahrain

Of the five countries covered by this study, Bahrain has the highest per capita Internet penetration, with 21 per cent of the population having access. The Internet was first made publicly available in 1995 and growth has been sharp since then. The number of users was projected to increase by 43 per cent between 2001 and 2002 alone.[41] Bahrain has a single ISP, Batelco, the national telecommunications company that is majority-owned by the state. Batelco provides a comprehensive portal to Internet services and web addresses. Internet access was initially provided in Bahrain to serve the business community. It is closely monitored by the state and, in the name of state security, the government has blocked access to some sites, including those of opposition groups, which it accuses of inciting sectarianism. In 1997, Sayyid Alawi Sayyid Sharaf, a Batelco engineer, was arrested and detained for two years without charge for allegedly using the Internet to transmit information to political opposition groups.[42]

In spite of some evidence of censorship and monitoring, the Internet is still a powerful force in business, education and entertainment in Bahrain. Bahrain University offers all of its students free e-mail accounts and access to the World Wide Web. Its Information Technology Centre provides access and training for students, faculty and staff. There are over 35 computer labs at the university and registration for courses is conducted online. Government high schools also encourage Internet use through a business qualification that requires training in Internet use and content development as well as other forms of IT literacy. Internet cafés are also popular gathering places for young people, some offering courses in web design and writing CVs as well as venues for meetings. The Idea Gallery, Bahrain's first Internet café, is also a full service restaurant, while Cyberzones has a restaurant and an early-learning centre with games for children. However, the hourly cost of access in Bahraini Internet cafés keeps the Internet out of reach of the poorer sections of society. Since the government continues to monopolize the ISP market in Bahrain, the cost of access is unlikely to drop until competition is allowed.

The sense that many women use the Internet regularly for work and leisure emerges strongly from the narrative of Haya, a government employee in her mid-twenties. Leisure uses include chatting, with less trepidation about negative aspects, perhaps because Bahrain has a somewhat different social environment from Saudi Arabia or Kuwait. What stands out from Haya's observations is that women's Internet access appears widespread:

> Most business women here are Internet savvy, as are many housewives and self-employed women. Internet in the workplace is an integral part of work (e-mail, research) so for business purposes it is widely used. Chatting is also hugely popular – from first-hand observation, the age range of 11–30 years I would say likes to chat on the net. [43]

Haya notes that for her personally, the Internet has 'just sped things up'. She celebrates the ability to stay in touch with people, whether for work or pleasure, and the ability to send and receive information with speed and ease. Discussing the impact on Bahraini society as a whole, Haya said:

> Socially, it is also interesting that there seems to be an undocumented rise in the number of marriages that start off as Internet romances … I think this is especially true in the Gulf and probably mainly for twenty-somethings, who don't have the opportunity to date all that much. E-mail is also used quite a bit as a chat-up method – it isn't uncommon to get random e-mails from strangers telling you that they have seen you somewhere and would like to get to know you (again, over e-mail!!). Instant messaging is also hugely popular.

Just as the tone of these comments distinguishes the Bahraini case, so does the rate at which Internet use is perceived to be spreading. Haya expressed this perception as follows:

> I think that what started off as a rich woman's technology is now becoming increasingly mainstreamed. I know that in Bahrain, a lot of schools are improving their connectivity – some at a faster rate than others – but we are getting there.

Fatima, a friend of Haya's, provided some insights as to why the Internet should be spreading so fast in Bahrain. Her comments indicated that e-commerce is not only possible but practical, and that unmetered access and broadband are available – at a price. Contextualizing her narrative of the Internet's use and impact in Bahrain in the terms of her own experience, she explained:

> Speaking only for myself, I use the Internet everyday at all times and for all purposes. I rarely chat. I book plane tickets and hotels, buy groceries, use it for work-related research, obtain directions, book movie tickets, buy theatre tickets, read news ... [My] uses are many and varied. I have an ADSL line so I can use it 24/7.[44]

Fatima's use patterns fit those of other professionals on the career ladder all over the world. Even so, she believes that e-commerce still has much room for growth in Bahrain, as most companies use their pages for advertising rather than transacting business. But Fatima is also level-headed about the prospects for Internet use among the less wealthy. She observed:

> My thoughts on Internet usage are that it is probably currently a phenomenon of the wealthy rather than the poor for the following reasons:
>
> 1. The high transaction costs associated with acquiring a computer/ getting and paying for an Internet phone line – Most Gulf countries do not have freely accessible and cheap/free broadband telephone networks and computer penetration, and literacy tends to be higher among the more educated.
>
> 2. The wealthier tend to have more ease with English (which is vital for Internet use); even those who can read Arabic may not know how to type Arabic quickly which would make computer usage more difficult.
>
> 3. Gulf countries tend to censor traditional media so to the extent that the usage is to obtain news, users would tend to be people who are politicized and/or are interested in obtaining several different points of view; I don't know how that cuts in terms of usage.
>
> 4. There are currently not many local Internet commerce opportunities (i.e. businesses treat their web pages as an advertisement, not as a medium to transact business), so I assume from that that the utility of the Internet is likewise somewhat curtailed.

The barriers to more widespread Internet use that Fatima identified match those cited by others in this analysis. They are primarily: cost, education and literacy, language barriers, and lack of public interest or demand except among isolated pockets of society, including the rich, the young and rich, the politically active and urban professionals. If such observations are being made about the second most wired state in the region (second only to the UAE, where per capita penetration is nearly 37 per cent) then for countries like Morocco and Egypt the road towards more generalized Internet access for women and the masses must be even steeper. Fatima's comments provide a sobering dose of realism, lest we be inspired by the narratives of connectivity and use reported in this chapter to think that the Internet is a generalized phenomenon. In its present state, even in Bahrain, connectivity is inhibited by all of the factors which prolong the digital divide worldwide. If we take Fatima's and Haya's narratives together, they present a balanced snapshot. They indicate that, for the elite, Internet use is widespread. For the underclass, use is limited.

Conclusion

The information presented in this chapter suggests that the Internet in the Arab world is still predominantly a male domain. The women interviewed, all Internet-active, tended to fit a common pattern in being part of an elite of educated, mid-career professionals or rich young graduates of private schools. Received wisdom about women's use of the Internet outside the Arab world highlights the medium's potential for giving women a global voice, along with access to information and connections to professional networks. Internet literacy is seen as enhancing women's job prospects and, in the private sphere, as a means of staying in touch with family and friends. The analysis in this chapter shows that women's Internet use in the Arab world fits the received wisdom in some respects but not in others, and that the variations have to do with local characteristics of individual countries. The women interviewed here barely mentioned the concept of the 'global voice'; the only specific online political activity noted was the campaign for women's suffrage in Kuwait. Meanwhile, leisure use of the Internet for shopping in the Gulf cannot be replicated in North African countries where credit cards and e-commerce are restricted and customs duties on imported goods remain high. Professional women in the Arab world, as elsewhere, use the Internet for networking, research, e-mail and work-related activities. Among the young, the most common use is for entertainment, which includes chatting, maybe with the opposite sex. Secondary applications include obtaining information or networking with family and friends.

The study highlighted the fact that Internet penetration statistics do not tell us all that we need to know about Internet access, since Internet cafés are important for providing training and technical support as well as access. All the case studies suggest that the cost of Internet use and lack of training remain real barriers to more widespread use of the Internet by women in the Arab world. Among those who had overcome these initial barriers, using the Internet had become an everyday activity, which most could not imagine doing without. This tends to undermine essentialist arguments about certain societies being inherently 'slow to change'. It puts the emphasis instead on institutional factors that are historically specific, such as national telecommunications policies. Most interviewees in this chapter envisioned a long-term positive impact of the Internet in the region, especially if the technology is used to give women more of a voice in society, more autonomy in the selection of a spouse, and more authority at work and abroad. One respondent in particular hoped that wired technologies could help to promote global understanding. As the policies of certain governments around the world render the norms and stabilizing institutions of the world system increasingly ineffective in containing international conflict, global outreach and dialogue among ordinary people are needed more than ever before.

10
Power, NGOs and Lebanese Television: a Case Study of Al-Manar TV and the Hezbollah Women's Association

Victoria Firmo-Fontan

Lebanon is at present in a state of negative peace, whereby its citizens live alongside one another without resorting to armed violence, but do not live together as a nation. More than ten years after the end of the civil war, and given the government's failure to address the war's socio-political causes, the pressing task of rebuilding Lebanon as an entity remains to be achieved. While the Lebanese people refuse to accept liability for their troubled past and their lack of a common future, blaming malevolent external influences for the difficulty of reaching a national civic consensus,[1] civil society has reinvented itself in a Lebanese context of 'retributive peace', a concept explored in this chapter. It has done so by promoting its own polarization and that of the people it is supposed to accommodate. Women's groups in Lebanon consequently appear to be deeply political, polarized and at times devoid of any common sense of sisterhood, their polarization occurring in parallel with that of the Lebanese media. The purpose of this chapter is to analyse approaches to social responsibility in post-war Lebanese civil society, focusing on relations between women's groups and the media and particularly links between Al-Manar TV and the Women's Association of the Hezbollah resistance movement that runs Al-Manar.

The study develops a definition of civil society in Lebanon in order to consider whether media organizations and their messages reinforce the existing power relations between women's non-governmental organizations (NGOs) and the media or challenge them. This analysis is conducted in the context of Lebanon's power-sharing arrangements based on religious affiliation, referred to within Lebanese studies as confessionalism. The relationship between Al-Manar TV and the Hezbollah Women's Association (HWA) is considered with a view to assessing whether Al-Manar TV constitutes a vector of social responsibility and national civic commitment, or alternatively may be held responsible for helping to perpetuate deep divisions within Lebanese civil society, especially among women's groups.

Civil society and NGOs in Lebanon

The concept of civil society is an elusive one, assuming different significance according to the environments within which it thrives. Two generic characterizations of civil society can be found. In one the term describes a realm outside the state and the private sector. In the other, civil society is located exclusively between the individual and the state.[2] While the two approaches differ with regard to the private sector, they concur in emphasizing the absence of the state; instead of 'top down', civil society is seen as 'bottom up'. Moreover, while the political sphere can be included in the characterization of civil society, its relevance and insertion within civil society depend on an unambiguous separation from the coercive machinery of the state. According to these definitions, NGOs and non-state media are part of civil society. In Lebanon, however, the notion of civil society has assumed a somewhat different meaning. Irene Lorfing notes that it plays the role of intermediary between society and the political authority, but defines it as an environment in which 'citizens and groups within the government, the market, and civil groups and organizations undertake initiatives for the common good' in order to influence 'power'.[3] Of importance in this definition is the clear departure from conventional definitions of civil society as excluding government institutions. Not only does Lebanese civil society organize itself to include these, it also perceives itself solely in relation to political power. As a result, the NGO sector uses the media as a means to influence power, by making its voice heard.[4] The media, meanwhile, follow the same confessional configuration as the centres of political power. Hence, while parts of the Lebanese academic community do not recognize the media as being integral to civil society, the media appear to have become *instrumentalized* by the NGO sector's quest to influence power (see Figure 10.1).[5]

Figure 10.1

Lorfing's schematization of the media, NGOs and power in Lebanon

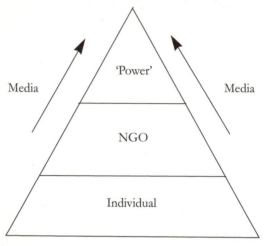

Since power seems to be central to the characterization of civil society in Lebanon, a study of relations between Lebanese women's NGOs and the Lebanese media must take into account the power dynamics that influence all civil society activity in the process of building post-war social responsibility. Conceptualizing these power dynamics, Lorfing goes so far as to place civil society, and the NGO sector in particular, at the centre of the democratic debate, describing NGOs as the potential upholders of Lebanon's democratic institutions.[6] Such a hierarchical view of civil society can be seen in the light of Steven Lukes's tri-dimensional characterization of power, which assigns different levels of importance to decision-making, partial retribution, and agenda-setting. In his model, agenda-setting supersedes other expressions of power because a decision cannot be made if it is not part of the political agenda.[7] When applied to Lebanon's civil society, the ranking in this model raises the question of who sets the public agenda and where the power to set it resides. If the media have agenda-setting capability, who is accountable for the political choices they make? Do the media challenge the government from outside its power structures, making them part of civil society in the conventional, non-Lebanese sense? Or are they in effect an arm of government, thus being counted as part of civil society only within a Lebanese setting?

To understand how the media and NGO sector relate to each other with regard to the status of women, it is necessary to examine particular characteristics of the Lebanese media. Although a fully comprehensive account would review a diverse range of outlets, this chapter concentrates specifically on television. This is because of its impact on a wide audience and because of the higher rate of illiteracy among the female population of Lebanon.[8]

Lebanese television: *'dis-moi qui tu hantes, je te dirai qui tu es'*?[9]

If it is hard to grasp the position of the Lebanese media in relation to civil society, it is partly because of sharp differences between Lebanese television and the terrestrial broadcasting outlets of neighbouring authoritarian states like Syria or Jordan. Compared with these, television in Lebanon appears to be a rather democratic, open and dialogical entity, by which is meant that it is geared towards an equal exchange between different actors.[10] In addition, the representation of women in Lebanese television, whether in soap operas or in other programmes, seems relatively liberal by regional standards.[11] However, comparison with television stations in the West highlights deep censorship in Lebanon's case, along with inefficiency and operations that appear detrimental to the establishment of social responsibility and sustainable peace.[12] Yet neither type of comparison helps clarify the nature of Lebanese television in its own terms. For that we need to look at the agenda-setting and lobbying patterns adopted by broadcasting agents.

Television in Lebanon started in the late 1950s, from a context of economic prosperity prompted by the strong growth of the business and finance sectors.[13] According to Nabil Dajani, the 'initiative to establish Lebanese television belongs to businessmen who had little experience in the requirements of television broadcasting'. As a result, the logic surrounding Lebanese television today stems from an ethos of commercialization, not one of fostering social responsibility.[14] After two years of negotiation with the Lebanese government, a licence was granted to La Compagnie Libanaise de Télévision to create two television channels. The licence allowed government scrutiny over programming, and forbade companies from broadcasting programmes that would jeopardize the consensual nature of Lebanon's existence as a multi-sectarian entity. Of importance under the terms of this licence was the political context in which television evolved. The Republic of Lebanon was artificially created after the Sykes–Picot Agreement of 1916, and validated by the establishment of a consociational constitution in 1926 (sharing power among confessional groups) and a proclamation of independence from the tutelage of the French Mandate in 1943.[15] At the centre of the newly-established nation was a consensus that recognized the existence of 17 religious sects and envisaged civil peace being maintained through a consociational form of government. Based on the Swiss model, this is characterized by a series of judicial arrangements geared to resolving potential conflicts among different sects. The government comprises a large coalition of politicians proportionally elected from all sectors of society, holding a mutual power of veto and autonomous from external influences.[16] According to Article 95 of the 1926 Constitution, this system of consociational democracy was supposed to be only '*à titre transitoire et dans une intention de justice et de concorde*': a provisional measure until such time as dissension among the diverse but newly united communities could be resolved.[17] This consensus gave birth to the concept of confessionalism, theoretically referring to the inter-sect power-sharing measures specific to Lebanon, whereby administrative and government appointments have to be shared equally among the different religious groups, while different communities are to be governed by their own religious law in such matters as marriage and inheritance.[18]

In practice, confessionalism evolved into a widespread system of granting socio-economic favours. Despite being conceived as a transitional measure, confessionalism still lies at the core of the Lebanese entity, and can be conceptualized as a control-matrix governing all aspects of the country's social, political and religious life. Held partly responsible for allowing the 1975–90 civil war to erupt through marginalization of individuals outside the confessional matrix, the political leadership present at the 1989 Taif peace negotiations ordered the establishment of a commission that would 'de-confessionalize' Lebanon.[19] More than a decade after the signing of the accord, such a commission remained to be appointed. Indeed, confessionalism is constantly blamed for the country's internal problems; according to one's stake in the privilege-gathering game, confessionalism will either be tolerated as a vector of one's economic survival, or be denounced as blatant corruption.[20] In fact, clientelism remains the most widespread expression of confessionalism within Lebanese society, whereby belonging to a political family or having what are commonly described in Lebanon as 'connections' will determine an individual's success in all things and at all levels, from finding a job to finding a parking space. Confessionalism is thus fundamental to any analysis of Lebanese television.

As a result of the war, and following the realization by warlords of the importance of broadcasting, television channels began to emerge de facto, representing the interests of the different warring factions. While the two initial broadcasting services were united under the auspices of the Lebanese television company, Télé-Liban, at the end of 1977, other television companies had to be regulated by the government at the end of the conflict. As a result, and in order to maintain the relative status quo pertaining to negative civil peace, the government in the mid-1990s legalized the most prominent of these television companies and granted them the special licence needed to broadcast news. The selection was made only on sectarian grounds and all licences were given to members of the government or their relatives, hence privileging sectarianism over professionalism.[21] Confessionalism in broadcasting became institutionalized. The stations that received a licence were: Murr Television (MTV), owned by the family of a former interior minister; the National Broadcasting Network (NBN), representing the Shia community and more specifically supporters of the speaker of the parliamentary assembly; the Lebanese Broadcasting Company International (LBCI), the strongest war-time television station originally established by the Christian militia and now owned by a group of businessmen-cum-politicians mainly from the Christian community; and Future Television, owned by relatives and associates of the Prime Minister, Rafiq Hariri.

An entirely privately-owned television sector has therefore emerged, favouring political bosses and/or religious groups' own broadcasting networks (see Table 10.1). The government licensing decision excluded Al-Manar TV, the broadcasting service of the Hezbollah resistance movement, and Télé-Lumière, belonging to the Maronite Christian Church. When neither station suspended its activities, and when other religiously oriented television stations were hastily established, the government finally granted a licence to both stations in an effort to dissuade other channels from following their subversive precedent. This decision can be seen as an effort by power holders to defuse a potentially threatening situation.[22] Although partial retribution might also have been used, the Lebanese government granted a licence to both stations in order to quell a growing public debate about the creation of other, more damaging, channels before the latter could begin to draw on a more substantial support base.

Table 10.1

Ownership of Lebanese television by confessional and political groupings

TV Station	Main owner	Ownership (%)	Confession
Al-Manar	Hezbollah Party	100	Shia
Télé-Lumière	Maronite Church	100	Maronite
Future TV	Hariri family and associates	60.69	Sunni
NBN	Berri family	55.82	Shia
MTV	Murr family	46.88	Orthodox
LBCI	Frangieh, Fares & Daher families	57.57	Maronite
Télé-Liban	State	100	State-owned

Source: Information International, *National Action for Fighting Corruption in Lebanon* (Beirut, 2001), p 25.

Who sets the agenda? power relations and the Lebanese media

Blatant confessionalization of the Lebanese media triggers concern as to whether particular media outlets only reflect or cater for the confessional group to which they are affiliated. In the case of Al-Manar TV, 100 per cent owned by the Shia Hezbollah (whose name translates as 'Party of God'), one might assume that its Islamic message is not necessarily intended to be received by Christian viewers. Were this so, it would reinforce an already dangerous process of polarization.[23] Moreover, applying Lukes's model of power dynamics to the confessionalization of the Lebanese media would suggest a strong influence over the crucial agenda-setting process in post-war Lebanon, sufficient to strip the NGO sector of its social responsibility function and leaving women's NGOs with no agenda-setting role. However, recent developments in Lebanese politics suggest that such an interpretation would be an over-simplification of confessionalism – one that underestimates the consensual nature of government in Lebanon and overlooks the latent alienation of 'power' within the Lebanese political scene.

Literature on the consociational nature of Lebanon is divided over the issue of the state's perceived weakness, as embodied for example in Syrian domination over Lebanon.[24] The consensual character of the Lebanese constitution – operated through a special electoral system based on the formation of multi-confessional coalitions – prevented the election of ethnically radical political figures and had the effect of moderating the public political narrative.[25] As a result, despite a confessionalized licensing system for the media, licensed television channels rarely engage in politically polarizing narrative, or in agenda-setting activities that would directly threaten the effective functioning of Lebanon as a confessional entity. While political analyses clearly diverge in relation to government policies, the discourse used by broadcasting services is invariably directed towards the government, and not a sect. MTV and LBCI illustrate this. In 2002, after they openly criticized the government and Syrian interference in Lebanese affairs, the information minister retaliated against them. In August 2002, the minister, Ghazi Aridi, reportedly tipped off the Sureté Générale to press charges against both channels. MTV was to be accused of 'disturbing Lebanon's ties with a fraternal state (Syria), impugning the president's dignity, slandering security agencies, and disturbing the country's general peace'. LBCI was accused of promoting 'sectarian strife' during its coverage of a shooting at the Beirut offices of the Private School Teachers Mutual Fund in July 2002.[26] On 4 September 2002, all broadcasting activities of MTV were suspended, the television channel's headquarters were evacuated and sealed *manu militari*.[27] This controversial action was seriously challenged by several other television channels, which decried the government's omnipotent role in regulating the opposition narrative presented through broadcasting. These channels came to the defence of their competitors, MTV and LBCI. Solidarity like this might even be described as inter-sectarian collaboration vis-à-vis the government, which is itself inter-sectarian.

However, the deeper issue at stake, that of the Syrian presence in Lebanon, has not been raised by television channels, which almost invariably remain cautious in their commentary and analysis for fear of experiencing the same treatment accorded to LCBI or MTV. Instances of inter-sectarian dissent within the Lebanese media at large are therefore confined to what Lukes calls two-dimensional power (decision-making and partial retribution), whereas the third dimension, the agenda-setting function, is reserved for what Lorfing elusively but accurately refers to as 'power'. The establishment of sustainable peace requires alternative voices to be expressed to prevent marginalization of the political opposition as happened in the 1970s. But the channels for alternative voices are obstructed by the pressure to maintain consensus. It might therefore be argued that, although the Lebanese broadcast media may appear deeply corrupt or biased, they do not openly encourage ethnic polarization through political discourse because this would lead to their broadcasting rights being challenged or rescinded by the government. It would seem safe to assert that the media's agenda-setting capabilities are virtually non-existent.

A thorough analysis of Lebanese television media should therefore take into account its unwillingness to voice a strong opposition to the Lebanese government, thus obliterating a major aspect of Lebanese political life that contributed to the resurgence of ethnic hatred in the country. The present government policy on peace-building and the media, claiming to foster the status quo through 'open censorship', can be understood as the direct rejection of what is identified as having caused the conflict. In the process, the circulation of ideas is constricted, which could threaten the country's longer-term stability.

The NGO sector and women's rights

As with the media, NGOs in Lebanon embody the confessional system; in extreme cases they are established for the political advancement of their patron. It is consequently very difficult to attribute any homogeneity to the NGO sector of civil society in post-war Lebanon. This was not always the case. Most welfare NGOs during the war were service-oriented, non-political and multi-confessional, aimed at addressing the pressing needs of the destitute population they came across.[28] However, the end of the conflict, and the withdrawal of international funds that had been geared towards the humanitarian alleviation of war-related poverty, left the government with the unattainable task of reshaping the Lebanese welfare system. The following paragraphs attempt to shed light on the diversification of the NGO sector with regard to women's issues and in the context of civil society's quest to influence power.

An assessment of women's NGOs in the post-war period carries numerous methodological problems. There is a dilemma as to whether to opt for a quantitative or qualitative approach. There is also the delicate task of naming certain organizations in what could (incorrectly) be understood as an implicit critique. To many of those involved, the exercise may appear subjective, although it could also be understood as an independent external evaluation of the type of relationship that exists between Lebanon's media and its women's NGOs. The predominantly confessional nature of Lebanon has shaped women's NGOs in its image, as a sector strongly influenced by the tensions experienced in political and sectarian life. At the same time, evaluating women's status in post-war Lebanon is subject to many pitfalls, the first of which could be the subjectivity of the researcher's own western background in relation to women's empowerment, as the empowerment criteria sought by the author might be different from those enjoyed by Lebanese women. Another difficulty concerns the high degree of heterogeneity among Lebanese women. Mona Khalaf, director of the Institute for Women's Studies in the Arab World, states:

> I always talk of Lebanese women rather than the Lebanese woman, because there is more than one stereotype of the Lebanese woman. It is very difficult to compare the Lebanese woman who lives in the South, and whose husband is a Hezbollah fighter, with the woman who teaches in the university, [or] with the woman who still lives as if nothing has happened in Lebanon: these ladies of *la haute société* who throw their parties every night and who have their massages during the day.[29]

In such a context, women's NGOs in Beirut are very different from women's NGOs in other parts of the country, especially southern Lebanon where women's NGOs are scarce. They are also a source of curiosity and sometimes contempt from women at the grassroots level, who do not identify with the 'futile' activities of some 'Beirut' women's gatherings. Quantifying women's NGOs is also fraught with complexity, as some organizations struggle to obtain a government permit to operate. While they are required to register with the Ministry of Interior to be issued a permit (a requirement not endorsed by any existing law), no precise registration figures are available as the Ministry's system for delivering permits remains obscure. Some NGOs complain that they have failed to obtain a permit more than eight years after submitting their request.[30] Other women's NGOs are offshoots of political parties or neo-feudal families, making it questionable whether they can be considered to be advancing women's rights per se. Before embarking on a deeper analysis of the Hezbollah Women's Association, one must therefore offer a Lebanese definition of the women's NGO sector, encompassing all the concerns identified here. As the sector's political nature represents a subjective minefield in which the author does not wish to step, it will be analysed instead in terms of monological and dialogical expressions of post-war civil society, and in relation to Lukes's conceptualization of power.[31]

Post-war civil society is indeed diversified, but also divided between two ethoses, respectively monological and dialogical. A monological ethos can be conceived as an absence of communication, embodied within the media by its inability to directly challenge governmental policies – an inability that allows alternative and challenging ideas to be marginalized, whether they are political or of another nature. Within the women's NGO sector the same ethos is embodied in an organization's inability or unwillingness to challenge the deeply embedded gender hierarchy pertaining to a patriarchy. The fact that the media and NGO sector operate in parallel, representing only one stratum of society at a time, is at the core of monological expression of post-war civil society. Within the women's NGO sector, this monological ethos can account for a stalemate that exists between an approach aimed at the development of one group of women and another aimed at the development of women as a whole. While one approach favours the establishment of a common expression of women's rights, the other dwells on the past to shape its own exclusive future, in which outsiders can have a place, but in a parallel structure rather than an integrated one. A very influential women's advocacy organization in Beirut can provide an example of this duality. The organization in question, headed at the time of writing by a woman MP, employed an Ethiopian girl aged approximately between 12 and 15 years to serve refreshments to guests and clean the offices.[32] In answer to a question about this girl, the author was told that she was fortunate to have found such a position in Beirut, having been extracted by her benefactors from a life of misery. The answer seemed to imply that the young girl was better off doing hard work as a servant than starving, for working in a respected establishment was the best she could hope for in a life pre-determined as that of an 'inferior' human being. Whatever the facts of the girl's life chances, this claim carries the hallmarks of a monological hierarchization of post-war Lebanese society.[33]

Indeed, while the organization advocates women's empowerment, only some Lebanese women seem to be eligible and others are excluded. This phenomenon of exclusion, repeated widely across post-war Lebanon, is symptomatic of a state of peace that can be characterized by its retributive nature. In a state of retributive peace, a post-war society first does not come to terms with its painful past, preferring to ignore it and apportion blame elsewhere, and secondly intensifies its hierarchical mechanisms, thus marginalizing certain social strata.[34] For example, the issue of modern slavery has been raised in the public sphere, through a series of press articles and campaigns by a small number of human rights activists and NGOs. Yet Lebanese public opinion has not put pressure on the government to legislate for the protection of migrant workers. Nor, at the time of writing, had the issue yet been addressed by a Lebanese television channel, partly perhaps because the practice of having a foreign maid in the household is considered normal and also because the phenomenon is exclusive to a certain economic class and is confined to cities.[35]

The most obvious reason for the lack of public interest is the widespread exploitation of Asian and African domestic workers in Lebanon, who are estimated to have exceeded 100,000 in number, based only on legally registered maids. Thus 'Other' women are exploited by Lebanese women according to a rationale stemming from the hierarchy that pertains to retributive peace.[36] For this state of affairs to be challenged would require that any agenda-setting capability on the part of the Lebanese media be supplemented by active campaigning by NGOs, subject to the monological/dialogical expressions of post-war civil society (see Figure 10.2). In other words, the situation of migrant domestic workers can be understood in relation to confessionalism in post-war Lebanon. Under confessionalism, part of the basis of 'power' seems to have shifted from government to political patrons, who are themselves in control of the broadcast media and partly in control of the NGO sector. While some media outlets and women's groups are able to raise the case of chronic violations of women's rights, as in the case of domestic migrant workers, the basis of 'power' will not choose to address it, as both 'power' and confessionally-bound Lebanese citizens benefit from the existing situation.[37] Moreover, the capacity of the women's NGO sector to address issues pertaining to the foundations of neo-patriarchy in Lebanon, itself embodied in the monological hierarchization of women, remains constrained by the self-sustaining confessional system.

Figure 10.2
NGOs, the media, 'power' and retributive peace

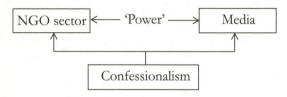

Post-war civil society in Lebanon, especially women's NGOs, appears to have been divided by the mechanisms of retributive peace, emerging through a monological expression of exclusive aid and representation, and facilitated by clientelism as a consequence of confessionalism. An analysis of the relationship between the women's NGO sector and the media in relation to 'power' therefore seems to indicate that, as with the media, women's NGOs will not challenge the foundations of the monological/hierarchical patriarchal system in Lebanon. Having established that neither the media nor women's NGOs are in a position to set the agenda in post-war Lebanon except under instruction from 'power', this chapter will now consider the two-dimensional power relationship between a broadcasting channel and a women's NGO. In analysing the relationship between Al-Manar TV and the HWA, it will address the issue of the representation of women in the media, in order to assess the social responsibility attributes of both institutions.

The HWA, Al-Manar TV and representation of women

The explicitly religious nature of Al-Manar TV and the HWA, offshoots of the Shia Muslim Hezbollah, might be assumed to place both organizations at the centre of the confessional debate in Lebanon. To a neophyte, western eye, the religious nature of the Hezbollah might imply that communication between Al-Manar TV and the HWA does not evolve outside the party's tight control, hence placing the power dynamic envisaged by Lorfing inside the realm of the party's political apparatus. A common supposition might also be that the audience for Al-Manar TV consists solely of Hezbollah members, hence reinforcing a sense of confessional polarization in which the television channel asserts and reasserts the party's political and religious message. This is a supposition that can be tested within a framework based on the concept of retributive peace. Here the monological or dialogical nature of both Al-Manar TV and the HWA will be analysed in relation to women's status within society, which can either be predetermined within a monological hierarchy or open-ended within an integrative dialogue fostering inter-sectarian collaboration. The power relations existing between Al-Manar TV and the HWA will be assessed in relation to the two-dimensional powers embedded within both organizations.

The HWA was founded in the early 1990s, in accordance with an ideology of complementarity between men and women, and as part of the rationalization process undergone by the Hezbollah Party after the 1992 Lebanese parliamentary elections.[38] Women, seen as the 'bearers of generations' by the party's mentor, Ayatollah Khomeini, were enabled to play an integral role in the revolutionary onset of the Hezbollah, through their participation in the struggle against Israeli occupation of South Lebanon until May 2000.[39] Although technically liable to become martyrs, very few women waged open warfare against Israeli or South Lebanon Army forces in the region, thus restricting their share of the authority derived from fighting. However, the women of the Hezbollah played a central role in the smuggling of weapons from caches to strategic positions. Furthermore, from the late 1980s they were encouraged to further their education, enter paid employment and take a more assertive role in the Islamic resistance against Israel, the latter symbolized by their prominent role as mothers responsible for the education of future members and devout Muslims.

Complementarity with men is an important aspect in the development of women within the Hezbollah, meaning that their empowerment is strongly encouraged as long as it does not hinder their family lives. The activities of the Women's Association, decided by the HWA leadership rather than the Council of Clerics or the Politburo, foster the development of women within the boundaries of their faith in Shia Islam. The HWA, headed by Rima Fakhri, an agricultural engineering graduate of the American University of Beirut, is strictly aimed at development of the individual. Women are given religious education, literacy classes and information technology tuition if they require it either as mothers or for their employment. In the summer, they are offered basic health and hygiene training to fend off heat-related diseases. They also regularly gather for social activities, thus reinforcing the ties that bound them within the Islamic resistance. While priority is given to the daughters of those who lost their lives as a result of the Israeli occupation of South Lebanon, girls are also socialized into a policy of individual development. They take part in summer camps, physical activities and supplementary education programs ranging from history to reproductive science for teenagers.

While the HWA clearly evolves under the auspices of patriarchy, one must apply caution before dismissing patriarchy as necessarily pejorative. Indeed, a post-modern outlook on Hezbollah women's dress code might find the encouraged wearing of the chadoor as de-objectifying for women.[40] While many Lebanese believe that the public display of the chadoor is rewarded with a monthly payment by the party, the action of wearing it cannot be dissociated from social mores in Lebanon, where women in non-conservative dress may be subject to sexual harassment in the absence of a male family member to defend their honour if threatened.[41] The image of women in Islam is potentially a vector of shame, implying that their appearance must be concealed to avoid the arousal of men.[42] Yet the preoccupation with honour and shame is by no means exclusive to Muslim areas in Lebanon and is seen by Germaine Tillion as a Mediterranean phenomenon rather than one linked to Islam.[43] An Ethiopian migrant worker recounted her experience while wearing modern dress outside her residence: '[w]hen we are walking in the streets, guys on motorcycles slap our asses and say nasty things'.[44] Rima Fakhri's view of the chadoor is that it allows women to engage in any kind of activity as equals with men.[45] However, representatives of other women's NGOs question this assertion, arguing that the chadoor gives women a licence to violate the code of sexual behaviour prescribed for Lebanese women in general. To reverse the attributes of 'virtue' in this way would appear to be a blatant expression of retributive peace and the monological hierarchization of Lebanese post-war society, whereby women compete in the ethnic hierarchy of sexual purity. Conversely, it must be noted that the HWA welcomes in its gatherings women who do not wear the chadoor. Instead of seeking to influence the agenda-setting dimension of power, the HWA seeks to empower women individually through equal representation with men. The question arising from this is whether Al-Manar TV's approach is consistent with that of the HWA, and whether it caters exclusively for a Shia audience.

The broadcasting service of the Lebanese Hezbollah, Al-Manar TV (Arabic for 'the lighthouse'), qualifies itself as a 'Lebanese TV station that aims to ... enhance the civilized role of the Arab and Islamic community', and as the 'first Arab establishment to stage an effective psychological warfare against the Zionist enemy'.[46] Al-Manar was created on 3 June 1991, in order for the Hezbollah to convey a message of 'love and tolerance ... of values, morals and goals ... to live in peace, support the oppressed and defend [the Lebanese people's] rights'.[47] This message was aimed at reaching the Lebanese public and the Arab world, as a means of countering the negative image of the party within Lebanon as a result of its pre-Musawi conservative leadership and close ties with Syria, and in an effort to mobilize the Lebanese against Israel's occupation of South Lebanon.[48] Via television aimed at unifying the Lebanese people, Al-Manar presented itself as a respectable broadcaster, safe for family viewing and unremitting in its denunciation of the Israeli occupation. It conveyed a strongly moral message aimed at eradicating 'instincts' provoked by other Lebanese television channels, where women are objectified and represented as 'belly-dancers and prostitutes'.[49]

On Al-Manar TV, female presenters wear the hejab, and no parts of the female body other than hands and face are exposed on any programme. The fact that women presenters wear the manteau and hejab, as opposed to the chadoor, can be interpreted as an initiative on the channel's part to avoid antagonizing more liberal viewers and to appeal to all sectors of the Lebanese population. Indeed, its former executive director, Nayef Krayem, declares that the channel is the third most watched TV channel in Lebanon, attracting 15 per cent of Lebanese people from all groups in society.[50] Among Hezbollah's main goals in 2002 were ending the alleged Israeli occupation of the Shebaa farms and actively supporting the Palestinian uprising, the Al-Aqsa intifada. In this context, Al-Manar's role was to raise awareness in Lebanon of the need to support the Palestinian population against the Israeli government. Opposition to the Israeli occupation of Arab land is the only point of consensus among the Lebanese people. After the beginning of the second intifada in 2000, Al-Manar chose to increase its airtime by 14 hours, reaching a total of 18 hours of programming per day. Since starting up in 1991, and especially since obtaining a broadcasting licence from the government in 1997, the channel has increased its audience share to the 15 per cent cited by Nayef Krayem. By concentrating on the Palestinian intifada, which is widely supported in Lebanon, and by welcoming speakers from all sectors of the Lebanese population onto its programmes, Al-Manar has tried to identify itself as a television channel fostering inter-sectarian collaboration. However, the Hezbollah stance on the intifada and the Shebaa farms is of concern to some Lebanese, especially since the 2002 State of the Union Address by the US president, George W. Bush, which named Hezbollah as a possible US target in its 'war on terrorism'. Al-Manar's constant bellicose rhetoric about waging 'psychological warfare' against Israel has been divisive of Lebanese public opinion, especially among the Christian community.[51]

While not specifically catering for women when it decided to increase its airtime in 2000, Al-Manar uses the services of women as journalists, commentators, editors and presenters on an equal footing with men. The channel's English-language broadcasting department has a majority of women working as reporters, presenters and political analysts. On the issue of women's representation in decision-making positions within Al-Manar, Fatmeh Berri argues that the channel thoroughly respects gender equality. She also states that Al-Manar respects women as human beings regardless of their physical appearance, implying that the Muslim dress code within television emphasizes a public image of women as intellectually viable.[52] Al-Manar lays claim to a wide following among Hezbollah women by offering a range of soap operas selected on moral grounds, a widely popular children's programme, *Al-Manar Al-Saghir* (Small Manar), talkshows, game shows and news, in all of which women are portrayed as de-objectified individuals. Female presenters include Safa Muslmany, Wafa Hoteit, Btoul Ayoub, Fatima Bdeir and Myriam Karnib, all playing a leading role in the development of the broadcasting channel. Among non-Hezbollah women, the following of Al-Manar TV is less obvious, but still significant, especially concerning news and children's programmes. Of importance when taking into account the television ratings for the whole of Lebanon is the predominance of Al-Manar TV as a substitution channel, not constantly watched by non-Hezbollah viewers, but frequently consulted for specific programmes, especially the news. As a result, the message of the HWA, while strictly within the boundaries set by patriarchy, is reiterated by Al-Manar TV, a message of intersectarian collaboration against a common Israeli enemy, and at times against the government's perceived anti-social policies. Moreover, Al-Manar TV's representation of women strictly adheres to the Shia religious message concerning the complementary place of women within society, itself a cardinal principle of the HWA.

Conclusion

Civil society and television in Lebanon can be seen to evolve in a one-way relationship with the realm of 'power'. The most they can do is to promote the existing social order in post-war Lebanon that is marked by polarization, retribution and a hierarchy in which success for groups and individuals is achieved at the expense of one's 'Other'. Social responsibility in Lebanon is as two-dimensional as the power exerted by the broadcasting media and women's NGOs. It evolves only within the boundaries of a pre-established order, maintaining a parallel status quo among different confessional communities. There are exceptions, however. The HWA does not use the services of imported maids, nor does it convey an objectified representation of women. This sets it apart from the norms prevailing in other sectors of Lebanese society, where women's emancipation is defined in terms that presuppose the presence of domestic servants. Power for Lebanese women and NGOs would be to adjust the social order that defines success for women in terms of their accomplishments as home-makers and socialites and makes this success dependent on the exploitation of another woman. For these reasons, one can safely assert that the HWA tends towards a dialogical mode, reinforcing its message through Al-Manar TV, in contrast to most other women's NGOs in Lebanon, which are trapped in the false pretences of a monological mode. *L'habit ne fait donc pas le moine.*[53]

Straddling Cultures: Arab Women Journalists at Home and Abroad

Magda Abu-Fadil

Reuters's Samia Nakhoul sustained serious head injuries when a US shell hit Baghdad's Palestine Hotel while she was covering the war on Iraq in 2003. Her miraculous recovery steeled her resolve to maintain her professional autonomy in the field. It also earned her more support to rise through the ranks. Yet not all Arab women journalists with stellar records of war reporting can count on promotion, or even freedom to meet the requirements of their profession.

Since the suicide attacks in the US on 11 September 2001, Arab leaders have openly acknowledged the need for Arab media outlets to face up to the challenge of media globalization and ensure that balanced and accurate media messages flow between Arab countries and the West. It is obvious that meeting this challenge requires an army of articulate communicators who can report credibly and succinctly, and who can address foreign news outlets in accessible language not laced with rhetoric. Less obvious is the fact that the Arab world has a reservoir of experienced multilingual women journalists, whose voices have the potential to surmount the wall of provocative bluster and help to bridge the knowledge gap between the Arab world and the West. This chapter identifies a few of these women. Based on interviews with them, it discusses their careers to date and their aspirations. Interviews ranged over subjects such as professionalism and promotion and gender-related aspects of being a journalist in the Arab world.

The interview questions were prompted in part by issues that have been shown to be relevant to media women worldwide. For example, workplace studies in many contexts have shown how a metaphorical glass ceiling somehow blocks media women on their way to senior jobs. In an article entitled 'After 9/11: where are the voices of women?', journalist and commentator Geneva Overholser reported a study showing that only five out of 88 op-eds in leading US dailies had been written by women. She referred to findings that women's rise to top editorial positions had stalled in the 1990s as a result of glass ceilings in their respective organizations, and how they had struggled to juggle professional and family priorities.[1] When work commitments are governed by the erratic and unpredictable schedules linked to breaking news, that struggle is universal, as the International Women's Media Foundation found from research it conducted in 100 countries in 1999. The Foundation found that the difficulty of balancing home and work was one of two basic, universal obstacles facing media women. The other was a lack of role models. This too is a phenomenon noted in the US. Board members of the American Society of Newspaper Editors (ASNE) have acknowledged that women's lack of progress in executive suites may be due to a lack of mentors and the fact that male newspaper executives do not feel comfortable grooming females for top jobs. Joy Buchanan of the *ASNE Reporter* wrote of one board member who advised women to advance their careers by 'breaking into the informal networks that men cultivate'.[2]

War reporting has also been seen as a route to advancement, although Nakhoul's shocking experience in Baghdad confirms how unglamorous it really is. After the 1991 Gulf War, Anne Sebba noted that a high proportion of the women who covered the war worked for television. She argued that war is given added drama when reported by a woman, whose presence on screen simultaneously distracts from the horror of the events themselves. According to Sebba, women reporters had recognized that by 'risking their lives for minor stations' they stood a better chance of landing a big story that would be taken up by major networks.[3] Nakhoul risked her life while working for one of the world's biggest news agencies.

The interviews recounted in this chapter broached some of these issues of career progression and glass ceilings. They probed the general and the particular in the experience of seven Arab media women. Before proceeding to their stories, the next section sets the interviews in context.

Alternative voices

The battle for the minds of Americans and Arabs went into overdrive soon after the events that shook the world on 11 September 2001. Print, broadcast and online media were mobilized at full throttle to report, analyse and explain. Globalization of the media meant instant bulletins feeding into an already frenzied news cycle, giving reporters and editors no time to assess what they were conveying. Media outlets needed a steady stream of 'experts', but US networks were hard put to find full-time political scientists at the nation's top universities with specialist knowledge of the Middle East or South Asia. Stephen Kotkin, writing in the *New York Times*, attributed the lack of such specialists to a rancorous and long-running debate over the best method for understanding the way the world works. On one hand, he said, is a belief that statistics and econometrics can identify universal patterns that underlie all economic and political systems. On the other is a preference for mastering the languages, cultures and institutions of a particular region.[4] In the turmoil, Arab men were approached for comment but the voices of Arab women journalists and commentators were sorely lacking.

In the aftermath of the initial shock, the next move in Washington was to target a media campaign at Arab and Muslim countries, to try to explain American values to their youth. These efforts eventually resulted in a new Arabic-language radio station, Radio Sawa, which started in March 2002, and a monthly magazine in Arabic, called *Hi*, launched in July 2003. Plans for a Middle East Television Network in Arabic, later dubbed Al-Hurra (The Free One), became public when the 2004 budget request was submitted to Congress in February 2003. One of those shaping the campaign in its early stages was Charlotte Beers, a Madison Avenue advertising executive who had progressed from the position of product manager for Uncle Ben's Rice to become chairman of the J. Walter Thompson and Ogilvy and Maher agencies. Appointed as under-secretary of state for public diplomacy and public affairs, Beers told a Congressional committee that the US should set up a training centre for Muslim journalists and help them to get direct interviews with US officials. 'We can turn the proven practice of English teaching into a story with even greater value through the use of pictures and music', she said.[5] It was Beers who suggested the US government work with leading Arab satellite television stations, including the Saudi-owned MBC, Lebanon's

LBC and Future channels, and Qatar's Al-Jazeera. She said the Public Broadcasting System (PBS) and Discovery channels, as well as Hollywood, had offered to provide material for Arab partners.

Success on the US side of the propaganda war is hard to gauge. Beers herself resigned a few months later in frustration and poor health. As a report in *The Washington Monthly* noted, attempts to enlist Hollywood producers would be more likely to succeed if they were aimed at boosting profits rather than particular government policies. But the same article also noted that George Bush Senior, the former president, along with figures from previous US administrations, including Henry Kissinger, James Baker, Brent Scowcroft and George Schultz, were setting up a non-profit organization called Al Haqiqa (The Truth) Television to 'create foreign language TV programmes to be broadcast in Muslim countries'. It seemed Hollywood had responded more favourably to efforts to work 'outside the bounds of government'.[6]

Arab leaders, for their part, shuffled and fiddled for months after 9/11, promising to launch one or more (state-backed) satellite channels to promote Arab culture and Islam and sever any link in people's minds between terrorism and Arabs or Muslims. By the time the US had started to implement its media plans, few of the Arab ideas had left the drawing-board. One exception, the 24-hour news channel Al-Arabiya, was apparently modelled on Al-Jazeera but with less editorial freedom. Saudi Arabia, home to 15 of the 19 hijackers responsible for the 9/11 atrocities, reportedly spent $14.6 million in 2002 on a public relations campaign in the US. This consisted mainly of television advertisements seeking to reassure Americans that Saudi Arabia was an ally in the war on terror.[7] Instead of the kingdom's image undergoing a real improvement, however, Saudi Arabia came under more criticism of its human rights record in the US Congress and elsewhere.

Lost in the cacophonous airwaves and cyberspace shuffle were the voices of Arab women journalists. The UAE government tried to remedy this in February 2002 by convening the first Arab Women's Media Forum under the title 'Women & Media: Towards An Interactive Media Sphere'. The forum, in Abu Dhabi, was long on gripes and short on practical solutions for today's woes. Most participants complained about stereotyping of women in the Arab media or stereotyping of Arabs and Muslims in western media. All agreed that women needed to be more involved in the shaping of perceptions about Arab and Islamic culture, but only a handful came up with how-to blueprints for countering the negative images or enabling women to play an active role in setting the record straight. The speakers with the most practical solutions chanted a steady chorus about how one of the easiest ways was through the Internet, with its plethora of websites dedicated to women, to media, or both. The Internet's potential was especially great, they said, in more conservative Arab societies where women had traversed borders through cyberspace from the privacy of their homes. Participants also recognized that they should maintain contacts with women in the West to minimize the damage of stereotyping and to reach common ground on issues not adequately tackled by male-dominated media.

The portraits that follow provide a glimpse of the Arab world's reservoir of women reporters and commentators whose knowledge, experience, talent, tenacity and humanity could be tapped to bring down the transatlantic decibel levels. The seven journalists interviewed for this chapter are all Lebanese, including two Lebanese Americans and three of Palestinian origin. Their multicultural – and by extension global – approach, coupled with an appreciation for individuals and their needs, would seem to make them ideal communicators and bridge builders. The question then is: what is stopping these media women and others like them from moving to the forefront of the Arab media scene?

Octavia Nasr

Octavia Nasr, senior editor for Arab affairs at CNN, started her media career in Lebanon. As a woman, that meant she had to deal with attitude problems and ignorance that overshadowed the pool of talent at the television station where her career was launched. Recruited to CNN by its founder, Ted Turner, Nasr joined what was then a trail-blazing network and took up a job at its headquarters in Atlanta, Georgia. 'I had a very successful career in Lebanon; I did achieve a lot, it's something to be proud of. But when the opportunity presented itself, of course I took it', she said.[8] As a contributor from Lebanon's LBC to CNN World Report, Nasr had been invited to attend a five-day annual conference in Atlanta, while the civil war raged back home. It turned into a five-year stay before she could even go back and visit her family. It was also a daunting challenge for the French-educated reporter who had until then broadcast in her native Arabic. But a drama degree at an American college in Lebanon, combined with experience of covering the country's civil war, made her even more determined to succeed. 'It was a dream come true. It was a life changing experience', she recalled of her debut as an international media star. But Nasr also had to learn new rules to the game. 'As a journalist you have to be first, you have to be accurate and to be open to criticism and feedback'. This was not always the case with media in Lebanon, she explained.

As senior international editor at CNN, anchor of *CNN World Report* and occasional anchor of *CNN International News* for many years, Nasr continued to deal with Lebanese television editors and reporters, as well as broadcast journalists and executives around the world. After 9/11 she assumed the role of bridge-builder, flying to Qatar to negotiate a deal with the Gulf-based pan-Arab news channel Al-Jazeera. Among other achievements, she secured retransmission of Al-Jazeera footage of US attacks on Kabul, as CNN's Nic Robertson had been asked to leave Afghanistan when the war began. Asked whether, given her current high profile, she would return to work in the Arab world, Nasr revealed her distrust of the way business is conducted there, citing a lack of job security. She would go, she said, 'as a consultant, on my own terms'.

As for a glass ceiling blocking career progression for media women, Nasr admitted suffering from it at one point or another, in both Lebanon and the US. Today, in contrast, she believes opportunities abound for her. 'At this stage in my career, I'm at a nice peak'. Has her talent been put to full use? 'I'd like to think so', she said. 'I'm doing all the fun jobs that I've always wanted to do. I enjoy exposure, acceptance and recognition from my peers. That's a great place to be'. Does she think she's compensated enough for her work? 'Not really. While I enjoy the day-to-day work and the assignments, I don't make as much as I'd like to in terms of material compensation'. Nasr quickly adds: 'I'm not in it for the money or the fame, that's for sure. I just love my job and I love the people I work with. If any of those change, I'll be out of here'.

Women, Nasr lamented, had to explain and fight ten times harder than men to advance. Tragically, she said, in the Middle East they do not always look out for other women to help them move up. So she took it upon herself as a woman to provide opportunities such as internships for aspiring journalists while they were still students. Asked whether she faced problems being an Arab American and a woman, especially after the 11 September attacks, Nasr said that she personally had not been adversely affected. But, she stressed, everything had changed since that historic day, not just in terms of ethnicity, but also with regard to ethics and morals. 'Post-9/11, people were on edge, and everybody had an opinion about everything'.

Nasr straddles different cultures with ease, feels comfortable switching languages, is telegenic and has a hard-to-miss media presence. Yet she is unassuming and approachable on a personal level and, like all good communicators, an engaging conversationalist. To bridge the cultural divide, she advises Arabs to be honest about themselves and proud of who they are. 'They have to bring in change within themselves and their own countries', she maintains. 'They should fight to have free media and elections, to establish democracies, and then spread the word about their culture'. Although Nasr believes there is still a long way to go to achieve these goals, she did praise Arab youth for demonstrating in support of change and expressed hope in the future generations. 'This could be a good start, but I urge Arabs to stay active in normal times as well, not just in times of crisis', Nasr insisted. As to her own future, she declared her biggest challenge to be her 'kids'. Married to a successful Arab-American landscape architect, and mother to two young daughters, Nasr said: 'All I want to prove is being a good mom'. 'I hope they get better opportunities and accomplish what I couldn't, and have choices in life that I didn't have'.

Tania Mehanna

Like Octavia Nasr, Tania Mehanna learned her profession at LBC. She is more than competent in covering the local scene and has also looked beyond it, becoming a national and international reporter and war correspondent. Her assignments have included stories on the US-led wars on Iraq and Afghanistan, the military build-up in Pakistan, UN sanctions on Iraq, the release of Abu Sayaf hostages in the Philippines and Libya, the conflict in South Lebanon, and a US tour by Lebanon's national basketball team. Closer to home, she reports on politics, human rights, women's issues and has a soft spot for human interest and social significance stories.

The award-winning Mehanna has degrees in political science and public administration and is good at languages. She speaks in staccato tones about the shortcomings of Arab media and US officials who, she said, have a long history of miscommunication. 'Why', she asked, 'can't we see that there are moderate people on both sides, that these people are against violence, that they are willing to work together to stop the extremists from taking over in this conflict?'.[9] She urged US officials to choose their words carefully to avoid misinterpretation when addressing non-American audiences but also asked Arab media to give more space to people who are not cheerleaders for governments. 'The ideal solution would be to get Arab-Americans to establish the link between the two civilizations and pick it up from there', she advised.

Being a single woman journalist has not been easy for Mehanna, who finds that a career in journalism is in itself a challenge in the Arab world. First, she said, a woman has to do twice as much to prove she is as professional as a male co-worker. Second, once that is established, a woman has to prove she is a good journalist. Mehanna's name is as well known as her male counterparts' in the local media, and for some, she is considered the Lebanese equivalent of CNN's famous correspondent Christiane Amanpour. Like her western colleagues, Mehanna also gets saddled with uninteresting stories that make little use of her experience and creativity. But she can sometimes persuade her top bosses to send her on serious and tough assignments. Mehanna, who constantly tries to circumvent restrictions that may exist for some women journalists, declares that being female can be advantageous in facilitating entry into homes and among families where male reporters would be barred. 'Also, in such a female-hostile environment, some people would hesitate to hit a woman or search her because of their religious beliefs. This can save the whole crew from trouble', she explained.

Mehanna's versatility is demonstrated by her contributions to the *CNN World Report* and her freelance work for NBC TV, as well as French and German TV stations during the Lebanese civil war. She said she would feel comfortable working for an international media giant in the US, but also noted that difficulties might arise in trying to communicate with people with limited international experience who are sometimes quite judgemental about situations and ideas. 'I find it difficult to accept intolerance towards other cultures', she said. She relies on the Internet for a good part of her research and is constantly soaking up information in a cross-cultural setting. She seeks common ground with western journalists in such matters as humanitarian values, freedom of expression, respect for other cultures and respect for traditions, but is also driven to help events move positively along more liberal lines.

While she would like to progress, Mehanna shuns desk jobs and does not aspire to the position of editor-in-chief. 'My ambition is to become a senior war correspondent in order to cover any conflict anywhere in the world, not only those related to the Middle East', she explained. Why, she asked, is it so difficult for decision-makers in media networks to make use of their reporters' experience of conflict situations (such as hers) to improve coverage elsewhere. A glass ceiling can be erected when editors consider certain assignments better suited for men, she said. 'Fortunately, and slowly, we have been proving as women war correspondents that we can be as tough, and at the same time more sensitive when it comes to humanitarian issues, without losing our femininity'. Mehanna is also lucky not to be second-guessed in these stories by her superiors. They only slam on the brakes if sensitive Lebanese political issues are at stake, since repercussions from coverage of these can extend well beyond the journalist who reports on them to jeopardize the entire organization. Asked about her aspirations, Mehanna said she hoped that, by the time she retired, she would look back and realize that she had contributed, if only modestly, to positive change or to have saved someone's life just by talking about it.

Raghida Dergham

Raghida Dergham is the senior diplomatic correspondent in the US for the pan-Arab daily *Al-Hayat*. She is known for her interviews with heads of state across the globe and is a regular guest on television shows and panels of experts on the Middle East. She is a member of the Council on Foreign Relations, a board member of the International Women's Media Foundation, a recipient of countless awards (as well as a letter bomb at her New York office) and a constant advocate of cross-cultural dialogue. Dergham was one of three people featured on an hour-long PBS TV documentary about Arab-Americans. Entitled *Caught in the Crossfire*, it marked the first anniversary of the 11 September attacks. 'Reason, moderation and sobriety are never more needed than in crisis', Dergham wrote in the international edition of *Newsweek* magazine. 'Yet seldom have such qualities been so absent, nowhere more so than in the media'.[10]

Dergham found troubling common denominators in both her worlds' media coverage after 9/11 – in the tenor of coverage that seemed destructive in intent and effect, and in a partisanship that she found irresponsible and harmful. 'Whether it's the sound-bite quality of American television or the "pontificator monologues" of Arab commentators, the result is similar: the erosion of the media's role in learning and then educating', she wrote. 'Its place has been usurped by a collective "us" versus "them"'. Celebrity as a correspondent and noted columnist, and infamy to her detractors who send hate mail, have helped Dergham to develop an appreciation for the media as a strategic component of policy. This, she said, is something the Arabs have yet to fully comprehend and utilize. All the kudos she has earned did not save the Beirut-born New Yorker and Lebanese-US national from the indignity of having her Lebanese passport revoked in June 2000. It appears she had angered the Beirut government by reporting certain news and by appearing at a public forum alongside an Israeli official. Although deemed by the Lebanese authorities to have been 'consorting with the enemy', Dergham had in fact appeared on the panel to defend her native country and the Arab cause.

It took a campaign involving the Committee to Protect Journalists, the International Press Institute and intervention by UN Secretary-General Kofi Annan, to name a few, to have the passport reinstated. The charges were eventually dropped in the military court that accused her of treason. But, as far as Dergham is concerned, there will be no closure 'as long as the media don't have full freedom', she said.[11] Dergham also faulted US officials for not being forthcoming in seeking exposure in Arab media before 9/11 and for treading conservatively after those events. But she described her interview with Secretary of State Colin Powell in the aftermath of the tragedy as a historical document that had helped explain US policy to Arab readers. She had also assured her American friends after 9/11 that all Arabs did not hate them but had legitimate qualms about US foreign policy objectives. She also told her Arab friends that Americans did not know them and only saw extremists and fundamentalists in their midst. 'Americans may act in the world, but they are not worldly', she wrote in *Newsweek*.

A go-getting pursuer of news and interviews, Dergham does not believe that being a woman has hindered her career. She enjoys writing a column that sways opinions or changes attitudes but acknowledges the role and influence of male decision-makers at the higher editorial levels of her profession in the Arab world. Faced with obstruction she has resorted to various tactics. 'At times I was confrontational, at others I gave in', she admitted, adding that there were also times when she did a mixture of both. Dergham does not desire a managerial position but would like to explore different ways of doing what she already does, including perhaps hosting her own television show for both her worlds – Arab and American. She has lived in the Big Apple since 1970. Armed with a degree in creative writing and journalism from the State University of New York at Plattsburgh, she made a conscious decision to become a commentator and write in Arabic. Her alma mater honoured her as a distinguished alumna and nominated her to its Hall of Fame.

Dergham's cosmopolitan outlook, impressive list of contacts, American modus operandi and speak-for-itself journalistic record complement strong ethnic roots and pride in being an Arab. And yet in the past she has hated being an Arab American. As a Lebanese, she has felt hurt and not at peace with the country of her birth, but continues to seek balanced and fair coverage and views. 'Fairness. That's the most important word in my life. What happened to me was totally unfair', she said of the passport incident. Is she paid enough for her work? Yes and no. Yes, by Arab standards. But 'no', it's not enough. At least her editorial judgement is hardly ever questioned, except when a column may prove troublesome. That's a freedom few Arab women journalists enjoy. Ever a supporter of the underdog, Dergham feels it is time to institute better working conditions for journalists and to consider that journalism is a high cost profession with a high level of burn-out. 'The media should be entitled to all benefits, to health plans, to vacations', she said ruefully. Yet she loves New York and loves having lived in the city all those years. She was never drawn to Washington, DC. Journalists are attracted to the power centres in Washington like moths to lights that eventually burn them; Arab journalists are considered second-class citizens at the White House, State Department, Pentagon, Capitol Hill and most major events.

Dergham is comfortable in her skin and feels no need to prove anything. 'God has blessed me with my daughter, family and friends', she said. That is a powerful statement for the unmarried, single mother who broke with Arab convention to do it her way. She would like to mentor newcomers in the profession and looks forward to writing a book. She regards it as her civic duty to go out on a limb and explain points of view.

Mona Ziade

Another articulate fighter who earned her stripes as a war-tested news agency correspondent is Mona Ziade. Ziade established herself first with United Press International and then Associated Press, both in Lebanon and globally. She later became Middle East editor for Lebanon's English-language paper, the *Daily Star*. Her assignments were not limited to conflicts but included in-depth reporting of regional Middle East issues, international summits and interviews with key world officials.

Ziade admits there were hardships for media women a quarter of a century ago. When interviewing an official by telephone she once heard chuckles upon introducing herself as a news agency reporter. 'But', she said, 'the contingent of female journalists grew rapidly in the 1980s, especially after so many of us had to share trenches with US Marines, Palestinian guerrillas and others during the Middle East conflict'.[12] Even so, had she been a man, Ziade thinks she might have had more career chances. Like many of her female contemporaries, Ziade has confronted a glass ceiling but she sees it more in financial than professional terms. 'For nearly 25 years I have found myself doing the same – and often much more – than my male peers, but have still been paid considerably less'. Today Ziade works with the World Bank. As a journalist, her ambition was to exist in a professionally comfortable structure with more experienced hands able to take some of her day-to-day load of supervising content, thereby leaving her more free to delve into writing and focus more on analysing issues of importance to readers. She would like to be financially secure to take the time to write a book.

Ziade's editorial judgement was seldom questioned and she appreciated the respect and flexibility afforded her on that score. She joined the ranks of the *Daily Star* in 1996 when the paper came out of mothballs following years of hiatus and war-imposed obscurity. But there was a price to pay. She had to stretch her schedule to spend time with her journalist husband and daughter and she kept odd hours as a newspaper editor, often coming home well after midnight. Previously, as a news agency correspondent, she was on call like an emergency room doctor. Days often ran into nights and deadlines could be a matter of seconds away when the pressure was on to beat the competition to get the story on the wires. Ziade has also experienced what it means to be a news agency desk editor. That requires a solid background, good instincts, a cool head and the ability to function like an orchestra conductor to handle incoming dispatches at varying speeds from a number of bureaux. It is a job she has done with aplomb on an international level and which has enabled her to straddle eastern and western cultures with no difficulty. As a trilingual communicator who studied political science in college, she complements news instincts with a solid knowledge base. Given her own background, Ziade advises aspiring journalists to acquire experience working for news agencies, which she called boot camps.

'It is amazing how sometimes I find myself defending the West and plunging into arguments with my own kin, even though I can't say I agree with US policies, especially not when it concerns the Israeli–Palestinian issue', she said. In fact, Ziade feels US officials have failed miserably in establishing credible communication channels with the Arabs on the media and diplomatic fronts. 'And where the channels do exist, the debate is often patronizing, rather than an attempt to understand the other side of the problem'. Washington's public diplomacy campaign was better late than never, she said, although she felt it may have been too late, compared to Europe's efforts at reaching out to Arabs and Muslims. Ziade elaborates:

> As for the Arabs, it is astounding that it took this long for the governments to understand the need to address western public opinion, and even now, after the terrible onslaught in the post-9/11 world, there's too much emphasis on trying to justify extremism, rather than promote moderates in the vast media outlets that are now reaching US households.

She urged interlocutors on both sides of the cultural divide to engage in a serious dialogue rather than just be satisfied with occasional conferences and talkshows. These, she said, only buttressed xenophobia.

Diana Moukalled

Journalism is a far cry from the medical career Diana Moukalled first thought she would pursue. Unconvinced of the rigours of medical training, she switched majors to journalism at university and went into broadcasting with relish, first as a general assignment reporter at Lebanon's New TV and a year later at Future TV, where she is a producer, news assignment editor and presenter of documentaries. Moukalled was the assignment editor of a newscast on Zein, a youth station owned by the Future TV group, and moved from there to Future's satellite channel later in 2002. She also writes freelance in-depth pieces for the London-based pan-Arab daily *Al-Hayat* and its weekly magazine *Al-Wasat*. What helped achieve this versatility was a year as a freelance news and documentary producer with Reuters TV and work for both German and Finnish TV. She also did a stint as a researcher and editor at the Lebanese Ministry of Information.

Moukalled's evolution and maturity are visible on Future TV's terrestrial and satellite channels, which attract Arabic-speaking viewers around the world. 'The first two years I was busy with myself, worrying how I looked on camera', she admitted, adding that she had received a superficial journalism education that focused on voice and appearance. From then on, however, she branched out. She became interested in features, children, women and social issues. Exposure to foreign documentaries plus a period of training at the BBC in London, with backing from Future TV, taught her volumes about technical aspects of shooting, the background of filming and the human side of media. It was after witnessing results of the gruesome Qana massacre in 1996, during Israel's Operation Grapes of Wrath, when Israeli forces bombed over 100 unarmed civilians sheltering at a United Nations post in south Lebanon, that Moukalled asked that she no longer be assigned to cover humdrum topics.

In 1998 she briefly left Future TV to work for a production company on documentaries in India, covering such topics as nuclear weapons, pollution and dowry crimes. She returned that same year with a desire to make documentaries and public affairs programmes and has made her mark with *Bi'l-Ain al-Mujarrada* (With the Naked Eye), which she shoots as a series of shows, usually three instalments per trip outside Lebanon. 'I've travelled to Iraq, Kurdistan, Iran, Algeria, the Western Sahara, Kuwait, Turkey, Jordan, Afghanistan during the Taliban's rule, Kashmir, Armenia, Karabakh, Russia, Yemen, Britain and the US', she recounted.[13] A series broadcast in 2002 had her trekking to the US in the wake of the 11 September attacks to interview Arabs, Arab Americans and non-Arab Americans and record their opinions, reactions and feelings on what had brought about these calamities, and how people viewed each other. In 2003 she was drawn again to Kurdistan to cover America's and Britain's war on Iraq. She complemented her programmes with a print series in

Al-Hayat newspaper to reach an even wider audience. Her themes were unmistakably geared to bridge-building and trying to create better under-standing of differences in cultures and perceptions and to humanize conflicts. All the while, however, Moukalled has been constantly reminded of hindrances on her side of the fence in the pre-censorship that Arab journalists must exercise if they wish to avoid harassment. 'From the time one applies for a visa (to Arab countries), one is being investigated and I've been turned down on many occasions', she said. Reporters must always have Ministry of Information guides or minders to accompany them when filming in Arab states. 'It differs from one country to another, but it's generally the same'.

Moukalled sees her gender as more of a social than an official obstacle. She agreed with Tania Mehanna that being a woman sometimes facili-tates contacts with other women. She cited coverage of rape crimes in Algeria, when thousands of women were violated by members of armed Islamist groups, or issues like the effects of tribal traditions on women. On one occasion her intrusiveness netted a rebuke from the Taliban to Lebanon's prime minister, Rafiq Hariri, whose family owns Future TV. But she took advantage of being a woman to penetrate further into Afghanistan's society. She visited women's hospitals there and even approached Taliban spiritual leaders in Pakistani *madrassas* (religious schools). 'I tried not to be maddened by their provocative behaviour, but to be understanding', she said, adding that she makes an effort not to be judgemental and to avoid clichés when describing situations in her scripts. This in turn requires extensive research. So she relies heavily on the Internet, devours books, magazines and newspapers and finds people who have travelled to her selected destinations. 'I write the primary script, I specify the stories and angles to be reflected in the reports, I contact a fixer to make arrangements, I send a proposal and ask where we can go', she said of the logistical details involved. Although some-times stumped by restrictive regulations in certain countries, Moukalled still hopes to produce a 30–60-minute documentary on social issues in the Arab world.

Fluent in Arabic and English, the Lebanese Moukalled was born in Saudi Arabia and graduated from high school at 17 before heading to college in Lebanon, where she described the public university curriculum as archaic and not practice-oriented. To fill in the academic gap, she took private lessons to improve her English and further her career. As a testament to her success, Moukalled's programmes have gone into re-runs, which are usually packaged into 12 premium shows and marketed widely. Moukalled, who loves to travel, realizes she is unlikely to make it to the managing editor's job. Her dream is to set up a research and documentary department at Future TV. Her journalist husband understands her ambition and determination.

Samia Nakhoul

What drives Samia Nakhoul is that, as she says, she is not bound by routine and that in journalism there are no borders, no time limits and that the work is multi-cultural. The risks are also global and not gender specific. Her near-death experience in Baghdad in April 2003 earned her Lebanon's Presidential Shield award for doing her job with valour.

'Since I was a child I've wanted to be a journalist. It's expanded my horizons; I didn't want to just work in one country', said the bureau chief of the Reuters news agency in the Gulf and previously in Lebanon and Syria. 'It's challenging, active and you feel you're at the centre of the world'.[14] Her passion stemmed from a desire to write about her own people and about others, she explained. At the age of 12 she knew she wanted to be a reporter and savour the adventures associated with the job and of always learning something new. She attributed her drive to a restless character and likened the experience to someone sitting for a daily exam. During her senior year in college, marked by Israel's invasion of Lebanon in 1982, she was an intern at Lebanon's leading Arabic-language daily *Al-Nahar*. She was armed with a BA in international affairs and a minor in journalism. Nakhoul then worked freelance and later moved to the English-language paper, the *Daily Star*, initially as a proof-reader, and also put in time as a reporter for United Press International in Beirut. She joined Reuters in 1987 and has been moving around with the agency since. 'I started as a local correspondent covering the Lebanese civil war and all the extras – Israeli incursions, hijackings, kidnappings, hostage-taking, car bombings, political assassinations, the Taif peace agreement and the ousting of General (Michel) Aoun from Lebanon', she recalled. 'In between, I covered the Iraqi invasion of Kuwait in 1990 and the Gulf War'.

The French-educated Nakhoul, who is just as comfortable functioning in English, also feels close to her Arab background. She straddles several cultures with ease, a prerequisite for an international news agency that in the 1980s began hiring more locals for key positions, instead of relying exclusively on British bureau chiefs. 'So there's motivation to go up the ladder', she said. She has not suffered from a glass ceiling because of her gender. She can apply for any job within the agency, and would probably get it if she were qualified. 'We're all Reuterized. No editor would say "you're biased towards the Arabs"', she said, describing the agency as very democratic. Her news judgement is rarely questioned and she is given significant latitude in her work. If she writes analysis, she can project. Otherwise, it's adherence to strict reporting guidelines. Being a woman also has its blessings and advantages, Nakhoul maintains. During Lebanon's civil war, for example, militiamen for the various factions did not take women reporters seriously; the combatants were not hostile to them, judging that they did not threaten anybody. She said that in the Middle East women fought until they proved their mettle and were seen as better than men, noting that in Bahrain and Dubai the professional atmosphere was more relaxed than elsewhere in the region. Saudis were very nice to women, she said, and she did not need to cover herself completely on visits to Saudi Arabia, although she sometimes wore the chadoor out of respect.

'They have to accept us', she said of Arab women journalists' credibility. 'I put a lot of effort into proving I can do the job as well as a man, but that also happens in the West'. If women journalists are persistent and consistent, they will secure respect, she said. Nakhoul worked hard while based in Cairo as a senior international correspondent, where her beat also included Libya and Sudan. 'It was a totally different experience – writing about the Arab–Israeli peace talks, Muslim fundamentalism and militant violence directed at foreign tourists and Egyptian officials', she said of her Cairo assignment. She has also been based in Nicosia as sub-editor on the Middle East and Africa desk and has lived for a year in India on sabbatical with her husband, a journalist for the *Financial Times*. They have no children. She would like to be in charge of news editing for the Middle East or land a more senior job in a few years, or become an editor in London. 'I would like to do more reporting. I still like fieldwork. I would like to use my expertise on the Middle East', she said.

May Kahale

May Kahale set a precedent when she became the first media advisor to a head of state in the Arab world – then Lebanese President Elias Hrawi. Once in, she set another precedent by allowing television cameras to film in the presidential palace and beam their reports by satellite and other links to their respective stations. In post-civil-war Lebanon it was an unusual occurrence. But viewers soon became accustomed to seeing the woman they had known earlier as a newspaper reporter and television interviewer standing alongside the country's leader or briefing journalists about affairs of state.

'Being a woman in the Arab world is a double-edged sword' Kahale said.[15] 'On the one hand we benefit from deep respect accorded women in a region where they represent the family's top values, as mothers or sisters. But we also suffer because there is little understanding of a woman's need to have a career, or to advance financially outside of traditional social criteria'. She is aware of differences in various parts of the Arab world but notes that, even in relatively liberal Lebanon, going from one region of the country to another may dictate how a woman dresses to seem 'decent' and not shock people. For Kahale, who was constantly in the spotlight during her time as presidential advisor, 'the toughest thing is to always adopt a professional attitude and to ensure that one's private life is compatible with the pressures of one's public life'. On a professional level, Kahale said, she also experienced jealousy from men because of what she had attained, because of her influence on the president, and because of fear that she would replace them. She did not face the same problem with other women in public office because none had reached such heights. To wit, only three women are legislators in a 128-member Chamber of Deputies in Lebanon and no woman is a member of the cabinet.

Kahale has known what a glass ceiling is, both in the press and as a media advisor to the president. She had expected promotion to a higher position in the administration at the time, but men were given preferential treatment, so she returned to her initial profession – journalism and political analysis. 'The price is always high for a woman, particularly if she insists on professionalism, so her private life is minimized. But what's hardest is limitations on progress and the intentional disregard for women's advancement within the system', said Kahale who is single.

Fortunately, Kahale has never had her judgement questioned by her editors at Saudi Arabia's daily *Al-Riyadh*, where she reports from Lebanon and writes columns and analyses.

While she does straddle the cultures, Kahale believes that events are a decisive factor in how reporters react and that journalists are always faced with preferences and feelings that may affect their sense of professional objectivity. 'We must accept our imperfections, otherwise we lose our humanity and all sense of dignity if we just think that we're products of a pure Arab culture and forget the benefits of western culture', she said, adding that a good mix was key. Fluent in Arabic and French and quite conversant in English, Kahale studied journalism in college and started, but never completed, a master's degree in history. She first worked as a translator for the National Commission on UNESCO, and then joined the ranks of *Al-Nahar* newspaper where she covered local politics for 16 years, including during Lebanon's civil war. During those years she also took on the challenge of working for television alongside her print journalism career, first with the privately owned (and at the time Christian militia-supported) LBC, and then with state-run Télé-Liban, and later back with the LBC, where she first met and interviewed Hrawi when he was a presidential candidate.

While capable of conveying the media message and articulating it to a foreign audience, she admits she would not be able to work for a strictly American or western news organization. 'Feelings are important to me as they denote truth as I live it, not as I see it from afar'. If a man dies, she said, he represents a citizen with a name and a family, whereas in the US media, unless he was American, he would be just another statistic. Kahale said it was obvious that the misunderstanding between the US administration and the Arabs was not limited to the media but also existed between governments and regimes. Some Arab regimes were considered America's allies but fully realized that Israel's interests far outweighed any of theirs, leading them to resort to double-speak, she said. 'They lambast the US for domestic consumption but are unconditionally allied to America in their foreign policy'. Since Arab media reflect the official policy, they are, in turn, anti-American on the domestic front. US officials realize the fact but make no attempt to remedy the situation, notably by understanding regional problems, with the situation in Palestine being at the core, she said. 'Arab media, on the other hand, and despite all the technological progress, are miles from understanding the political language of other powers'. She continued: 'The media also lack freedom and the ability to analyse, which would enhance the masses' understanding'.

In Kahale's view, the real handicap to mutual understanding was that the US had for years disregarded dialogue with Arab citizens, in favour of close talks with regimes. Meanwhile the Arab media that tried to loosen the shackles of their regimes still could not reach their citizens, much less the Americans. But she remained optimistic about getting her message across and still hopes to take on new challenges. 'A journalist never stops learning and upgrading his/her knowledge and style'. One of her dreams, time permitting, is to write a book about her nine years as a presidential media advisor.

Conclusion

In the post-9/11 world, could Arab women journalists help to turn the tide of stereotyping and misunderstanding? The interviews presented here contain ample evidence that they could. So what is it that stops them from becoming household names? Again, on the evidence collected, it remains doubtful whether the Arab media, mostly state-run and patriarchal, are ready even to tackle the job of explaining the Arabs to themselves, let alone to a suspicious and uncertain world.

The journalists profiled in this chapter are no novices when it comes to understanding bureaucratese and government double-speak, whether in their own countries or the West. They know first-hand how far the Arab media have yet to travel to engage in meaningful dialogue or establish transparent employment practices. But all are practised in the art of bridge-building and cross-cultural communication and are not only motivated but well-equipped to clear up misconceptions about cultures on both sides of the post-9/11 divide. Their strength is drawn from experiencing the horrors of the Lebanese civil war, which was formative for them and contributed to their insight, stamina and humanity. They are multilingual, widely-travelled and their track records show them to be in possession of the professional and technical skills needed to make it into print, broadcast or online.

Yet obstacles remain. Two of the most senior women interviewed have pursued their careers in non-Arab companies and a third, although working for an Arab employer, is based in the US. Four of the seven have no children and three are single. Although more and more women have become news anchors and reporters in Arab media outlets over the past decade, few can aspire to top editorial or managerial positions under present conditions. Perhaps a handful of Arab women journalists can hope to reach the heights that Octavia Nasr did. Privately, Arab women reporters and editors concede that they face various types of harassment on the job. If they are attractive, it makes the challenge of proving themselves doubly difficult. Jealousy by co-workers from both sexes is no different from western models, with the added disadvantage that male colleagues in Arab corporations (who have less experience of working with women in senior positions) may tend to be more chauvinistic and patronizing. Accurate figures are lacking on how many Arab women work in the media and in what jobs.[16] But more critical still is that the definition of a journalist is itself controversial in the Arab world, pitting trade associations and officially-designated journalists' syndicates against reporters who may not fit the narrow definitions set by monopolistic heads, who are out of touch with the times and who are in collusion with the region's governments.

Given the climate of mistrust and miscommunication between the Arab-Muslim world and the West, it would seem that Arab women journalists have a dual responsibility: to cater to their own readers, viewers and listeners and to reach out to share their knowledge with people in the West, including their female counterparts who also struggle for advancement and recognition in their profession. The knowledge gap they need to fill is clearly not restricted to so-called 'women's issues'. Knowing how to relate foreign news to ethno-centric or ill-informed audiences is a major challenge. The women interviewed here have proven versatility, having worked on many different kinds of stories for a range of national and international media.

Aware of the need for mentors and role models, some of the women featured in this chapter felt they had a duty to help others entering the profession. Some had mentored budding young reporters and others were eager to do so. They also regarded self-improvement as a high priority and one that is especially needed in the globalized twenty-first-century world, where good writing and editing skills and general knowledge are essential. Acquiring the habit of featuring women professionals, whether physicians, economists, athletes or airline pilots, is likewise something that mentoring can promote. Overcoming corporate and gender obstacles, and eventually bridging the cultural divide, requires media literacy and a concerted effort to educate oneself and others. Arab women reporters, editors and executives should capitalize on all manner of networks to reach out beyond their national and regional borders to foster rational discourse.

Notes

1 Women–media interaction in the Middle East

1 Over the years MBC has received funding and direction from King Fahd bin Abdel-Aziz and his youngest son, Prince Abdel-Aziz.

2 Raid Qusti, 'Women's rights in Saudi Arabia', *Arab News*, 18 June 2003. *Arab News* is published by Saudi Research and Marketing, founded by Prince Ahmad bin Salman bin Abdel-Aziz, son of the governor of Riyadh, and taken over on Prince Ahmad's death by his brother, Prince Faisal bin Salman.

3 Peter Golding and Graham Murdock, 'Culture, communications and political economy', in J. Curran and M. Gurevitch (eds), *Mass Media and Society* (London, 2000), p 70.

4 For more on the phases and nature of development see Naomi Sakr, *Satellite Realms: Transnational Television, Globalization and the Middle East* (London, 2001) and Naomi Sakr, 'Maverick or model? Al-Jazeera's impact on Arab satellite television', in J. Chalaby (ed.), *Transnational Television Worldwide* (London, 2004), pp 66–95.

5 *Arab News* website, 11 June 2003.

6 E.g. *Lexington Herald, Monterey County Herald, Philadelphia Inquirer, Chicago Sun Times*, all on 27 June 2003.

7 The practicalities of life for female employees in Saudi Arabia are discussed in Eleanor Abdella Doumato, 'Education in Saudi Arabia: gender, jobs and the price of religion', in E. Doumato and M. Posusney (eds), *Women and Globalization in the Arab Middle East: Gender, Economy & Society* (Boulder, CO, 2003), pp 250–2. Plans to form an association for employed journalists were announced in December 2001.

8 An MBC-FM programme on unemployment was discussed in *Arab News* by a writer who identified herself as a 'Saudi woman from Najd' and proposed ways to increase the number of Saudi women in the workforce. Moodhy Al-Khalaf, 'Jobless Saudi women: problem grows worse', *Arab News*, 2 June 2003.

9 Intertextuality is discussed in general terms by John Fiske in *Television Culture* (London, 1987), pp 108–27 and in terms of gendered meanings by Charlotte Hooper in *Manly States: Masculinities, International Relations and Gender Politics* (New York, 2001), pp 122–5 and 212–17.

10 Liesbet Van Zoonen, *Feminist Media Studies* (London, 1994), p 4.

11 United Nations Development Progamme, *Arab Human Development Report 2002* (New York, 2002), pp 27–8.

12 Martha Lauzen and David Dozier, 'The role of women on screen and behind the scenes in the television and film industries: review of a program of research', *Journal of Communication Inquiry*, 23/4 (October 1999), pp 355–6.

13 Study conducted by Ann Selzer for the American Press Institute and Pew Center for Civic Journalism, reported online at editorandpublisher.com, 27 September 2002.

14 Caroline Millington, 'Getting in and getting on: women and radio management at the BBC', in Caroline Mitchell (ed.), *Women and Radio: Airing Differences* (London, 2000), pp 211–12.

15 Jane Arthurs, 'Women and television', in S. Hood (ed.), *Behind the Screens: The Structure of British Television* (London, 1994), pp 93 and 99.

16 Susan Reed, 'The value of women journalists', *Nieman Reports*, 56/1 (Spring 2002), p 63.

17 Broadcasting Standards Council, *Perspectives of Women in Television* (London, 1994) pp 24–7.

18 Christy Bulkeley, 'A pioneering generation marked the path for women journalists', *Nieman Reports*, 56/1 (Spring 2002), p 62.

19 Carolyn Byerly, 'Gender and the political economy of newsmaking: a case study of human rights coverage', in E. Meehan and E. Riordan (eds), *Sex and Money: Feminism and Political Economy in the Media*, (Minneapolis, 2002), pp 137–8.

20 Annabelle Sreberny-Mohammadi, 'Introduction', *Journal of International Communication*, 3/1 (1996), online at www.mucic.mq.edu.au/JIC.

21 Teresita Hermano and Anna Turley, 'Who makes the news?', *Nieman Reports*, 55/4 (Winter 2001), pp 78–9.

22 Margaret Gallagher, *Gender Setting: New Agendas for Media Monitoring and Advocacy*, (London, 2001), p 194.

23 Margaret Gallagher, *An Unfinished Story: Gender Patterns in Media Employment* (Paris, 1995).

24 Rebecca J. Cook, 'State accountability under the Convention on the Elimination of All Forms of Discrimination Against Women', in R. Cook (ed.), *Human Rights of Women: National and International Perspectives* (Philadelphia, 1994), pp 234–5.

25 Stuart Hall, 'Old and new identities, old and new ethnicities', in A. King (ed.), *Culture, Globalisation and the World System* (Basingstoke, 1991), p 57.

26 Particularly notable in this regard is Chandra Mohanty's work in her edited collection *Third World Women and the Politics of Feminism* (Bloomington and Indianapolis, 1991). See also Andrea Press, 'Recent developments in feminist communication theory: difference, public sphere, body and technology', in J. Curran and M. Gurevitch (eds), *Mass Media and Society* (London, 2000), pp 29–30. For discussion of enduring 'East–West essentialism' see Nadje Al-Ali, *Secularism, Gender and the State in the Middle East: The Egyptian Women's Movement* (Cambridge, 2000), pp 22–6.

27 H. Leslie Steeves, 'Creating imagined communities: development communication and the challenge of feminism', *Journal of Communication*, 43/4 (Summer 1993), p 222.

28 Karin Werner, '"Coming close to God" through the media: a phenomenology of the media practices of Islamist women in Egypt', in K. Hafez (ed.), *Mass Media, Politics and Society in the Middle East* (Cresskill, NJ, 2001), pp 213–14.

29 Kay Mills, 'What difference do women journalists make?', in P. Norris (ed.), *Women, Media, and Politics* (Oxford, 1997), pp 45–7.

30 Mills: 'What difference', p 49.

31 Mieke De Clercq, 'A critical mass: does it make a difference? Women journalists in Flanders', paper presented to a symposium on 'Cultures of Journalism' at Goldsmiths College, University of London, 24 April 2003.

32 Lauzen and Dozier: 'The role of women on screen'.

33 E.g. David Weaver, 'Women as journalists', in P. Norris (ed.), *Women, Media, and Politics* (Oxford, 1997), p 37.

34 Liesbet Van Zoonen, 'One of the girls? the changing gender of journalism', in C. Carter, G. Branston and S. Allan, *News, Gender and Power* (London, 1998), p 35.

35 James Napoli, Hussein Amin and Richard Boylan, 'Assessment of the Egyptian print and electronic media', report submitted to the United States Agency for International Development (Cairo, 1995), pp 171–2.

36 Raymond Baker, 'Combative cultural politics: film art and political spaces in Egypt', *Alif Journal of Comparative Poetics*, 15 (1995), pp 19–32; Nicole Khouri, 'La politique antiterroriste de l'état Egyptien à la télévision en 1994', *Revue Tiers-Monde*, 37 (April–June 1996), pp 263–83.

37 Lila Abu Lughod, 'Women on women: television feminism and village lives', in S. Joseph and S. Slyomovics (eds), *Women and Power in the Middle East* (Philadelphia, 2001), p 103.

38 A 2001 report published in the UAE said that women accounted for three-quarters and half the heads of ERTU radio and television stations respectively. Zayed Center for Coordination and Follow-up, *Al-Mar'a wa al-Ilam al-Arabi* (Women and the Arab Media) (Abu Dhabi, October 2001), p 60.

39 International Federation of Journalists, *Equality and Quality: Setting Standards for Women in Journalism* (Brussels, June 2001), pp 15 and 17. The Washington-based International Women's Media Foundation reported on its website (iwmf.org) in 1999 that the two biggest obstacles facing women journalists worldwide were the difficulty of balancing work and family obligations and a lack of role models.

40 The workings of the JPA are described in Article 19, *Blaming the Press: Jordan's Democratization Process in Crisis* (London, October 1997), pp 34–9 and 91–4.

41 Naomi Sakr, 'Media reform in Jordan: the stop-go transition', in M. Price, B. Rozumilowicz and S. Verhulst (eds), *Media Reform: Democratizing the Media, Democratizing the State* (London, 2002), pp 115–16.

42 Article 19: *Blaming the Press*, p 92.

43 Tiare Rath, 'Jordanian entrepreneur gives women a helping hand', *Daily Star*, 29 May 2002.

44 Francesa Sawalha, 'Friedrich Naumann Foundation celebrates 20 years of close cooperation with Jordan', *Jordan Times*, 6 November 2002.

45 Ghada Elnajjar, 'Jordanian woman journalist receives international press award', *Washington File*, 13 October 2002.

46 Shirin Rai, 'Women and the state in the Third World', in H. Afshar (ed.), *Women and Politics in the Third World* (London, 1996), p 34.

47 Rai: 'Women and the state', p 34.

48 Craig Calhoun, 'Introduction: Habermas and the public sphere', in C. Calhoun (ed.), *Habermas and the Public Sphere* (Cambridge, MA, 1992), p 10.

49 This is Nancy Fraser's formulation in 'Rethinking the public sphere: a contribution to the critique of actually existing democracy', in C. Calhoun (ed.), *Habermas and the Public Sphere* (Cambridge, MA, 1992), pp 110–11.

50 For a summary of the concept and its development, see James Curran, *Media and Power* (London, 2002), pp 232–6.

51 Lisa McGlaughlin, 'From excess to access: feminist political agency in the public sphere', *Javnost/The Public*, 2/4 (1995), p 37.

52 Fraser: 'Rethinking the public sphere', p 119.

53 Fraser: 'Rethinking the public sphere', pp 122–9. Emphasis in original, p 129.

54 For examples see Naomi Sakr, 'Seen and starting to be heard: women and the Arab media in a decade of change', *Social Research*, 69/3 (Fall 2002), pp 834–40.

2 The Women's Press in Contemporary Iran

1 Shadi Sadr's interview with Iranian community radio in Stockholm, *Radio Hambastegi* (Solidarity) on 16 June 2002 available from http://home.bip.net/radiohambastegi/mosahebe_6.html.

2 Annabelle Sreberny-Mohammadi and Ali Mohammadi, *Small Media, Big Revolution: Communication, Culture, and the Iranian revolution* (Minneapolis, 1994), p 54.

3 Mitra Bagherian, 'Economic analysis of women journalistic activities', *Zanan*, 1/3 (1993); Masoumeh Keyhani, 'How women-oriented issues are reflected in the Tehran newspapers', *Rasaneh*, 13/2 (2002); Omid Massoudi, 'A glance at the early experience of Iranian women journalists', *Rasaneh*, 9/1 (1998).

4 Keyhani: 'How women-oriented', p 67.

5 Keyhani: 'How women-oriented'.

6 Mohammad Sadr-Hashemi, *History of Iranian Press and Magazines*, vol. 2 (Isfahan, 1985), pp 181–5.

7 Bagherian also mentions a daily *Aftab-e Shargh* (Eastern Sun), edited by Narjes Amouzegar. Bagherian, 'Economic analysis', p 20.

8 Keyhani: 'How women-oriented'.

9   Farid Qasemi, *Iranian Press in Twentieth Century* (Tehran, 2001).

10 Bagherian: 'Economic analysis'.

11 Keyhani: 'How women-oriented'.

12 Parvin Ardalan, 'Zanan introduces women's press: Zan-e Rouz', *Zanan*, 52 (1999), pp 2–6.

13 Centre for Cultural and International Studies, *The Cultural Viewpoints of the Leader of the Islamic Revolution of Iran, Ayatollah Seyed-Ali Khamenei* (Tehran, 2000).

14 Maryam Poya, *Women, Work & Islamism: Ideology and Resistance in Iran* (London, 1999).

15 Noushin Ahmadi-Khorasani, *Women Under the Shadow of Patriarchs* (Tehran, 2001), p 166.

16 Nira Yuval-Davis, *Gender and Nation* (London, 1997).

17 Olivier Roy, *The Failure of Political Islam* (London, 1994).

18 Asghar Schirazi, *The Constitution of Iran: Politics and the State in the Islamic Republic* (London, 1998), pp 141–3.

19 Azadeh Kian, 'Women and politics in post-Islamist Iran: the gender conscious drive to change', *British Journal of Middle Eastern Studies*, 24/1 (1997), p 76.

20 Ali Barzegar, 'Who are in search of civil society?', *Political & Economic Ettela'at*, 13/135–6 (1999), pp 28–33.

21 Haleh Afshar, 'Competing interests: democracy, Islamicisation and women politicians in Iran', *Parliamentary Affairs*, 55 (2002); Poya: *Women, Work & Islamism*.

22 Valentine Moghadam, *Women, Work and Economic Reform in the Middle East and North Africa* (Boulder, CO, 1998); Poya: *Women, Work & Islamism*.

23 Haideh Moghissi, *Populist Feminism and Islamic Feminism: A Critique of Neo-Conservative Tendencies among Iranian Feminists in the West* (Toronto, 1998).

24 Haleh Afshar, 'Women and work in Iran', *Political Studies*, 45 (1997).

25 Kian: 'Women and politics'; Afshar: 'Competing interests'; Poya: *Women, Work & Islamism*; Ziba Mir-Hosseini, 'Feminist movements in the Islamic Republic', www.hamta.co.uk/feminist.htm.

26 Azar Tabari and Nahid Yeganeh (eds), *In the Shadow of Islam: The Women's Movement in Iran* (London, 1982).

27 Kian: 'Women and politics'.

28 Kian: 'Women and politics'; Afshar: 'Competing interests'.

29 Valentine Moghadam, 'Islamic feminism and its discontents: towards a resolution of the debate', *Sign: Journal of Women in Culture and Society*, 27/4 (2002).

30 Janet Afary, 'The war against feminism in the name of the Almighty: making sense of gender and Muslim fundamentalism', *New Left Review*, 224 (1997); Haleh Afshar, 'Islam and feminism: an analysis of political strategies', in M. Yamani (ed.), *Feminism & Islam: Legal and Literary Perspectives* (New York, 1996); Kian: 'Women and politics'.

31 Ziba Mir-Hosseini, 'Stretching the limits: a feminist reading of the Shari'a in post-Khomeini Iran', in M. Yamani (ed.), *Feminism & Islam: Legal and Literary Perspectives* (New York, 1996).

32 Shahrzad Mojab, 'Theorizing the politics of "Islamic feminism"', *Feminist Review*, 69 (2001); Moghissi: *Populist Feminism and Islamic Feminism*.

33 Moghadam: 'Islamic feminism', p 1165.

34 Mir-Hosseini: 'Feminist movements'.

35 Lily Farhadpour, *Berlin Women* (Tehran, 2000).

36 The main firms in Iran are regarded as 'public property', and their managing directors are selected and appointed by the supreme leader.

37 Mohammad Ghouchani, *Godfather and the Young Left: The Struggle for Critique of Power* (Tehran, 2000).

38 Ardalan: 'Zanan introduces … Zan-e Rouz'.

39 Elham Gheytanchi, 'Civil society in Iran: politics of motherhood and the public sphere', *International Sociology*, 16/4 (2001), p 563.

40 Mir-Hosseini: 'Feminist movements'; Mir-Hosseini: 'Stretching the limits'; Afshar: 'Islam and feminism'.

41 The 'Iran After the Elections' conference was held 7–9 April in Berlin by the Heinrich Boll Institute, an organization associated with the German Green Party. It aimed to promote understanding and informed political opinion and intended to bring together critical voices from both secular and Islamic reformist groups. Some prominent writers and publishers, as well as reformist politicians and journalists, were invited to speak. A large demonstration of some Iranian political groups in exile, however, disrupted the proceedings and a woman danced in her underwear to protest the Islamic dress code in Iran. Rafsanjani later condemned these people for shameful conduct. Iranian national television, controlled by the supreme leader Ali Khamenei, showed a highly biased and selective film of the conference, cynically skewed to inflame religious opinion and paint the participants in an anti-Islamic light. A number of participants, including two women, Mehrangiz Kar, a human rights lawyer, and Shahla Lahiji, an independent publisher, together with Alireza Afshar, secretary of the Office of Consolidation of Unity, the largest student association, and Akbar Ganji, a reformist and well-known investigative journalist, were all arrested and sent to jail, charged with acts against national security by making propaganda against the Islamic Republic of Iran.

42 www.badjens.com/fourthedition/kar.htm.

43 Elaheh Rostami Povey, 'Feminist contestations of institutional domains in Iran', *Feminist Review*, 69 (2001).

44 www.pbs.org/adventuredivas/iran/divas.

45 Parvin Ardalan, 'Zanan introduces women's press: Farzaneh', *Zanan*, 69 (2000).

46 Shadi Sadr, *Justice from the Point of View of a Third Person* (Tehran, 2000).

47 Ahmadi-Khorasani: *Women Under the Shadow of Patriarchs*, pp 158–65.

48 Parvin Ardalan, 'Zanan introduces women's press: Payam-e Zan', *Zanan*, 62 (2000).

49 Parvin Ardalan, 'Zanan introduces women's press: Neda', *Zanan*, 55 (1999).

50 www.iranwomen.org.

51 Parvin Ardalan, 'Zanan introduces women's press: Faslnameh', *Zanan*, 80 (2001).

52 Ahmadi-Khorasani published the journal without a licence. It was published in a book format by Ahmadi-Khorasani's own publication firm. The regime was alarmed when *Jens-e Dovom* appeared with numbers and ordered the editor, who was hoping to get away with it by pretending that the journal was a book, to close it.

53 Poya: *Women, Work & Islamism*, p 138.

54 www.badjens.com/fourthedition/lahiji.htm.

55 Cinema is of course another area in which Iranian women have made great headway. In contrast to only two women directors in pre-1979 period, there are at least 11 women directors in Iran now. Some are internationally known and well-received in international film festivals and, despite the limitations imposed by the Islamic Republic, have managed to produce movies of astonishing quality dealing with 'women's questions' with spectacular effect. See Hamid Nafisi, 'Veiled vision/powerful presence: women in post revolutionary Iranian cinema', in Mahnaz Afkhami, and Erica Friedl (eds), *In the Eye of Storm: Women in Post-Revolutionary Iran* (London, 1994). Some – for example, Tahmineh Millani – have even been imprisoned for their movies. According to one report, in the years before the revolution only three women made a feature film in Iran, one in 1956 and the other two in the late 1970s. Of 11 women film directors in post-revolution Iran, the majority have made more than one film and four have made at least four or five movies, which are made distinctive by their focus on gender issues. Reza Tahami, 'Iranian women make films', *Film International Quarterly*, 2/3 (1994).

56 Nazanin Shah-Rokni, 'Women journalists: life of another kind', *Zanan*, 45 (1998); Parvin Ardalan, 'Women journalists are still second sex', *Jens-e Dovom*, 2 (1999).

57 www.badjens.com/11_21_00/farhadpour.htm.

58 Elina Vuola, 'Remaking universal? Transnational feminism(s) challenging fundamental ecumenism', *Theory, Culture & Society*, 19/1–2 (2002).

59 Gholam Khiabany and Annabelle Sreberny 'The Iranian press and the continuing struggle over civil society 1998–2000', *Gazette*, 62/2–3 (2001). Since then the number of banned publications has increased to over 80. The total number of executions in Iran in 2001 was 131, second only to China, *Guardian Education*, 21 January 2003, p 64.

3 'Till I Become a Minister'

1 Margot Badran, 'Epilogue', in H. Shaarawi, *Harem Years: The Memoirs of an Egyptian Feminist*, translated and introduced by Margot Badran (London, 1986), p 112.

2 Cynthia Nelson, *Doria Shafik, Egyptian Feminist: A Woman Apart* (Gainesville, FL, 1996).

3 Cynthia Nelson, 'Biography and women's history: on interpreting Doria Shafik', in N. Keddie and B. Baron (eds), *Women in Middle Eastern History: Shifting Boundaries in Sex and Gender* (New Haven and London, 1991), pp 313–14.

4 Nelson: 'Biography and women's history', p 314.

5 Beth Baron, *The Women's Awakening in Egypt: Culture, Society and the Press* (New Haven and London, 1994).

6 The title in Arabic is *Al-Durr al-Manthur fi Tabaqat Rabbat al-Khudur*. For more on this work see Marilyn Booth, *May Her Likes Be Multiplied: Biography and Gender Politics in Egypt* (Berkeley and Los Angeles, 2001).

7 Leila Ahmed, *Women and Gender in Islam: Historical Roots of a Modern Debate* (New Haven and London, 1992), p 141.

8 Ahmed: *Women and Gender in Islam*, p 141; Ismail Ibrahim, *Sahafiyat Tha'irat* [Revolutionary Women Journalists] (Cairo, 1997), pp 16–20.

9 Iglal Khalifa, *Al-Harakah al-Nissa'iyyah al-Haditha* (Cairo, 1973), pp 20–30.

10 Ahmed: *Women and Gender in Islam*, p 139.

11 Mohammed Omara, *Qasim Amin wa Tahrir al-Mar'a fi Misr* [Qasim Amin and Women's Liberation in Egypt] (Cairo, 1988).

12 Thomas Philipp, 'Feminism and nationalist politics in Egypt', in L. Beck and N. Keddie (eds), *Women in the Muslim World* (Cambridge, MA, 1978), p 279.

13 Ahmed Khaky, *Qasim Amin and his Work* (Cairo, 1973), pp 89–100.

14 Sometimes translated as 'The Intimate Companion', or 'The Sociable Companion'.

15 Philipp, in 'Feminism and nationalist politics in Egypt' (p 280), cites secondary sources to give the start date of *Al-A'ila* as 1904. Baron, in *The Women's Awakening* (p 21), states that it lasted from 1899 at least until 1904 and possibly 1907.

16 Philipp: 'Feminism and nationalist politics in Egypt', p 282.

17 Khalifa: *Al-Haraka al-Nissa'iyya al-Haditha*, pp 29–40.

18 Philipp: 'Feminism and nationalist politics in Egypt', pp 283–4.

19 Afaf Lutfi al-Sayyid, *Egypt and Cromer: A Study in Anglo-Egyptian Relations* (London, 1968), pp 169–72.

20 Baron: *The Women's Awakening*, p 131.

21 Selma Botman, *Engendering Citizenship in Egypt* (New York, 1999), p 34.

22 Magd El Din Hifni, 'Athar Bahithat el-Badiyya' [The influence of the Seeker of the Desert], in *El-Mawsouaa el-Misriyya el-Amma* [General Egyptian Encyclopedia] (Cairo, 1962).

23 'Malak Hifni Nassef', in Women and Memory Forum (ed.), *Nissa'iyyat* (Cairo, 1998), pp 60–1

24 Philipp: 'Feminism and nationalist politics in Egypt', p 286.

25 Margot Badran, 'Independent women: more than a century of feminism in Egypt', in J. Tucker (ed.), *Arab Women: Old Boundaries, New Frontiers* (Bloomington and Indianapolis, 1993), pp 130–1.

26 Badran: 'Epilogue', p 118.

27 In Arabic: *Lagnat al-Wafd al-Markaziyya lil Sayyidat*.

28 The 1881 Press Law, imposed by Egypt's Turco-Circassian governing elite but scarcely invoked since 1894, was reactivated by the British administrator Eldon Gorst in 1909, allowing newspapers to be suspended and editorial staff to be sent into exile. See P. J. Vatikiotis, *The History of Egypt From Muhammad Ali to Sadat*, 2nd edn (London, 1980), p 207.

29 Badran: 'Epilogue', pp 129–30.

30 Irène Fenoglio Abdel-Aal, 'Feminisme et politique en Egypte', *Peuples méditerranéens*, 48–9 (July–December 1989), pp 155 and 160–2.

31 The charge, made by Inji Aflatun in her 1949 book *Nahnu ... al-Nissa' al-Misriyat* [We, the Egyptian Women] (p 105) is quoted in Hind Wassef and Nadia Wassef, 'Introduction', in H. Wassef and N. Wassef (eds), *Daughters of the Nile: Photographs of Egyptian Women's Movements, 1900–1960* (Cairo, 2001), p 11.

32 Amal Kamel Bayoumi El-Sobki, *Al-Haraka al-Nissa'iyya fi Misr bain Thawratain 1919–1925* (Cairo, 1986), pp 100 and 120.

33 Fenoglio Abdel-Aal: 'Feminisme et politique', p 156.

34 Booth: *May Her Likes be Multiplied*, p xxiv.

35 Khalifa: *Al-Haraka al-Nissa'iyya al-Haditha*, p 132.

36 *Al-Ahram*, 3 March, 1924.

37 *Al-Balagh*, 9 April, 1924.

38 Mounira Thabet, *Thawra fi'l-Bourg al-Aagi* (Cairo, 1945), p 27.

39 Thabet: *Thawra fi'l-Bourg al-Aagi*, p 29.

40 *Al-Ahram*, 9 June, 1938.

41 Thabet: *Thawra f'il-Bourg al-Aagi*, p 4.

42 Nelson: *Doria Shafik*, pp 88–9.

43 Nelson: *Doria Shafik*, pp 98–9.

44 Nelson: 'Biography and women's history', p 318.

45 Nelson: 'Biography and women's history', p 321.

46 Nelson: 'Biography and women's history', p 332, n22.

47 Doreya Shafiq, *Al-Mar'a al-Misriyya* [The Egyptian Woman] (Cairo, 1955), p 31.

48 Shafiq: *Al-Mar'a al-Misriyya*, p 44.

49 Nelson: 'Biography and women's history', p 317.

50 Shafiq: *Al-Mar'a al-Misriyya*, p 47.

51 Shafiq: *Al-Mar'a al-Misriyya*, p 185.

52 *Al-Ethnein*, 23 May 1948; Shafiq: *Al-Mar'a al-Misriyya*, p 195.

53 Shafiq: *Al-Mar'a al-Misriyya*, pp 196–9.

54 Doreya Shafiq, 'Ahdafuna wa wasa'ilna' [Our goals and means], *Bint el-Nil*, 63 (February 1951).

55 Shafiq: *Al-Mar'a al-Misriyya*, pp 201–5.

56 Shafiq: *Al-Mar'a al-Misriyya*, p 242.

57 Sonia Dabous, 'Nasser and the Egyptian press', in C. Tripp (ed.), *Contemporary Egypt: Through Egyptian Eyes* (London, 1993), p 107.

4 Maghrebi Women Film-makers and
the Challenge of Modernity

1 Antoine Galland published his multi-volume translation of *The Thousand and One Nights* between 1704 and 1717.

2 Zahia Smail Salhi, 'Stereotyping, prejudice and race: colonial encounters East and West', in P. Smith (ed.), *Aesthetic Encounters* (London, forthcoming).

3 Malek Alloula, *The Colonial Harem* (Manchester, 1987), p 5.

4 Alloula: *The Colonial Harem*, p 31.

5 Dina Sherzer, 'Introduction', in D. Sherzer (ed.), *Cinema, Colonialism, Post-colonialism: Perspectives from the French and Francophone Worlds* (Austin, TX, 1996), p 3.

6 Sherzer: 'Introduction', p 3.

7 Sherzer: 'Introduction', p 4. Emphasis added.

8 See Zahia Salhi, *Politics, Poetics and the Algerian Novel* (Lampeter, 1999).

9 One example is S. Ben Ali and Rene Potier Paris, *La Tente noire: roman saharien* (Paris, 1833) by Les Oeuvres Representatives. Another is S. Ben Ibrahim and Etienne Dinet, *Khadra, la danseuse des Ouled Nail* (Paris, 1910).

10 Sherzer: 'Introduction', p 5.

11 Quoted in Sherzer: 'Introduction', p 7.

12 Taos Amrouche, *Jacinthe Noire* (Paris, 1947).

13 Djamila Debeche, *Aziza* (Algiers, 1955).

14 Assia Djebar, *Ces voix qui m'assiègent* (Paris, 1999), pp 25–7.

15 Valérie Budig-Markin, 'Writing and filming the cries of silence', *World Literature Today*, 70/4 (Autumn 1996), p 893.

16 A good example here is the image of the Algerian woman in Kateb Yacine's *Nedjma*. For more details see Salhi: *Politics, Poetics and the Algerian Novel.*

17 Algeria was the last Maghreb country to win its independence in 1962. It was preceded by Tunisia and Morocco in 1956. The first Maghrebi feature film is *Al-Layl Yakhaf Al-Shams* (*The Night is Afraid of the Sun*) by the Algerian Mustapha Badie, in 1965. The first Tunisian feature, *Al-Fajr* (*The Dawn*) by Omar Khlifi, appeared in 1966. It was followed two years later by the first Moroccan feature, *Intissar al-Hayat* (*Conquer to Live*), by Mohammed B. A. Tazi and Ahmed Mesnaoui, in 1968.

18 Farid Boughedir, *Caméra arabe* (film), La Médiathèque des trois mondes, 1987.

19 Boughedir: *Caméra arabe.*

20 See Zahia Salhi, 'Wounded smile: women, politics, and the culture of betrayal', *Critique*, 18 (Spring 2001), pp 101–19.

21 Mildred Mortimer, 'Reappropriating the gaze in Assia Djebar's fiction and film', *World Literature Today*, 70/4 (Autumn 1996), p 859.

22 Although *Reed Dolls* has a male director, the story of the film was written by Farida Benlyazid, who is also the film's scriptwriter.

23 *La Nouba des Femmes du Mont Chenoua*, Assia Djebar (1978, 16mm, colour, 115 mins). This film won first prize at the Venice Film Festival in 1979.

24 For more details see Zahia Salhi, 'Gender and national identity in the work of Assia Djebar', in Y. Suleiman and I. Muhawi (eds), *Articulating the Nation: Literary Landscapes from the Middle East and North Africa* (Edinburgh, forthcoming).

25 Salhi: 'Gender and national identity'.

26 Ibrahim Fawal, *Youssef Chahine* (London, 2001), pp 81–8.

27 Evelyn Accad, 'Assia Djebar's contribution to Arab women's literature: rebellion, maturity, vision', *World Literature Today*, 70/4 (Autumn 1996), p 809.

28 Budig-Markin: 'Writing and filming the cries of silence', p 898.

29 Accad: 'Assia Djebar's contribution', p 809.

30 Mortimer: 'Reappropriating the gaze', p 861.

31 *Reed Dolls*, Djilali Ferhati, screenplay and story by Farida Benlyazid, (1981, 35mm, colour, 88 minutes).

32 See: Alison Baker, *Voices of Resistance: Oral Histories of Moroccan Women* (New York, 1998).

33 Emphasis added.

34 Emphasis added.

35 Emphasis added.

36 According to 1988 statistics, Morocco had the highest rate of all Arab countries at 78.3%, with Algeria at 63.1%. See Fatima Mernissi, *Women's Rebellion and Islamic Memory* (London, 1996).

37 *Les Silences du Palais*, Moufida Tlatli, (1994, 35mm, colour, 127 minutes). This film won the Grand Prix (Golden Tanit) at the Carthage Film Festival in 1994 and was voted Best First Feature at the 1994 Chicago International Film Festival.

38 Lizzie Francke, 'Revolution on the quiet', *Guardian*, 6 April, 1994.

39 Francke: 'Revolution on the quiet'.

40 Djebar: *Ces voix qui m'assiégent*.

5 The Orient and its Others

1 Deniz Kandiyoti, 'Identity and its discontents: women and the nation', in P. Williams and L. Chrisman (eds), *Colonial Discourse and Post-Colonial Theory: A Reader* (London, 1994), p 377.

2 V. Spike Peterson, 'Sexing political identities/nationalism as heterosexism', *International Feminist Journal of Politics*, 1/1, (1999), p 48.

3 Floya Anthias and Nira Yuval-Davis, 'Introduction', in N. Yuval-Davis and F. Anthias (eds), *Woman–Nation–State* (London, 1989), pp 1–15.

4 Anthias and Yuval-Davis: 'Introduction', p 7.

5 Chandra Talpade Mohanty, 'Under western eyes: feminist scholarship and colonial discourses', in P. Williams and L. Chrisman (eds), *Colonial Discourse and Post-Colonial Theory: A Reader* (London, 1994), p 196.

6 Mohanty: 'Under western eyes', p 202.

7 Kandiyoti: 'Identity and its discontents', p 377.

8 Kandiyoti: 'Identity and its discontents', p 377.

9 Kandiyoti: 'Identity and its discontents', p 376.

10 E. Ann Kaplan, *Motherhood and Representation: The Mother in Popular Culture and Melodrama* (London, 1992), p 79.

11 Kaplan: *Motherhood and Representation*, p 124.

12 Kaplan: *Motherhood and Representation*, p 124.

13 Mervat Hatem, 'Toward the development of post-Islamic and post nationalist feminist discourses in the Middle East', in J. Tucker (ed.), *Arab Women: Old Boundaries, New Frontiers* (Bloomington and Indianapolis, 1993), p 39.

14 Hatem: 'Toward the development', p 39.

15 Margot Badran, 'Independent women: more than a century of feminism in Egypt', in J. Tucker (ed.), *Arab Women: Old Boundaries, New Frontiers* (Bloomington and Indianapolis, 1993), pp 129–48.

16 Anouar Majid, 'The politics of feminism in Islam', *Signs: Journal of Women in Culture and Society*, 23/2 (Winter 1998), p 327.

17 Majid: 'The politics of feminism in Islam', p 327.

18 Shahnaz Khan, 'Muslim women: negotiations in the Third Space', *Signs: Journal of Women in Culture and Society*, 23/1 (Winter 1998), p 468.

19 Quoted in Rick Wilford, 'Women, ethnicity and nationalism: surveying the ground', in R. Wilford and R. L. Miller (eds), *Women, Ethnicity and Nationalism: The Politics of Transition* (London, 1998), p 6.

20 Anthias and Yuval-Davis: 'Introduction'; Suad Joseph, 'Women between nation and state in Lebanon', in C. Kaplan, N. Alarcon and M. Minoo (eds), *Between Woman and Nation: Nationalisms, Transnational Feminisms, and the State* (Durham, NC, 1999), pp 162–81; Wilford: 'Women, ethnicity and nationalism'.

21 Carol Delaney, 'Father state, motherland, and the birth of modern Turkey', in S. Yanagisako and C. Delaney (eds), *Naturalizing Power: Essays in Feminist Cultural Analysis* (London, 1995), pp 177–200, p 190. Italics in original.

22 Simona Sharoni, *Gender and the Israeli-Palestinian Conflict* (Syracuse, NY, 1995).

23 Sita Ranchod-Nilsson and Mary Ann Tétreault, 'Gender and nationalism: moving beyond fragmented conversations', in S. Ranchod-Nilsson and M. Tétreault (eds), *Women, States and Nationalism: At Home in the Nation?* (London, 2000), pp 1–17.

24 Anthias and Yuval-Davis: 'Introduction'.

25 Peterson: 'Sexing politial identities/nationalism as heterosexism', p 49.

26 Jan Jindy Pettman, *Women, Nationalism and the State: Towards an International Feminist Perspective*, Occasional Paper 4 in Gender and Development Studies, Asian Institute of Technology (Bangkok, 1992), pp 5–6.

27 Judith E. Tucker, 'The Arab family in history: "Otherness" and the study of the family', in J. Tucker (ed.), *Arab Women: Old Boundaries, New Frontiers* (Bloomington and Indianapolis, 1993), pp 195–207; Efrat Tseelon, *The Masque of Femininity: The Presentation of Woman in Everyday Life* (London, 1995).

28 Peterson: 'Sexing political identities/nationalism as heterosexism', p 48.
29 Kaplan: *Motherhood and Representation*; Laura Mulvey, 'Visual pleasure and narrative cinema', in S. Thornham (ed.), *Feminist Film Theory: A Reader* (Edinburgh, 1999), pp 58–69.
30 Laura Mulvey, *Visual and Other Pleasures* (London, 1989), p 57.
31 Mulvey: 'Visual pleasure and narrative cinema', p 60.
32 Mulvey: 'Visual pleasure and narrative cinema'; Tseelon: *The Masque of Femininity*.
33 Tseelon: *The Masque of Femininity*.
34 Eleanore Kofman, 'Feminism, gender relations and geopolitics: problematic closures and opening strategies', in E. Kofman and G. Youngs, *Globalization: Theory and Practice* (London, 1996), pp 209–24.
35 Tseelon: *The Masque of Femininity*, p 68.
36 Tseelon: *The Masque of Femininity*, pp 68–9.
37 Tseelon: *The Masque of Femininity*, p 68.
38 Zillah Eisenstein, 'Writing bodies on the nation for the globe', in S. Ranchod-Nilsson and M. Tétreault (eds), *Women, States and Nationalism: At Home in the Nation?* (London, 2000), p 38.
39 Haleh Afshar, 'Women and the politics of fundamentalism in Iran', in H. Afshar (ed.), *Women and Politics in the Third World* (London, 1996).
40 Malek Alloula, *The Colonial Harem* (Minneapolis, 1986).
41 Khan: 'Muslim women: negotiations in the Third Space', p 469.
42 Fadwa Guindi, *Veil: Modesty, Privacy and Resistance* (Oxford, 1999).
43 Nawal El Saadawi, *The Nawal El Saadawi Reader* (London, 1997), p 95. My emphasis.
44 Anne McClintock, '"No longer in future heaven": gender, race and nationalism', in A. McClintock, A. Mufti and E. Shohat (eds), *Dangerous Liaisons: Gender, Nation, and Postcolonial Perspectives* (Minneapolis, 1997), p 89.
45 Kandiyoti: 'Identity and its discontents', p 382.
46 Georgina Waylen, *Gender in Third World Politics* (Buckingham, 1996).
47 Kandiyoti: 'Identity and its discontents', p 379.
48 Jean Franco, 'Beyond ethnocentrism: gender, power and the Third-World intelligentsia', in P. Williams and L. Chrisman (eds), *Colonial Discourse and Post-Colonial Theory: A Reader* (London, 1994), p 366.
49 Mulvey: *Visual and Other Pleasures*.
50 Cynthia Enloe, *Bananas, Beaches & Bases: Making Feminist Sense of International Politics* (Berkeley, 1990).
51 Meyda Yegenoglu, *Colonial Fantasies: Towards a Feminist Reading of Orientalism* (Cambridge, 1998), p 123.
52 Yegenoglu: *Colonial Fantasies*.
53 Souad Dajani, 'Palestinian women under Israeli occupation', in J. Tucker (ed.), *Arab Women: Old Boundaries, New Frontiers* (Bloomington and Indianapolis, 1993), p 114.
54 Maria Holt, 'Palestinian women and the Intifada: an exploration of images and realities', in H. Afshar (ed.), *Women and Politics in the Third World* (London, 1996), p 190.

55 Rosemary Sayigh, 'Palestinian women and politics in Lebanon', in J. Tucker (ed.), *Arab Women: Old Boundaries, New Frontiers* (Bloomington and Indianapolis, 1993), p 176.

56 Sayigh: 'Palestinian women and politics in Lebanon'.

57 Majid: 'The politics of feminism in Islam', p 351.

58 Nahla Abdo, 'Nationalism and feminism: Palestinian women and the Intifada – No going back?', in V. Moghadam (ed.), *Gender and National Identity* (London, 1994), p 162.

59 Wilford: 'Women, ethnicity and nationalism', p 3.

60 Yvonne Tasker, *Spectacular Bodies: Gender, Genre and the Action Cinema* (London, 1993).

61 Sherrie A. Inness, *Tough Girls: Women Warriors and Wonder Women in Popular Culture* (Philadelphia, 1999), p 46.

62 Anthias and Yuval-Davis: 'Introduction', p 10.

63 Inness: *Tough Girls*, p 98.

64 Tasker: *Spectacular Bodies*; Yvonne Tasker, *Working Girls: Gender and Sexuality in Popular Cinema* (London, 1998).

65 Mary Ann Doane, '*Caught* and *Rebecca*: the inscription of femininity as absence', in S. Thornham (ed.), *Feminist Film Theory: A Reader* (Edinburgh, 1999), p 71.

66 Jackie Stacey, 'Feminine fascinations: forms of identification in star-audience relations', in S. Thornham (ed.), *Feminist Film Theory: A Reader* (Edinburgh, 1999), p 201.

67 Tasker: *Spectacular Bodies*, p 26.

68 Tasker: *Spectacular Bodies*, p 14.

69 Inness: *Tough Girls*.

70 Inness: *Tough Girls*.

71 Tasker: *Working Girls*.

72 Inness: *Tough Girls*, p 97.

73 Tasker: *Spectacular Bodies*, p 19.

74 Inness: *Tough Girls*.

75 Inness: *Tough Girls*, p 35.

76 Enloe: *Bananas, Beaches and Bases*.

77 Kirsten Schulze, 'Communal violence, civil war and foreign occupation: women in Lebanon', in R. Wilford and R. L. Miller (eds), *Women, Ethnicity and Nationalism: The Politics of Transition*, (London, 1998), p 159.

78 McClintock: 'No longer in future heaven', p 89.

79 Ranchod-Nilsson and Tétreault: 'Gender and nationalism', p 5.

80 Valentine Moghadam, 'Introduction and overview: gender dynamics of nationalism, revolution and Islamization', in V. Moghadam (ed.), *Gender and National Identity* (London, 1994), pp 1–17.

81 McClintock: 'No longer in future heaven', p 90.

82 Sara Suleri, 'Woman skin deep: feminism and the postcolonial condition', in B. Ashcroft. G. Griffiths and H. Tiffin (eds), *The Post-Colonial Studies Reader* (London, 1995), p 273.

6 Multiple Literacies, Multiple Identities

1 Liesbet Van Zoonen, *Feminist Media Studies* (London, 1994), pp 148–9.
2 Laila Abdel-Migeed, *Women and Electronic Media: An Annotated Selected Bibliography 1983–1993* (Cairo, 1995).
3 Kubi Sakamoto, 'Reading Japanese women's magazines: the construction of new identities in the 1970s and 1980s', *Media, Culture and Society*, 21/2 (1999), p 173.
4 David Morley, *Television, Audiences and Cultural Studies* (London, 1992).
5 Mona el-Hadeedy, 'Egyptian women in radio and television's social programmes', *Art of Broadcasting*, 105 (1985), pp 21–2.
6 Van Zoonen: *Feminist Media Studies*, p 105.
7 Adli Reda, *The Image of Father and Mother in Arabic Soap Operas* (Cairo, 1988); Abdel-Fattah Abdel-Nabi, *The Future of the Egyptian Village: Communication Patterns in Rural Egypt* (Cairo, 1995).
8 Caroline Moser, *Gender Planning and Development: Theory, Practice and Training* (London, 1993), p 27.
9 Stuart Hall, 'Encoding/decoding', in S. Hall, D. Hobson, A. Lowe and P. Willis (eds), *Culture, Media, Language: Working Papers in Cultural Studies 1972–1979* (London, 1980), pp 128–30.
10 Mary Hamilton, 'Introduction: signposts', in M. Hamilton, D. Barton and R. Ivanic (eds), *Worlds of Literacy* (Clevedon, 1994), p 9.
11 Hall: 'Encoding/decoding', p 134.
12 Paul Davies, Stella Fitzpatrick, Victor Grenko and Roz Ivanic, 'Literacy, strength and identity', in M. Hamilton, D. Barton and R. Ivanic (eds), *Worlds of Literacy* (Clevedon, 1994), p 166.
13 Valerie Walkerdine, 'Some day my prince will come: young girls and the preparation for adolescent sexuality', in A. McRobbie and M. Nava (eds), *Gender and Generation* (London, 1984). pp 183–4.
14 Shirley Cornes, 'Gender-engendered literacy needs', in M. Hamilton, D. Barton and R. Ivanic (eds), *Worlds of Literacy* (Clevedon, 1994), p 105.
15 Hamilton: 'Introduction: signposts', p 10.
16 Marie Gillespie, *Television, Ethnicity and Cultural Change* (London, 1995).
17 Rosemary Deem, *All Work and No Play: The Sociology of Women and Leisure* (Milton Keynes, 1986).
18 Barbara Adam, *Time Watch* (Cambridge, 1995).
19 Everett Rogers, *Communication and Development* (California, 1976).
20 Tricia Hartley, 'Generations of literacy among women in a bilingual community', in M. Hamilton, D. Barton and R. Ivanic (eds), *Worlds of Literacy* (Clevedon, 1994), pp 29–40
21 Hamilton: 'Introduction: signposts', p 5.
22 Gillespie: *Television, Ethnicity and Cultural Change*, p 16.
23 John Fiske, *Television Culture* (London, 1987), p 178.
24 Andrea Press, *Women Watching Television: Gender, Class and Generation in the American Television Experience* (Philadelphia, 1991).

25 Walkerdine: 'Some day my prince will come', p 164.

26 Walkerdine: 'Some day my prince will come', p 167.

27 Walkerdine: 'Some day my prince will come', pp 164–5.

28 Fiske: *Television Culture*, p 15.

29 Brian Street, 'Struggles over the meaning(s) of literacy', in M. Hamilton, D. Barton and R. Ivanic (eds), *Worlds of Literacy* (Clevedon, 1994), p 15.

30 Sonia Livingstone, *Making Sense of Television: The Psychology of Audience Interpretation* (London, 1990), pp 180–2.

31 Walkerdine: 'Some day my prince will come', p 174.

32 Walkerdine: 'Some day my prince will come', p 174.

33 Fiske: *Television Culture*, pp 62–3.

34 Livingstone: *Making Sense of Television*, p 182.

35 Hall: 'Encoding/decoding', p 131.

36 Cary Bazalgette and David Buckingham, *In Front of the Children* (London, 1995).

37 Gillespie: *Television, Ethnicity and Cultural Change*, p 5.

38 Hamilton: 'Introduction: signposts', p 5.

39 Lawrence Grossberg, 'Identity and cultural studies: is that all there is?', in S. Hall and P. du Gay (eds), *Questions of Cultural Identity* (London, 1996), p 92.

40 Gillespie: *Television, Ethnicity and Cultural Change*, p 5.

41 Grossberg: 'Identity and cultural studies', p 99.

42 Livingstone: *Making Sense of Television*, p 24.

43 Hartley: 'Generations of literacy', p 32.

44 Ann Gray, *Video Playtime: The Gendering of a Leisure Technology* (London, 1992).

45 Livingstone: *Making Sense of Television*.

46 Hall: 'Encoding/decoding', pp 136–8.

47 Grossberg: 'Identity and cultural studies', p 91.

48 Stuart Hall, 'Introduction to part III', in J. Evans and S. Hall (eds), *Visual Culture: A Reader* (London, 1999), pp 312–13.

49 Hall: 'Introduction to part III', p 311.

50 Street: 'Struggles over the meaning(s) of literacy', p 20.

51 Street: 'Struggles over the meaning(s) of literacy', p 15.

52 David Barton, 'Preface: literacy practices and literacy events', in M. Hamilton, D. Barton and R. Ivanic (eds), *Worlds of Literacy* (Clevedon, 1994), p x.

53 Hamilton: 'Introduction: signposts'.

54 Street: 'Struggles over the meaning(s) of literacy'.

55 Gillespie: *Television, Ethnicity and Cultural Change*, p 25.

7 Echoes: Gender and Media Challenges in Palestine

1 Rosemary Sayigh, 'Palestinian women: triple burden, single struggle', *Peuples méditerranéens*, 44–5 (July–December 1998), p 251.

2 Sayigh: 'Palestinian women', p 253.

3 Heba Assaf, *Dur al-Mar'a fi'l-Ilam al-Filistini: Dirasa Mujaza* [The Role of Women in the Palestinian Media: A Brief Study] (Ramallah, 2001).

4 Assaf: *Dur al-Mar'a fi'l-Ilam al-Filistini.*

5 Jerusalem Media and Communication Centre, *Israeli Military Orders in the Occupied Palestinian West Bank 1967–92* (East Jerusalem, 1993).

6 Daoud Kuttab, 'Palestinian diaries: grass roots TV production in the Occupied Territories', in T. Dowmunt (ed.), *Channels of Resistance: Global Television and Local Empowerment* (London, 1993), pp 139–40.

7 Kuttab: 'Palestinian diaries', p 140.

8 Islah Abdul Jawwad, 'The evolution of the political role of the Palestinian women's movement in the uprising', in M. Hudson (ed.), *The Palestinians: New Directions* (Washington, DC, 1990), p 69.

9 Eileen Kuttab, 'Women's studies program in Palestine: between criticism and new vision', *Cairo Papers in Social Science*, 20/3, (1998), pp 119–21.

10 Suheir Azzoumi, 'Lobbying for citizenship rights: the Palestinian case and the role of the Women's Affairs Technical Committee', paper presented to the Third Mediterranean Development Forum (Cairo, March 2000), p 2.

11 Benaz Somiry-Batrawi, 'Waqaa al-Mar'a fi'l-Amal al-Tilifiziyuniyya wa'l-Izaiyya fi Filistin' [The situation of women in television and radio work in Palestine], paper presented to the First Conference of Arab Media Women (Amman, June 2001), p 16.

12 Walid Batrawi, 'Private television in Palestine', MA dissertation, University of Leicester (April, 2001). Online at http://www.amin.org/views/walid_batrawi/2002/nov2002.html.

13 Batrawi: 'Private television in Palestine'.

14 Azzoumi: 'Lobbying for citizenship rights'.

15 Batrawi: 'Private television in Palestine'.

16 Editor's note: Nabil Khatib, MBC Bureau Chief in Jerusalem, told an audience in Amman in February 2002 about a phone call he and an Al-Jazeera correspondent had received from a Palestinian woman who wanted help from the Arab satellite channels to ensure that her son would receive severance pay from his employer. Khatib said many Palestinians looked on the Arab satellite stations as 'ombudsmen'.

17 Somiry-Batrawi: 'Waqaa al-Mar'a', p 9.

18 Assaf: *Dur al-Mar'a fi'l-Ilam al-Filistini.*

19 Assaf, *Dur al-Mar'a fi'l-Ilam al-Filistini.*

20 Unicef, 'Al-Mar'a wa'l-Tifl fi'l-Ilam al-Filistini' [Women and children in Palestinian media], unpublished study (Jerusalem, 2000).

21 Kuttab: 'Palestinian diaries', p 144.

22 Daoud Kuttab, 'A word from the director', in Institute of Modern Media brochure (Ramallah, 2000).

23 Institute Of Modern Media brochure.

24 The project is one of those highlighted in WomenAction, *Women and Media for Social Change: Communications Initiatives Worldwide* (Montreal, 2001), pp 101–2.

25 Joel Campagna/Committee to Protect Journalists, *Picking Up the Pieces* (New York, June 2002), p 3.
26 Quoted in Campagna/Committee to Protect Journalists: *Picking Up the Pieces*, p 3.
27 Wasim Abdullah, 'Sledgehammer treatment', *Middle East International*, 673 (19 April 2002), p 8. Also online at http://www.geocities.com/wramallah/sledgehammer_treatment_for_pales.htm.
28 Institute of Modern Media, *Report on the Events of April 2002: Losses, Plans for the Future* (Al-Bireh/Ramallah, 2002).
29 Campagna/Committee to Protect Journalists: *Picking Up the Pieces*, p 3.
30 Campagna/Committee to Protect Journalists: *Picking Up the Pieces*, p 3.
31 Abdullah: 'Sledgehammer treatment'.

8 Engagement in the Public Sphere

1 Lance Bennett, *News: The Politics of Illusion*, 4th edn (New York, 2001); Pierre Bourdieu, *On Television*, trans. Priscilla Parkhurst Ferguson (New York, 1998).
2 Benedict Anderson, *Imagined Communities: Reflections on the Origin and Spread of Nationalism*, 2nd edn (London, 1991).
3 Liah Greenfeld, *Nationalism: Five Roads to Modernity* (Cambridge, MA, 1992).
4 Anderson: *Imagined Communities*, p 44.
5 Bennett: *News: The Politics of Illusion*; Bourdieu: *On Television*.
6 Bennett: *News: The Politics of Illusion*.
7 Daniel C. Hallin, 'The media, the war in Vietnam and political support: a critique of the thesis of an oppositional media', *Journal of Politics*, 46/1 (February 1984), pp 2–24.
8 Mary Ann Tétreault, *Stories of Democracy: Politics and Society in Contemporary Kuwait* (New York, 2000).
9 Jean Edward Smith, *George Bush's War* (New York, 1992), p 51.
10 'Eisa Bu Yabis, interview with Mary Ann Tétreault, September 1992 in Kuwait.
11 Article 19 of the International Covenant on Civil and Political Rights (ICCPR) guarantees all individuals 'the freedom to seek, receive and impart information and ideas of all kinds, regardless of frontiers'. See Human Rights Watch, 'Kuwaiti court ruling limits free expression: writers, journalists, academics, and publishers at risk', press release, 27 March 2000, website accessed 15 January 2003, http://www.hrw.org/reports/2000/kuwait/kuwait_03.htm.
12 Tétreault: *Stories of Democracy*, pp 107–10.
13 Tétreault: *Stories of Democracy*, p 71.
14 Mary Ann Tétreault, 'Bringing in the last Bedouins?', *Current History*, 99/633 (January 2000), pp 27–32.

15 Human Rights Watch, 'Kuwaiti court ruling'; Ilene Prusher, 'Pushing the boundaries on Islam and women', *Christian Science Monitor*, 11 August 2000 (Gulf2000 archive).

16 Prusher: 'Pushing the boundaries'.

17 Muhammed Rumaihi, *Beyond Oil* (London, 1986), p 99.

18 Mary Ann Tétreault, *The Kuwait Petroleum Corporation and the Economics of the New World Order* (Westport, CT, 1995); Tétreault: *Stories of Democracy*.

19 Haya al-Mughni, *Women in Kuwait: The Politics of Gender*, 2nd edn (London, 2001); Mary Ann Tétreault, 'A state of two minds: state cultures, women, and politics in Kuwait', *International Journal of Middle East Studies*, 33/2 (May 2001), pp 203–20.

20 Nouria al-Sadani, *Al-Masira al-Tarikhiya lil Huquq Siyasiya lil Mar'a al-Kuwaytiya fi fatra ma bain, 1971–1982* [The history of the Kuwaiti women's movement for political rights, 1971–1982] (Kuwait, 1983), p 284, translation by Haya al-Mughni.

21 Peter Mansfield, *Kuwait: Vanguard of the Gulf* (London, 1990), p 113.

22 Kamla Nath, 'Education and employment among Kuwaiti women', in L. Beck and N. Keddie (eds), *Women in the Muslim World* (Cambridge, MA, 1978), pp 172–88.

23 *Arab Times* (Kuwait), 23–4 June 1994.

24 Coverage of such issues remains a problem throughout the Arab world. See the report published by the Centre for Media Freedom, Middle East and North Africa (CMF-MENA), *Women's Rights and the Arab Media* (London, November 2000).

25 BBC, 'Kuwaiti policeman faces hanging', 8 June 2002, 15:44 GMT (Gulf2000 archive).

26 Associated Press (AP), 'Kuwaiti journalist dies in shooting', 20 March 2001 (Gulf2000 archive).

27 BBC, 'Confession in murder of Kuwaiti editor', 22 March 2001, 10:54 GMT (Gulf2000 archive).

28 Compare AP: 'Kuwaiti journalist dies in shooting' to BBC: 'Kuwaiti policeman faces hanging'.

29 Reuters, 'Kuwaiti policeman denies murdering woman editor', 16 April 2001 (Gulf2000 archive).

30 *Manbar al-Taleba* (Kuwait), September 1981. The translation from Arabic in this paragraph is by Haya al-Mughni.

31 Haya al-Mughni, 'Women's movements and the autonomy of civil society in Kuwait', in R. L. Teske and M. Tétreault (eds), *Conscious Acts and the Politics of Social Change*, (Columbia, SC, 2000), pp 170–87; also, Al-Mughni: *Women in Kuwait*, 2nd edn.

32 Fatma Al-Abdali, interview by Haya al-Mughni and Mary Ann Tétreault, 5 January 2002 in Kuwait.

33 Khawla Al-Attiqi, interview by Haya al-Mughni and Mary Ann Tétreault, 5 January 2001 in Kuwait.

34 Haya al-Mughni, *Women in Kuwait: The Politics of Gender*, 1st edn (London, 1993); al-Mughni: *Women in Kuwait*, 2nd edn.

35 Al-Mughni: *Women in Kuwait*, 1st and 2nd edns.

36 Interviews by Mary Ann Tétreault with Kuwaiti candidates for parliament, in Kuwait, September–October 1992.

37 Al-Mughni: *Women in Kuwait*, 2nd edn.

38 Bourdieu: *On Television*, p 21. Emphasis in the original.

39 Bourdieu: *On Television*, p 47.

40 Al-Mughni: *Women in Kuwait*, 1st and 2nd edns; Tétreault: *Stories of Democracy*; Tétreault: 'A state of two minds'.

41 Personal e-mail communication from Abdullah al-Shayeji, November 1999.

42 Deborah Wheeler, 'New media, globalization and Kuwaiti national identity', *Middle East Journal*, 54/3 (Summer 2000), pp 432–44. See also Chapter 9 of this volume.

43 Bourdieu: *On Television*.

44 For example, Susan Bordo, *Unbearable Weight: Feminism, Western Culture, and the Body* (Berkeley, 1993); also Fatima Mernissi, *Scheherazade Goes West: Different Cultures, Different Harems* (New York, 2001).

9 Blessing and Curses

1 Minister Ben Ngubane, Chair of the Board of COMNET, in a keynote address to the Sixth Olympiad of the Mind, Paris, 16–17 November 2000.

2 Quoted in Minke Valk, Henk van Dam and Sarah Cummings, 'Celebrating the power, diversity and strength of African women's networks', in Oxfam (ed.), *Women's Information Services and Networks: A Global Source Book* (Oxford, 1999), p 27.

3 Nancy Hafkin and Nancy Taggart, *Gender, Information Technology and Developing Countries: An Analytic Study* (Washington, DC, 2001), p 16.

4 Robyn Greenspan, 'Web continues to spread', *CyberAtlas*, www.internet.com/big_picture/geographics/print/0,,5911_1556641,00.html.

5 www.www.cybergeography.org/atlas/geographic.html.

6 Miral Fahmy, 'Arabs jeopardise economic future by lagging on IT', Reuters, 20 May 2000, arabia.com/article/0,1690,Business|20744,00.htm.

7 UNDP, *Arab Human Development Report 2002*, (New York, 2002), p 10, www.undp.org/rbas/ahdr.

8 ITU, online at www.itu.ch.

9 Dale Spender, *Nattering on the Net* (Toronto, 1995), p xvi.

10 'Queen launches Arab Women's Summit', *Jordan Times*, 5 November 2002.

11 www.womenswire.org/opinion.htm.

12 Amal Bouhabib, 'Wooing women into the World Wide Web', *Daily Star*, www3.estart.com/arab/women/www.html (downloaded 28 January 2003).

13 Manuel Castells, *The Internet Galaxy: Reflections on Internet, Business and Society* (Oxford, 2001), p 7.

14 March 2003 data, contained in UNDP, *Human Development Report 2003* (New York, 2003), pp 328–9. The other percentages were 1.3 in Jordan, 2.3 in Lebanon, 2.4 in Egypt, 6.2 in Algeria, 9.7 in Sudan, 10.4 in Syria and 10.8 in Morocco.

15 UNDP: *Human Development Report 2003*, pp 310–12 and 325.

16 The names of all interviewees in this chapter have been changed to protect their identities. The online interviews were arranged by people known personally to the author to guarantee the reliability of the data. Thanks are due to Loubna Skalli , who helped with the interviews in Morocco.

17 UNDP: *Human Development Report 2003*, pp 276, 272 and 312.

18 Interview with the author, 31 July 2000.

19 Interview with the author, 10 April 2000.

20 Interview with the author, 13 June 2000.

21 Jacques Ellul, *The Technological Society* (New York, 1965), p 1.

22 Interview with the author, 2 August 2000.

23 See Deborah Wheeler, 'Building an information society for international development: a look at the Egyptian experiment, *Review of African Political Economy* (forthcoming), and Deborah Wheeler, 'Living at e-speed: a look at Egypt's e-readiness', in Economic Research Forum (ed.), *Economic Challenges and Opportunities in the MENA Region* (Cairo, forthcoming).

24 Interview with the author, 15 August 2000.

25 Najat Rochdi, 'Morocco using Internet to enter global economy', *Afro News*, 17 June 2001, p 1, www.afrol.com/News2001/mor005_web_econ omy.htm.

26 Michael Pastore, 'Morocco's online population', *CyberAtlas*, 21 May 2001, http://cyberatlas.internet.com/big_picture/geographics/article/ 0,1323,5911_166081,00.html.

27 Rochdi: 'Morocco using Internet'.

28 Rochdi: 'Morocco using Internet'.

29 UNDP: *Human Development Report 2003*, p 312.

30 Interview with the author, 11 November 2002.

31 World Press Freedom Review 2001, www.freemedia.at/wpfr.

32 See www.aljamaa.com and www.yassine.net.

33 Interview with the author, 11 November 2002.

34 Deborah Wheeler, 'New media, globalization and Kuwaiti national identity', *Middle East Journal*, 54/3 (Summer 2000), pp 432–44.

35 Deborah Wheeler, 'New technologies, old culture: a look at women, gender and the Internet in Kuwait', in C. Ess and F. Sudweeks (eds), *Culture, Technology Communication: Towards an Intercultural Global Village* (New York, 2001), pp 187–212.

36 Interview with the author, 29 October 2001.

37 Interview with the author, 30 November 2001.

38 Interview with the author, December 2002.

39 For more on censorship of the web in the Arab world see Human Rights Watch/Eric Goldstein, *The Internet in the Mideast and North Africa: Free*

Expression and Censorship (New York 1999), www.hrw.org/advocacy/internet/mena.

40 Joshua Teitelbaum, 'Dueling for daawa: state vs society on the Saudi Internet', *Middle East Journal*, 56/2 (Spring 2002), p 7.

41 Joseph Braude and Guy Zibi, *Capacity and Content: Internet Opportunities in the Arab Middle East* (Cambridge, MA, 2001), p 3.

42 Human Rights Watch/Goldstein: *The Internet in the Mideast and North Africa*, p 42.

43 Interview with the author, 15 April 2002.

44 Interview with the author, 10 April 2002.

10 Power, NGOs and Lebanese Television

1 Samir Khalaf, *Civil and Uncivil Violence in Lebanon* (New York, 2002), p 9.

2 Adam Seligman, *The Idea of Civil Society* (New York, 1992), p 58.

3 United Nations Development Programme (UNDP), *Development Co-operation Report: Lebanon 2000* (Beirut, 2000), p 20; and Irene Lorfing, 'Civil society: concept, principles, indicators and methods', in A. Messara, I. Lorfing and A. Kahi (eds), *Promoting Civil Society in Lebanon* (Beirut, 2000), p 123.

4 Irene Lorfing, 'Civil society and the media: a partnership for the promotion of democracy and sustainable development', in A. Messara, I. Lorfing and A. Kahi (eds), *Promoting Civil Society in Lebanon* (Beirut, 2000), p 547.

5 Lebanese Centre for Policy Studies, 'A mapping of civil society and its connection with governance' (Beirut, 1999), obtained on http://www.ids.ac.uk/ids/civsoc/docs/leb.doc, 12 August 2002.

6 Lorfing: 'Civil society and the media', p 547.

7 Steven Lukes, *Power, A Radical View* (London and Basingstoke, 1974), pp 36–45.

8 The illiteracy rate in Lebanon is 7.9 per cent for the adult male population, and 19.7 per cent of the female population, according to the World Bank, *World Development Indicators Database: Lebanon* (accessed on 13 August 2002 on http://devdata.worldbank.org/external/). The female population of Lebanon is highly heterogeneous: some women in rural areas have not had access to long-term education, while others have neither the time nor the inclination to engage in the daily reading of major newspapers. For these women, television seems to be the most available media outlet for consultation.

9 'Tell me who you mix with and I'll tell you who you are'.

10 Lebanese Centre for Policy Studies: 'A mapping of civil society', p 22.

11 Dina Toufic Hakim, 'Family relations and physical encounters in Arab soap operas', *Al-Raida*, 17/88 (2000), pp 15–17; Dima Dabbous-Sensenig, 'Portrayal of women in the media', *Al-Raida*, 17/88 (2000), p 26.

12 Information International, *National Action for Fighting Corruption in Lebanon* (Beirut, 2001), p 14.

13 Nabil Dajani, 'The confessional scene in Lebanese television', paper presented at the Carsten Niebuhr Institute of Near Eastern Studies workshop on Islam on TV (Copenhagen, December 1999), p 2.

14 Dajani: 'The confessional scene in Lebanese television', p 2.

15 Michael Johnson, *All Honourable Men: The Social Origins of War in Lebanon* (London and New York: 2001), pp 142–6.

16 Antoine Nasri Messarra, *Théorie générale du système politique Libanais: essai comparé sur les fondements et perspectives d'évolution d'un système consensuel de gouvernement* (Paris, 1994), p 27.

17 Fabiola Azar, *Construction identitaire et appartenance confessionnelle au Liban: approche pluridisciplinaire* (Paris, 1999), p 69.

18 Azar: *Construction identitaire*, p 37.

19 Author's recorded interview with the former prime minister, Salim el-Hoss, 3 September 2002.

20 Information International: *Fighting Corruption in Lebanon*, p 4.

21 Dajani: 'The confessional scene in Lebanese television', pp 8–9.

22 Lukes: *Power, A Radical View*, p 37.

23 Dajani: 'The confessional scene in Lebanese television', pp 11–12.

24 Fadia Kiwan, 'Lebanon's strength and weaknesses', communication presented at the *Observatoire de la Paix Civile au Liban 2002* (Ayia Napa, Cyprus, 25–8 August 2002).

25 Albert Hourani, 'Lebanon: the development of a political society', in L. Binder (ed.), *Politics in Lebanon* (New York, 1966), p 26. At the time of writing, a debate has emerged concerning possible reform of the electoral system into a one-list system, marginalizing political dissidents even more and strengthening the already important Syrian input into Lebanon's political affairs.

26 Sabine Darrous, 'TV prosecutions questioned: "settling of scores" allegedly behind charges against LBCI, MTV', *Daily Star*, 13 August 2001.

27 Ziad Makhoul, 'Suite et fin d'une chronique annoncée: de la cire rouge pour sceller les portes de la MTV', *L'Orient Le Jour* (Beirut), 5 September 2002, p 2.

28 Lebanese Centre for Policy Studies: 'A mapping of civil society', p 3.

29 Author's recorded interview with Mona Khalaf, Lebanese American University, Beirut, 17 July 2001.

30 Information International: *Fighting Corruption in Lebanon*, p 27.

31 Victoria Firmo-Fontan, 'Civil peace in Lebanon: endogenous patriarchy and social humiliation as dynamics in a developing re-creation process', PhD thesis, University of Limerick, 2003.

32 The servant's presence was remarked on during an interview carried out by the author in February 2001.

33 An analysis of the widespread issue of modern slavery in Lebanon can be found in: Ray Jureidini and Nayla Moukarbel, 'Female Sri Lankan domestic labour in Lebanon: contractual, slavery-like practices and conditions',

unpublished manuscript, Department of Social and Behavioural Sciences, American University of Beirut, n.d.

34 Firmo-Fontan: *Civil Peace in Lebanon*, p 187.

35 While a case in which a Lebanese child-maid was tortured received coverage on Lebanese television, it is assumed that the treatment of foreign maids would not raise public interest. See Julie Hannouche, 'Modern-day slavery: a maid in Lebanon', *Daily Star* (Beirut), 21 October 1998.

36 Robert Tuttle, 'New foreign labour laws unlikely to have much effect', *Daily Star* (Beirut), 2 September 1998.

37 A human rights activist states: 'My job has become public awareness. Don't beat them. Don't rape them. Everyone in Lebanon has someone powerful behind them. The law can't reach them', in Reem Haddad, 'Housekeeper says policemen tried to beat confession out of her', *Daily Star* (Beirut), 6 October 1998.

38 Data in this section was gathered during a participant observation initiative that took place between June and August 2001.

39 Maria Holt, 'Lebanese Shi'a women and Islamism: a response to war', in Lamia Rustum Shehadeh (ed.), *Women and War in Lebanon* (Gainesville, FL, 1999), pp 186–7.

40 The chadoor consists of a black headscarf and a loose black overcoat also covering the head, showing only the woman's face and hands. The *manteau* is an overcoat from the neck to the feet of any non-fluorescent colouring, supplemented by a hejab or headscarf and gloves when appropriate. Both wrists and neck are strictly hidden in both dress codes.

41 For an account of the honour system pertaining to Lebanon, see Johnson: *All Honourable Men*, pp 31–3.

42 Fatima Mernissi, *Women's Rebellion in Islamic Memory* (London, 1996).

43 Germaine Tillion, *The Republic of Cousins* (London, 1983), p 175.

44 Alia al-Zoughi, 'The streets of slaves on Lebanon's road to slavery', unpublished manuscript, Beirut, 2002, p 9.

45 Author's recorded interview with Rima Fakhri, 26 June 2001.

46 See http://www.manartv.com.

47 Recorded interview with Ibrahim Musawi, Al-Manar TV official, 21 June 2002.

48 Victoria Firmo-Fontan, 'Al-Manar TV's narrative in a 9/11 context: a vector of Hezbollah's *glasnost?*', paper presented at the University of Sussex conference 'Media Representations of Islamic Societies and War' (Falmer, July 2002), p 5.

49 Dabbous-Sensenig: 'Portrayal of women in the media', p 26.

50 Author's recorded interview with Nayef Krayem, 3 September 2002. (Editor's note: Data collated from various advertising agencies in Lebanon put 'yesterday's reach' for Al-Manar at 17 per cent of Lebanese viewers in 2001).

51 Cilina Nasser, 'Qornet Shehwan claims Hizbullah is endangering Lebanon', *Daily Star* (Beirut), 28 December 2001.

52 Dania Sinno, 'Summary of conference papers' *Al-Raida*, 17/88 (2000), p 34.
53 'Wearing a habit doesn't make you a monk'.

11 Straddling cultures

1 Geneva Overholser, 'After 9/11: where are the voices of women?', *Columbia Journalism Review* (March/April 2002), p 67, online at www.cjr.org/year/02/2/overholser.asp.
2 Joy Buchanan, 'Survey finds women aren't progressing in newsroom management', *ASNE Reporter*, online at www.asne.org/2002/Friday/women12.html.
3 Anne Sebba, *Battling for News: The Rise of the Woman Reporter* (London, 1994), p 277. Quoted in Margaret Gallagher, *An Unfinished Story: Gender Patterns in Media Employment* (Paris, 1995), p 2.
4 Stephen Kotkin, 'A world war among professors', *New York Times*, 7 September 2002, online at www.nytimes.com/2002/09/07/arts/07AREA.html.
5 Charlotte Beers, 'Public diplomacy plans for the future', statement before the Senate Foreign Relations Committee (Washington, DC, 11 June 2002), http://state.gov/r/us/12170.htm.
6 Nina Teicholz, 'Privatizing propaganda', *The Washington Monthly Online*, December 2002, http://www.washingtonmonthly.com/features/2002/0212.teicholz.html.
7 Timothy Starks, 'Saudi Arabia spent $14.6 million on PR', *New York Sun*, 30 December 2002, http://nysun.com/sunarticle.asp?artID=440.
8 Octavia Nasr, interview with the author, Atlanta, 18 June 2002.
9 Tania Mehanna, interview with the author, Beirut, 18 July 2002.
10 Raghida Dergham, 'Divided lives: an Arab journalist living in America reflects on terrorism', *Newsweek International*, 15 October 2001, p 54.
11 Raghida Dergham, interview with the author, New York, 17 June 2002.
12 Mona Ziade, interview with the author, Beirut, 9 September 2002.
13 Diana Moukalled, interview with the author, Beirut, 14 May 2002.
14 Samia Nakhoul, interview with the author, Beirut, 14 May 2002.
15 May Kahale, interview with the author, Beirut, 27 May 2002.
16 Arab countries were not covered in Margaret Gallagher's 1995 study for UNESCO (Gallagher: *An Unfinished Story*). For discussion of data-gathering by the International Federation of Journalists, see Chapter 1.

Bibliography

Abdel-Migeed, Laila, *Women and Electronic Media: An Annotated Selected Bibliography 1983–1993* (Cairo, 1995)

Abdel-Nabi, Abdel-Fattah, *The Future of the Egyptian Village: Communication Patterns in Rural Egypt* (Cairo, 1995)

Abdo, Nahla, 'Nationalism and feminism: Palestinian women and the Intifada—No going back?', in V. Moghadam (ed.), *Gender and National Identity* (London, 1994), pp 148–73

Abdul Jawwad, Islah, 'The evolution of the political role of the Palestinian women's movement in the uprising', in M. Hudson (ed.), *The Palestinians: New Directions* (Washington DC, 1990), pp 63–76

Abu Lughod, Lila, 'Women on women: television feminism and village lives', in S. Joseph and S. Slyomovics (eds), *Women and Power in the Middle East* (Philadelphia, 2001), pp 103–14

Accad, Evelyn, 'Assia Djebar's contribution to Arab women's literature: rebellion, maturity, vision', in *World Literature Today*, 70/4 (Autumn 1996), pp 801–12

Adam, Barbara, *Time Watch* (Cambridge, 1995)

Afary, Janet, 'The war against feminism in the name of the Almighty: making sense of gender and Muslim fundamentalism', *New Left Review*, 224 (July–August 1997), pp 89–110

Afshar, Haleh, 'Islam and feminism: an analysis of political strategies', in Mai Yamani (ed.), *Feminism & Islam: Legal and Literary Perspectives* (New York, 1996), pp 197–216

——, 'Women and the politics of fundamentalism in Iran', in H. Afshar (ed.), *Women and Politics in the Third World* (London, 1996), pp 121–41

——, 'Women and work in Iran', *Political Studies*, XLV (1997), pp 755–67

——, 'Competing interests: democracy, Islamification and women politicians in Iran', *Parliamentary Affairs*, 55 (2002), pp 109–18

Ahmadi-Khorasani, Noushin, *Women Under the Shadow of Patriarchs* (Tehran, 2001)

Ahmed, Leila, *Women and Gender in Islam: Historical Roots of a Modern Debate* (New Haven and London, 1992)

Al-Ali, Nadje, *Secularism, Gender and the State in the Middle East: The Egyptian Women's Movement* (Cambridge, 2000)

Alloula, Malek, *The Colonial Harem*, translated by Myrna Godzich and Wlad Godzich (Minneapolis, 1986, and Manchester, 1987)

Al-Mughni, Haya, *Women in Kuwait: The Politics of Gender* (London, 1993)

——, 'Women's movements and the autonomy of civil society in Kuwait', in R. Teske and M. Tétreault (eds), *Conscious Acts and the Politics of Social Change* (Columbia SC, 2000), pp 170–87

——, *Women in Kuwait: The Politics of Gender*, 2nd rev. edn (London, 2001)

Al-Sadani, Nouria, *Al-Masira al-Tarikhiya lil Huquq Siyasiya lil Mar'a al-Kuwaytiya fi Fatra ma bain, 1971–1982* [The History of the Kuwaiti Women's Movement for Political Rights, 1971–1982] (Kuwait, 1983)

Al-Sayyid, Afaf Lutfi, *Egypt and Cromer: A Study in Anglo-Egyptian Relations* (London, 1968)

Amrouche, Taos, *Jacinthe Noire* (Paris, 1947)

Anderson, Benedict, *Imagined Communities: Reflections on the Origin and Spread of Nationalism,* 2nd edn (London, 1991)

Anthias, Floya, and Yuval-Davis, Nira, 'Introduction' in N. Yuval-Davis and F. Anthias (eds), *Woman-Nation-State* (London, 1989), pp 1–15

Ardalan, Parvin, 'Women journalists are still second sex', *Jens-e Dovom*, 2 (1999), pp 127–31

——, 'Zanan introduces the women's press: Zan-e Rouz', *Zanan*, 52 (1999), pp 2–6

——, 'Zanan introduces the women's press: Payam-e Hajar', *Zanan*, 53 (1999), pp 14–17

——, 'Zanan introduces the women's press: Neda', *Zanan*, 55 (1999), pp 16–19

——, 'Zanan introduces the women's press: Payam-e Zan', *Zanan*, 62 (2000), pp 8–13

——, 'Zanan introduces the women's press: Farzaneh', *Zanan*, 69 (2000), pp 10–13

——, 'Zanan introduces the women's press: Faslnameh', *Zanan*, 80 (2001), pp 20–5

Arthurs, Jane, 'Women and television', in S. Hood (ed.), *Behind the Screens: The Structure of British Television* (London, 1994)

Article 19, *Blaming the Press: Jordan's Democratization Process in Crisis* (London, October 1997)

Assaf, Heba, *Dur al-Mar'a fi'l-Ilam al-Filistini: Dirasa Mujaza* [The Role of Women in the Palestinian Media: A Brief Study] (Ramallah, 2001)

Azar, Fabiola, *Construction Identitaire et Appartenance Confessionnelle au Liban : approche pluridisciplinaire* (Paris, 1999)

Azzoumi, Suheir, 'Lobbying for citizenship rights: the Palestinian case and the role of the Women's Affairs Technical Committee', paper presented to the Third Mediterranean Development Forum (Cairo, March 2000)

Badran, Margot, 'Epilogue', in Huda Shaarawi, *Harem Years: The Memoirs of an Egyptian Feminist*, translated and introduced by Margot Badran (London, 1986), pp 112–37

——, 'Independent women: more than a century of feminism in Egypt', in J. Tucker (ed.), *Arab Women: Old Boundaries, New Frontiers* (Bloomington and Indianapolis, 1993), pp 129–48

Bagherian, Mitra, 'Economic analysis of women's journalistic activities', *Zanan*, 3 (1992), pp 18–25

Baker, Alison, *Voices of Resistance: Oral Histories of Moroccan Women* (New York, 1998)

Baker, Raymond, 'Combative cultural politics: film art and political spaces in Egypt', *Alif Journal of Comparative Poetics*, 15 (1995), pp 19–32

Baron, Beth, *The Women's Awakening in Egypt: Culture, Society and the Press* (New Haven and London, 1994)

Barton, David, 'Preface: literacy practices and literacy events', in M. Hamilton, D. Barton and R. Ivanic (eds), *Worlds of Literacy* (Clevedon, 1994), pp vii–x

Barzegar, Ali, 'Who are in search of civil society?', *Political & Economic Ettela'at*, 13/135–6 (1999), pp 28–33

Batrawi, Walid, 'Private television in Palestine', MA dissertation, University of Leicester (April, 2001). Online at http://www.amin.org/views/walid_batrawi /2002/nov2002.html

Bazalgette, Cary, and Buckingham, David, *In Front of the Children* (London, 1995)

Bennett, W. Lance, *News: The Politics of Illusion*, 4th edn (New York, 2001)

Booth, Marilyn, *May Her Likes Be Multiplied: Biography and Gender Politics in Egypt* (Berkeley and Los Angeles, 2001)

Bordo, Susan, *Unbearable Weight: Feminism, Western Culture, and the Body* (Berkeley, 1993)

Botman, Selma, *Engendering Citizenship in Egypt* (New York, 1999)

Bourdieu, Pierre, *On Television,* translated by Priscilla Parkhurst Ferguson (New York, 1998)

Braude, Joseph, and Zibi, Guy, *Capacity and Content: Internet Opportunities in the Arab Middle East* (Cambridge, MA, 2001)

Broadcasting Standards Council, *Perspectives of Women in Television* (London: 1994)

Budig-Markin, Valérie, 'Writing and filming the cries of silence', *World Literature Today*, 70/4 (Autumn 1996), pp 893–904

Bulkeley, Christy, 'A pioneering generation marked the path for women journalists', *Nieman Reports*, 56/1 (Spring 2002), p 62

Byerly, Carolyn, 'Gender and the political economy of newsmaking: a case study of human rights coverage', in E. Meehan and E. Riordan (eds), *Sex and Money: Feminism and Political Economy in the Media* (Minneapolis, 2002), pp 130–44

Campagna, Joel/Committee to Protect Journalists, *Picking Up the Pieces* (New York, June 2002)

Castells, Manuel, *The Internet Galaxy: Reflections on Internet, Business and Society* (Oxford, 2001)

Centre for Cultural and International Studies, *The Cultural Viewpoints of the Leader of the Islamic Revolution of Iran, Ayatollah Seyed-Ali Khamenei* (Tehran, 2000)

CMF-MENA/Naomi Sakr, *Women's Rights and the Arab Media* (London, November 2000)

Cook, Rebecca J., 'State accountability under the Convention on the Elimination of All forms of Discrimination against Women', in R. Cook (ed.), *Human Rights of Women: National and International Perspectives* (Philadelphia, 1994), pp 228–56

Cornes, Shirley, 'Gender-engendered literacy needs', in M. Hamilton, D. Barton and R. Ivanic (eds), *Worlds of Literacy* (Clevedon, 1994), pp 105–19

Curran, James, *Media and Power* (London, 2002)

Dabbous-Sensenig, Dima, 'Portrayal of women in the media', *Al-Raida*, 17/88 (2000), p 26

Dabous, Sonia, 'Nasser and the Egyptian press', in C. Tripp (ed.), *Contemporary Egypt: Through Egyptian Eyes* (London, 1993), pp 100–21

Dajani, Nabil H., 'The confessional scene in Lebanese television', paper presented at the Carsten Niebuhr Institute of Near Eastern Studies seminar on Islam on TV (Copenhagen, December 1999)

Dajani, Souad, 'Palestinian women under Israeli occupation', in J. Tucker (ed.), *Arab Women: Old Boundaries, New Frontiers* (Bloomington and Indianapolis, 1993), pp 102–26

Davies, Paul, Fitzpatrick, Stella, Grenko, Victor, and Ivanic, Roz, 'Literacy, strength and identity', in M. Hamilton, D. Barton and R. Ivanic, (eds), *Worlds of Literacy* (Clevedon, 1994), pp 157–66

Débèche, Djamila, *Aziza* (Alger, 1955)

De Clercq, Mieke, 'A critical mass: does it make a difference? Women journalists in Flanders', paper presented to a symposium on cultures of journalism at Goldsmiths College (London, April 2003)

Deem, Rosemary, *All Work and No Play: The Sociology of Women and Leisure* (Milton Keynes, 1986)

Delaney, Carol, 'Father state, motherland, and the birth of modern Turkey', in S. Yanagisako and C. Delaney (eds), *Naturalizing Power: Essays in Feminist Cultural Analysis* (London, 1995), pp 177–200

Djebar, Assia, *Femmes d'Alger dans leur appartement* (Paris, 1980)

——, *Ces voix qui m'assiégent* (Paris, 1999)

Doane, Mary Ann, '*Caught* and *Rebecca*: the inscription of femininity as absence', in S. Thornham (ed.), *Feminist Film Theory: A Reader* (Edinburgh, 1999), pp 70–82

Doumato, Eleanor Abdella, 'Education in Saudi Arabia: gender, jobs and the price of religion', in E. Doumato and M. Posusney (eds), *Women and Globalization in the Arab Middle East: Gender, Economy & Society* (Boulder, CO, 2003), pp 239–57

Eisenstein, Zillah, 'Writing bodies on the nation for the globe', in S. Ranchod-Nilsson and M. Tétreault (eds), *Women, States and Nationalism: At Home in the Nation?* (London, 2000), pp 35–53

El Guindi, Fadwa, *Veil: Modesty, Privacy and Resistance* (Oxford, 1999)

El-Hadeedy, Mona, 'Egyptian women in radio and television's social programmes', *Art of Broadcasting*, 105 (1985), pp 21–30

Ellul, Jacques, *The Technological Society* (New York, 1965)

El Saadawi, Nawal, *The Nawal El Saadawi Reader* (London, 1997)

El-Sobki, Amal Kamel Bayoumi, *Al-Haraka al-Nissa'iyya fi Misr bain Thawratain 1919–1952* (The Women's Movement in Egypt between Two Revolutions 1919–1952) (Cairo, 1986)

Enloe, Cynthia, *Bananas, Beaches & Bases: Making Feminist Sense of International Politics* (Berkeley, 1990)

Farhadpour, Lily, *Berlin Women* (Tehran, 2000).

Fawal, Ibrahim, *Youssef Chahine* (London, 2001)

Fenoglio Abdel-Aal, Irène, 'Feminisme et politique en Egypte', *Peuples méditerranéens*, 48–9 (July–December 1989), pp 151–62

Fiske, John, *Television Culture* (London, 1987)

Firmo-Fontan, Victoria, 'Civil peace in Lebanon: endogenous patriarchy and social humiliation as dynamics in a developing re-creation process', PhD thesis, University of Limerick, 2003.

——, 'Al-Manar TV's narrative in a 9/11 context: a vector of Hezbollah's *glasnost?*', paper presented at the University of Sussex conference 'Media Representations of Islamic Societies and War' (Falmer, July 2002)

Franco, Jean, 'Beyond ethnocentrism: gender, power and the Third-World intelligentsia', in P. Williams and L. Chrisman (eds), *Colonial Discourse and Post-Colonial Theory: A Reader* (London, 1994), pp 359–69

Gallagher, Margaret, *An Unfinished Story: Gender Patterns in Media Employment* (Paris, 1995)

——, *Gender Setting: New Agendas for Media Monitoring and Advocacy* (London, 2001)

Gheytanchi, Elham, 'Civil society in Iran: politics of motherhood and the public sphere', *International Sociology*, 16/4 (2001), pp 557–76

Ghouchani, Mohammad, *Godfather and the Young Left: The Struggle for Critique of Power* (Tehran, 2000)

Gillespie, Marie, *Television, Ethnicity and Cultural Change* (London, 1995)

Golding, Peter and Murdock, Graham, 'Culture, communications and political economy', in J. Curran and M. Gurevitch (eds), *Mass Media and Society* (London, 2000), pp 70–92

Gray, Ann, *Video Playtime: The Gendering of a Leisure Technology* (London, 1992)

Greenfeld, Liah, *Nationalism: Five Roads to Modernity* (Cambridge, MA, 1992)

Grossberg, Lawrence, 'Identity and cultural studies: is that all there is?', in S. Hall and P. du Gay (eds), *Questions of Cultural Identity* (London, 1996), pp 87–107

Hafkin, Nancy and Taggart, Nancy, *Gender, Information Technology, and Developing Countries: An Analytic Study* (Washington, DC, 2001)

Hakim, Dina Toufic, 'Family relations and physical encounters in Arab soap operas', *Al-Raida*, 17/88 (2000), pp 15–17

Hall, Stuart, 'Encoding/deconding', in S. Hall, D. Hobson, A. Lowe and P. Willis (eds), *Culture, Media, Language: Working Papers in Cultural Studies 1972–1979* (London, 1980), pp 128–38

——, 'Old and new identities, old and new ethnicities', in A. King (ed.), *Culture, Globalisation and the World System* (Basingstoke, 1991), pp 41–68

——, 'Introduction to Part III', in J. Evans and S.Hall (eds), *Visual Culture: A Reader* (London, 1999), pp 309–14

Hallin, Daniel C., 'The media, the war in Vietnam and political support: a critique of the thesis of an oppositional media', *Journal of Politics*, 46/1 (February 1984), pp 2–24.

Hamilton, Mary, 'Introduction: signposts', in M. Hamilton, D. Barton, and R. Ivanic (eds), *Worlds of Literacy* (Clevedon, 1994), pp 1–11

Hartley, Tricia, 'Generations of literacy among women in a bilingual community', in M. Hamilton, D. Barton and R. Ivanic (eds), *Worlds of Literacy* (Clevedon, 1994), pp 29–40

Hatem, Mervat, 'Toward the development of post-Islamic and post-nationalist feminist discourses in the Middle East', in J. Tucker (ed.), *Arab Women: Old Boundaries, New Frontiers* (Bloomington and Indianapolis, 1993), pp 3–29

Hermano, Teresita, and Turley, Anna, 'Who makes the news?', *Nieman Reports*, 55/4 (Winter 2001), pp 78–9

Hifni, Magd El Din, 'Athar Bahithat el-Badiyya' [The influence of the Seeker of the Desert], in *El-Mawsouaa El-Misriyya El-Amma* [General Egyptian Encyclopaedia] (Cairo, 1962)

Holt, Maria, 'Palestinian women and the Intifada: an exploration of images and realities', in H. Afshar (ed.), *Women and Politics in the Third World* (London, 1996), pp 186–203

——, 'Lebanese Shi'a women and Islamism: a response to war', in L. Rustum Shehadeh (ed.), *Women and War in Lebanon* (Gainesville, FL, 1999)

Hooper, Charlotte, *Manly States: Masculinities, International Relations and Gender Politics* (New York, 2001)

Hourani, Albert, 'Lebanon: the development of a political society', in L. Binder (ed.), *Politics in Lebanon* (New York, 1966)

Human Rights Watch/Eric Goldstein, *The Internet in the Mideast and North Africa: Free Expression and Censorship* (New York, 1999)

Ibrahim, Ismail, *Sahafiyat Tha'irat* [Revolutionary Women Journalists] (Cairo, 1997)

Information International, *National Action for Fighting Corruption in Lebanon* (Beirut, 2001)

Inness, Sherrie A., *Tough Girls: Women Warriors and Wonder Women in Popular Culture* (Philadelphia, 1999)

International Federation of Journalists, *Equality and Quality: Setting Standards for Women in Journalism* (Brussels, June 2001)

Institute of Modern Media, *Report on the Events of April 2002: Losses, Plans for the Future* (Al-Bireh/Ramallah, 2002)

Jerusalem Media and Communication Centre, *Israeli Military Orders in the Occupied Palestinian West Bank 1967–92* (East Jerusalem, 1993)

Johnson, Michael, *All Honourable Men: The Social Origins of War in Lebanon* (London and New York, 2001)

Joseph, Suad, 'Women between nation and state in Lebanon', in C. Kaplan, N. Alarcon and M. Minoo (eds), *Between Woman and Nation: Nationalisms, Transnational Feminisms, and the State* (Durham, NC, 1999), pp 162–81

Jureidini, Ray, and Moukarbel, Nayla, 'Female Sri Lankan domestic labour in Lebanon: contractual, slavery-like practices and conditions', unpublished manuscript (Department of Social and Behavioural Sciences, American University of Beirut, n.d.)

Kandiyoti, Deniz, 'Identity and its discontents: women and the nation', in P. Williams and L. Chrisman (eds), *Colonial Discourse and Post-Colonial Theory: A Reader* (London, 1994), pp 376–91

Kaplan, E. Ann, *Motherhood and Representation: The Mother in Popular Culture and Melodrama* (London, 1992)

Keyhani, Masoumeh, 'A glance at the early women's press in Iran', *Kelk*, 34 (1993), pp 73–91

——, 'How women-oriented issues are reflected in the Tehran nwspapers', *Rasaneh*, 13/2 (2002), pp 64–77

Khaky, Ahmed, *Qasim Amin and his Work* (Cairo, 1973)

Khalaf, Mona, 'The institute for women's studies in the Arab world', in C. Nelson and S. Altorki (eds), *Arab Regional Women's Studies Workshop*, Cairo Papers in Social Science, 20/3 (1998), pp 132–9

Khalaf, Samir, *Civil and Uncivil Violence in Lebanon* (New York, 2002)

Khalifa, Iglal, *Al-Haraka al-Nissa'iyya al-Haditha* [The Modern Women's Movement] (Cairo, 1973)

Khan, Shahnaz, 'Muslim women: negotiations in the third space', *Signs: Journal of Women in Culture and Society*, 23/1 (Winter 1998), pp 463–94

Khiabany, Gholam, and Sreberny, Annabelle, 'The Iranian press and the continuing struggle over civil society 1998–2000', in *Gazette*, 62/2–3 (May 2001), pp 203–23

Khouri, Nicole, 'La politique antiterroriste de l'état Egyptien à la télévision en 1994', *Revue Tiers-Monde*, 37 (April–June 1996), pp 263–83

Kian, Azadeh, 'Women and politics in post-Islamist Iran: the gender conscious drive to change', *British Journal of Middle Eastern Studies*, 24/1 (May 1997), pp 75–96

Kofman, Eleanore, 'Feminism, gender relations and geopolitics: problematic closures and opening strategies', in E. Kofman and G. Youngs, *Globalization: Theory and Practice* (London, 1996), pp 209–24

Kuttab, Daoud, 'Palestinian diaries: grass roots TV production in the Occupied Territories', in T. Dowmunt (ed.), *Channels of Resistance: Global Television and Local Empowerment* (London, 1993), pp 138–45

Kuttab, Eileen, 'Women's studies program in Palestine: between criticism and new vision', *Cairo Papers in Social Science*, 20/3 (1998), pp 118–31

Lauzen, Martha, and Dozier, David, 'The role of women on screen and behind the scenes in the television and film industries: review of a program of research', *Journal of Communication Inquiry*, 23/4 (October 1999), pp 355–73

Livingstone, Sonia, *Making Sense of Television: The Psychology of Audience Interpretation* (London, 1990)

Lorfing, Irene, 'Civil society: concept, principles, indicators and methods', in A. Mesarra, I. Lorfing and A. Kahi (eds), *Promoting Civil Society in Lebanon* (Beirut, 2000), pp 123–44

——, 'Civil society and the media: a partnership for the promotion of democracy and sustainable development', in Antoine Mesarra, Irene Lorfing and Abdo Kahi (eds), *Promoting Civil Society in Lebanon* (Beirut, 2000), pp 547–8

Lukes, Steven, *Power, A Radical View* (London and Basingstoke, 1974)

McClintock, Anne, '"No longer in future heaven": gender, race and nationalism', in A. McClintock, A Mufti and E. Shohat (eds), *Dangerous Liaisons: Gender, Nation, and Postcolonial Perspectives* (Minneapolis, 1997), pp 89–112

McGlaughlin, Lisa, ' From excess to access: feminist political agency in the public sphere', *Javnost/ The Public*, 2/4 (1995), pp 37–49

Madar Research, 'PC penetration vs. Internet user penetration in GCC countries', *Madar Research Journal: Knowledge, Economy and Research on the Middle East*, 1/0 (October 2002), pp 1–31

Majid, Anouar, 'The politics of feminism in Islam', *Signs: Journal of Women in Culture and Society*, 23/2 (Winter 1998), pp 321–61

Mansfield, Peter, *Kuwait: Vanguard of the Gulf* (London, 1990)

Massoudi, Omid, 'A glance at the early experience of Iranian women journalists', *Rasaneh*, 9/1 (1998), pp 56–62

Mernissi, Fatima, *Women's Rebellion in Islamic Memory* (London: 1996)

———, *Scheherazade Goes West: Different Cultures, Different Harems* (New York, 2001)

Messarra, Antoine Nasri, *Théorie Générale du Système Politique Libanais: essai comparé sur les fondements et perspectives d'évolution d'un système consensuel de gouvernement* (Paris, 1994)

Millington, Caroline, 'Getting in and getting on: women and radio management at the BBC', in Caroline Mitchell (ed.), *Women and Radio: Airing Differences* (London, 2000), pp 209–18

Mills, Kay, 'What difference do women journalists make?', in P. Norris (ed.), *Women, Media, and Politics* (Oxford, 1997), pp 41–55

Mir-Hosseini, Ziba, 'Stretching the limits: a feminist reading of the Shari'a in post-Khomeini Iran', in M. Yamani (ed.), *Feminism and Islam: Legal and Literary Perspectives* (New York, 1996), pp 285–319

Moghadam, Valentine, 'Introduction and overview: gender dynamics of nationalism, revolution and Islamization', in V. Moghadam (ed.), *Gender and National Identity* (London, 1994), pp 1–17

———, *Women, Work and Economic Reform in the Middle East and North Africa* (Boulder, CO, 1998)

———, 'Islamic feminism and its discontents: towards a resolution of the debate', *Sign: Journal of Women in Culture and Society*, 27/4 (2002), pp 1135–71

Moghissi, Haideh, *Populist Feminism and Islamic Feminism: A Critique of Neo-Conservative Tendencies among Iranian Feminists in the West* (Toronto, 1998)

———, *Feminism and Islamic Fundamentalism: The Limits of Postmodern Analysis* (London, 1999)

Mohanty, Chandra Talpade, (ed.), *Third World Women and the Politics of Feminism* (Bloomington and Indianapolis, 1991)

———, 'Under Western eyes: feminist scholarship and colonial discourses', in P. Williams and L. Chrisman (eds), *Colonial Discourse and Post-Colonial Theory: A Reader* (London, 1994), pp 89–112

Mojab, Shahrzad, 'Theorizing the Politics of "Islamic Feminism"', *Feminist Review*, 69 (Autumn 2001), pp 124–46

Morley, David, *Television, Audiences and Cultural Studies* (London, 1992)

Mortimer, Mildred, 'Reappropriating the gaze in Assia Djebar's fiction and film', *World Literature Today* 70/4 (Autumn, 1996), pp 859–66

Moser, Caroline, *Gender Planning and Development: Theory, Practice and Training* (London, 1993)

Mulvey, Laura, *Visual and Other Pleasures* (London, 1989)

——, 'Visual pleasure and narrative cinema', in S. Thornham (ed.), *Feminist Film Theory: A Reader* (Edinburgh, 1999), pp 58–69

Nafisi, Hamid, 'Veiled vision/powerful presence: women in post-revolutionary Iranian cinema', in M. Afkhami and E. Friedl (eds), *In the Eye of Storm: Women in Post-Revolutionary Iran* (London, 1994)

Napoli, James, Amin, Hussein, and Boylan, Richard, 'Assessment of the Egyptian print and electronic media', report submitted to the United States Agency for International Development (Cairo, 1995), pp 171–2

Nath, Kamla, 'Education and employment among Kuwaiti women', in L. Beck and N. Keddie (eds), *Women in the Muslim World* (Cambridge, MA, 1978), pp 172–88

Nelson, Cynthia, 'Biography and women's history: on interpreting Doria Shafik', in N. Keddie and B. Baron (eds), *Women in Middle Eastern History: Shifting Boundaries in Sex and Gender* (New Haven and London, 1991), pp 310–33

——, *Doria Shafik, Egyptian Feminist: A Woman Apart* (Gainesville, FL, 1996)

Omara, Mohammed, *Qasim Amin wa Tahrir al-Mar'a fi Misr* [Qasim Amin and Women's Liberation in Egypt] (Cairo, 1988)

Overholser, Geneva, 'After 9/11: where are the voices of women?', *Columbia Journalism Review* (March/April 2002), p 67

Pettman, Jan Jindy 'Women, nationalism and the state: towards an international feminist perspective', *Occasional Paper 4 in Gender and Development Studies, Asian Institute of Technology* (Bangkok, 1992)

Philipp, Thomas, 'Feminism and nationalist politics in Egypt', in L. Beck and N. Keddie (eds), *Women in the Muslim World* (Cambridge, MA, 1978), pp 277–94

Poya, Maryam, *Women, Work & Islamism: Ideology and Resistance in Iran* (London, 1999)

Press, Andrea, *Women Watching Television: Gender, Class and Generation in the American Television Experience* (Philadelphia, 1991)

——, 'Recent developments in feminist communication theory: difference, public sphere, body and technology', in J. Curran and M. Gurevitch (eds), *Mass Media and Society* (London, 2000), pp 27–43

Qasemi, Farid, *Iranian Press in the Twentieth Century* (Tehran, 2001)

Rai, Shirin, 'Women and the state in the Third World', in H. Afshar (ed.), *Women and Politics in the Third World* (London, 1996), pp 24–39

Ranchod-Nilsson, Sita and Tétreault, Mary Ann, 'Gender and nationalism: moving beyond fragmented conversations', in S. Ranchod-Nilsson and M. Tétreault (eds), *Women, States and Nationalism: At Home in the Nation?* (London, 2000), pp 1–17

Reda, Adli, *The Image of Father and Mother in Arabic Soap Operas* (Cairo, 1988)

Reed, Susan, 'The value of women journalists', *Nieman Reports*, 56/1 (Spring 2002), pp 63–5

Rogers, Everett, *Communication and Development* (California, 1976)

Rostami Povey, Elaheh, 'Feminist contestations of institutional domains in Iran', *Feminist Review*, 69 (Winter 2001), pp 44–72

Roy, Olivier, *The Failure of Political Islam* (London, 1994)

Rumaihi, Muhammed, *Beyond Oil* (London, 1986)

Sadr, Shadi, *Justice from the Point of View of a Third Person* (Tehran, 2000)

Sadr-Hashemi, Mohammad, *History of Iranian Press and Magazines*, vol. 2 (Isfahan, 1985)

Sakamoto, Kubi, 'Reading Japanese women's magazines: the construction of new identities in the 1970s and 1980s', *Media, Culture and Society*, 21/2 (1999), pp 173–93

Sakr, Naomi, *Satellite Realms: Transnational Television, Globalization and the Middle East* (London, 2001)

——, 'Media reform in Jordan: the stop-go transition', in M. Price, B. Rozumilowicz and S. Verhulst (eds), *Media Reform: Democratizing the Media, Democratizing the State* (London, 2002), pp 107–32

——, 'Seen and starting to be heard: women and the Arab media in a decade of change', *Social Research*, 69/3 (Fall 2002), pp 821–50

——, 'Maverick or model?: Al-Jazeera's impact on Arab satellite television', in J. Chalaby (ed.), *Transnational Television Worldwide* (London, 2004), pp 66–95

Salhi, Zahia Smail, *Politics, Poetics and the Algerian Novel* (Lampeter, 1999)

——, 'Wounded smile: women, politics, and the culture of betrayal', *Critique*, 18 (Spring 2001), pp 101–19

——, 'Gender and national identity in the work of Assia Djebar', in Y. Suleiman and I. Muhawi (eds), *Articulating the Nation: Literary Landscapes from the Middle East and North Africa* (Edinburgh, forthcoming)

——, 'Stereotyping, prejudice and race: colonial encounters East and West', in Piers Smith (ed.), *Aesthetic Encounters* (London, forthcoming)

Sayigh, Rosemary, 'Palestinian women: triple burden, single struggle', *Peuples méditerranéens*, 44–5 (July–December 1988), pp 247–68

——, 'Palestinian women and politics in Lebanon', in J. Tucker (ed.), *Arab Women: Old Boundaries, New Frontiers* (Bloomington and Indianapolis, 1993), pp 175–92

Schirazi, Asghar, *The Constitution of Iran: Politics and the State in the Islamic Republic* (London, 1998)

Schulze, Kirsten, 'Communal violence, civil war and foreign occupation: women in Lebanon', in R. Wilford and R. L. Miller (eds), *Women, Ethnicity and Nationalism: The Politics of Transition* (London, 1998), pp 150–69

Sebba, Anne, *Battling for News: The Rise of the Woman Reporter* (London, 1994)

Seligman, Adam, *The Idea of Civil Society* (New York, 1992)

Shafiq, Doreya, *Al-Mar'a al-Misriyya* [The Egyptian Woman] (Cairo, 1955)

Shah-Rokni, Nazanin, 'Women journalists: life of another kind', *Zanan*, 45 (1998), pp 2–7

Sharoni, Simona, *Gender and the Israeli-Palestinian Conflict* (Syracuse, NY, 1995)

Sherzer, Dina, (ed.), *Cinema, Colonialism, Post colonialism: Perspectives from the French and Francophone Worlds* (Austin, TX, 1996)

Sinno, Dania, 'Summary of Conference Papers', *Al-Raida*, 17/88 (2000), pp 34–7

Smith, Jean Edward, *George Bush's War* (New York, 1992)

Somiry-Batrawi, Benaz, 'Waqaa al-Mar'a fi'l-Amal al-Tilifiziyuniyya wa'l-Izaiyya fi Filistin' [The situation of women in television and radio work in Palestine], paper presented to the First Conference of Arab Media Women (Amman, June 2001)

Spender, Dale, *Nattering on the Net* (Toronto, 1995)

Spike Peterson, V., 'Sexing political identities/nationalism as heterosexism', *International Feminist Journal of Politics*, 1/1 (1999), pp 34–65.

Sreberny, Annabelle, 'Mediated culture in the Middle East: diffusion, democracy, difficulties', in *Gazette*, 62/2–3 (May 2001), pp 203–23

Sreberny-Mohammadi, Annabelle, and Mohammadi, Ali, *Small Media, Big Revolution: Communication, Culture, and the Iranian revolution* (Minneapolis, 1994)

——, 'Introduction', *Journal of International Communication*, 3/1 (1996), pp 1–4

Stacey, Jackie, 'Feminine fascinations: forms of identification in star-audience relations', in S. Thornham (ed.), *Feminist Film Theory: A Reader* (Edinburgh, 1999), pp 196–209

Steeves, H. Leslie, 'Creating imagined communities: development communication and the challenge of feminism', *Journal of Communication*, 43/4 (Summer 1993), pp 218–99

Street, Brian, 'Struggles over the meaning(s) of literacy', in M. Hamilton, D. Barton and R. Ivanic (eds), *Worlds of Literacy* (Clevedon, 1994), pp 15–20

Suleri, Sara, 'Woman skin deep: feminism and the postcolonial condition', in B. Ashcroft, G. Griffiths and H. Tiffin (eds), *The Post-Colonial Studies Reader* (London, 1995), pp 273–80

Tabari, Azar, and Yeganeh, Nahid, (eds), *In the Shadow of Islam: The Women's Movement in Iran* (London, 1982)

Tahami, Reza, 'Iranian women make films', *Film International Quarterly*, 2/3 (1994), pp 4–13

Tasker, Yvonne, *Spectacular Bodies: Gender, Genre and the Action Cinema* (London, 1993)

——, *Working Girls: Gender and Sexuality in Popular Cinema* (London, 1998)

Teitelbaum, Joshua, 'Dueling for daawa: state vs society on the Saudi Internet', *Middle East Journal*, 56/2 (Spring, 2002), pp 1–18

Tétreault, Mary Ann, *The Kuwait Petroleum Corporation and the Economics of the New World Order* (Westport, CN, 1995)

——, *Stories of Democracy: Politics and Society in Contemporary Kuwait* (New York, 2000)

——, 'Women's rights in Kuwait: bringing in the last Bedouins?', *Current History*, 99/633 (January 2000), pp 27–32

——, 'A state of two minds: state cultures, women, and politics in Kuwait', *International Journal of Middle East Studies*, 33/2 (May 2001), pp 203–20

Thabet, Mounira, *Thawra fi'l-Bourg al-Aagi* [Revolution in the Ivory Tower] (Cairo, 1945)

Tillion, Germaine, *The Republic of Cousins* (London, 1983)

Tseelon, Efrat, *The Masque of Femininity: The Presentation of Woman in Everyday Life* (London, 1995)

Tucker, Judith E., 'The Arab family in history: 'Otherness' and the study of the family', in J. Tucker (ed.), *Arab Women: Old Boundaries, New Frontiers*, (Bloomington and Indianapolis, 1993), pp 195–207

Unicef, 'Al-Mar'a w'al-Tifl fi'l-Ilam al-Filistini' [Women and children in Palestinian media], unpublished study (Jerusalem, 2000)

United Nations Development Programme (UNDP), *Development Co-operation Report: Lebanon 2000* (Beirut, 2000)

——, *Human Development Report 2002* (New York and Oxford, 2002)

——, *Arab Human Development Report 2002* (New York, 2002)

Valk, Minke, van Dam, Henk, and Cummings, Sarah, 'Celebrating the power, diversity, and strength of African women's networks', in Oxfam (ed.), *Women's Information Services and Networks: A Global Source Book* (Oxford, 1999), pp 21–9

Van Zoonen, Liesbet, *Feminist Media Studies* (London, 1994)

——, 'One of the girls? The changing gender of journalism', in C. Carter, G. Branston and S. Allan, *News, Gender and Power* (London, 1998), pp 33–46

Vatikiotis, P. J., *The History of Egypt From Muhammad Ali to Sadat*, 2nd edn (London, 1980), p 207

Vuola, Elina, 'Remaking universal? Transnational feminism(s) challenging fundamental ecumenism', *Theory, Culture & Society*, 19/1–2 (2002), pp 175–95

Walkerdine, Valerie, 'Some day my prince will come: young girls and the preparation for adolescent sexuality', in A. McRobbie and M. Nava (eds), *Gender and Generation* (London, 1984), pp 162–84

Wassef, Hind, and Wassef, Nadia, 'Introduction', in H. Wassef and N. Wassef (eds), *Daughters of the Nile: Photographs of Egyptian Women's Movements, 1900–1960* (Cairo, 2001), pp 1–13

Waylen, Georgina, *Gender in Third World Politics* (Buckingham, 1996)

Weaver, David, 'Women as journalists', in P. Norris (ed.), *Women, Media, and Politics* (Oxford, 1997), pp 21–40

Werner, Karin, '"Coming close to God" through the media: a phenomenology of the media practices of Islamist women in Egypt', in K. Hafez (ed.), *Mass Media, Politics and Society in the Middle East* (Cresskill, NJ, 2001), pp 199–216

Wheeler, Deborah L., 'New media, globalization and Kuwaiti national identity', *Middle East Journal*, 54/3 (Summer 2000), pp 432–44

——, 'New technologies, old culture: a look at women, gender and the Internet in Kuwait', in C. Ess and F. Sudweeks (eds), *Culture, Technology, Communication: Towards an Intercultural Global Village* (New York, 2001), pp 187–212

——, 'Building an information society for international development: a look at the Egyptian experiment', *Review of African Political Economy* (forthcoming)

——, 'Living at e-speed: a look at Egypt's e-readiness', in Economic Research Forum (ed.), *Economic Challenges and Opportunities in the MENA Region* (Cairo, forthcoming)

Wilford, Rick, 'Women, ethnicity and nationalism: surveying the ground', in R. Wilford and R. L. Miller (eds), *Women, Ethnicity and Nationalism: The Politics of Transition* (London, 1998), pp 1–22

WomenAction, *Women and Media for Social Change: Communications Initiatives Worldwide* (Montreal, 2001)

Women and Memory Forum (ed.), *Nissa'iyyat* (Cairo, 1998)

Yegenoglu, Meyda, *Colonial Fantasies: Towards a Feminist Reading of Orientalism* (Cambridge, 1998)

Yuval-Davis, Nira, *Gender and Nation* (London, 1997)

Zayed Center for Coordination and Follow-up, *Al-Mar'a wa al-I'lam al-Arabi* [Women and the Arab Media] (Abu Dhabi, October 2001)

Index